W9-COZ-014

Herbert Read: A Memorial Symposium

JACOB KRAMER: *The Young Herbert Read*

Herbert Read

A MEMORIAL SYMPOSIUM

Edited by

ROBIN SKELTON

Professor of English in the University of Victoria,
British Columbia, Canada

METHUEN & CO LTD
11 NEW FETTER LANE · LONDON EC4

First issued as the January 1969 number
of *The Malahat Review, An International
Quarterly of Life and Letters*, published by
the University of Victoria, British Columbia,
Canada.
This edition first published in 1970
by Methuen & Co Ltd,
11 New Fetter Lane, London EC4.
© 1968 by *The Malahat Review*
Text printed offset in Great Britain
by The Camelot Press Ltd,
London and Southampton
Illustrations printed
by W. & J. Mackay & Co Ltd, Chatham

SBN 416 15120 5

Distributed in the U.S.A.
by Barnes & Noble Inc.

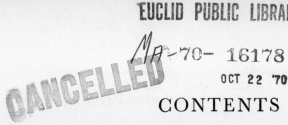
CONTENTS

Preface

No SINGLE BOOK could pay adequate tribute to the many ways in which Sir Herbert Read vitalized the culture of his time, and no one symposium could represent more than a very few of the many writers and artists whom he encouraged, assisted and inspired. He confessed, in an essay published in *Twentieth Century* shortly before his death, " ... in dissipating my talents in half-a-dozen fields I have made it difficult for my contemporaries to recognize the underlying unity of my purpose and my practice. I am left with the hope that someday someone will take the trouble to trace 'the figure in the carpet'." The following pages cannot pretend to do more than begin the study he wished for and deserves; they are simply an attempt by one of many who profited from his advice and encouragement at a time when advice and encouragement were most needed to gather together a selection of essays, poems, and pictures which may indicate a few of those qualities of his life and work which made him one of the truly great men of our civilization. They are also an attempt to say thank you.

In editing this symposium I have been greatly assisted by many people. I must thank, first of all, Lady Read and Mr. Benedict Read for their kindness, generosity, and advice during a difficult and distressful time. I must also thank Liam Miller, Peter Kahn, and Donald Harvey for making a number of useful suggestions, and Mr. Harold Billings for his assistance with the Edward Dahlberg correspondence. Most of all, however, I would like to express my gratitude to the contributors who, on receiving my invitation, dropped all other work in order to provide me as soon as possible with the material I desired. No editor can have been less disturbed by the rapid approach of his deadline. Mr. Howard Gerwing demands special thanks. He has, in the middle of an extremely busy life, contrived to produce an enormous body of work in an exceedingly short time; he has accomplished this by working hours which would have felled a lesser man. Finally, I must thank the University of Victoria Publications Committee which made a special grant to *The Malahat Review* in order to make the creation of this symposium possible.

R.S.

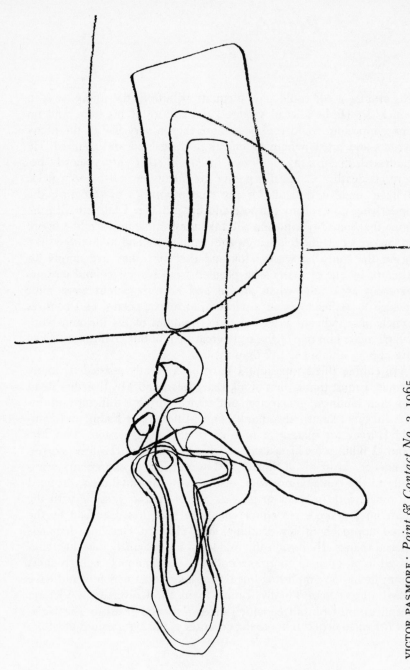

VICTOR PASMORE: *Point & Contact No. 3.* 1965.

GEORGE BARKER

Whipmawhopmagate

(In memory of Herbert Read)

I walked down Whipmawhopmagate
 one morning in the winter
("The death of man stands up inside him
 like a heron in water.")

I saw an old friend staring into
 the rain that ran in the gutter:
("Death is a hole in the ground, my dear.
 I am the dirty water.")

I thought to speak, but I could feel
 the cancer in his throat.
He turned and, lifting his hand, walked up
 through Whipmawhopmagate.

There is a silence we hear when
 the lonely heron cries:
the silence that falls when death itself
 mourns what dies.

Denise Levertov

HERBERT READ: A MEMOIR

I HAD BEGUN TO READ some of Herbert Read's books on art when I was 14 or 15; then his poems, and perhaps *The Green Child*, though that may have been a little later. So that, in 1939, when I was 16, and the ballet school at which I was a full-time student was evacuated to Seer Green, Buckinghamshire, it was tremendously exciting to find that the Reads lived at the next house up the road. My first visit there, with some other ballet students, was, I think, part of an expedition to sell tickets for our first local recital. I said not a word, but used every minute to scan the wonderful paintings — one was a Miro, I recall — and the bookshelves, which, even though I had grown up in a house full of books, were the most enticing I had ever seen. Before long Mrs. Read was kindly filling in as class accompanist when the regular pianist was ill; and I believe she once played for one of our recitals. I seized every opportunity to be the bearer of messages from my teacher to Mrs. Read, in order to return to that magical house, thatched with Norfolk Reeds, in which the world of contemporary art and poetry, which I already dreamed of entering (as a painter as well as a writer, in those ambitious days — yes, and a ballerina as well, though I never really believed that part would come true). Sometimes Mr. Read would appear, and I would gaze at him, my hero, so intensely that it must have embarrassed him had he not been too modest to notice it. At least once the senior students — five or six of us — were invited to dinner at the Reads, which gave me the chance to go upstairs to wash, and peer at more paintings and sculptures, more beautifully arranged, brightbacked books. But I

10

never, during that whole year, had courage to say to Herbert Read, "I draw and paint and write poems and I've read your books and I long to talk with you."

I remember one day in the summer of 1940, during the "Battle of Britain" when sudden explosions of white cloud in the blue skies would reveal the reality of a war that still didn't seem quite real: a day when the ballet school gave a garden party to mark the opening of an art exhibition in our dance studio. The artist was a child prodigy, Plato Chan, who with his mother and sister was a member of the strange assemblage of dancers, evacuees, refugees, Russian exiles, and misfits that formed our household; and Herbert Read had consented to give a short speech on the exhibit. After he'd done so, I escaped from the crowded room filled with local gentry. But the garden was full of them too. Shy and lonely, and imagining Mr. Read to be somewhere among them having a brilliant conversation I wished I were privileged to overhear, I retreated to the garden's furthest edge and slipped behind the tall hedge to be by myself and moon over my poems — and who should I find there but Herbert Read himself, with his little boy, then about two. They were hiding! He too had escaped! I'll never forget the guilty, embarrassed look he gave me. I fled, with a startled "Sorry!" — and said nothing when, back in the crowd, with a tray of glasses thrust into my hand to pass round, I heard people chattering, "Where is Herbert? Where can Mr. Read be?" ... I was happy in my sense of complicity.

That fall, when the bombing began, I went back to London to be with my parents, and I did not see him again for several years. But when I was 18 I wrote to him, sending some poems and asking for criticism. He wrote back encouraging me, giving quite detailed comments, and gently reproving me for never having spoken to him when I was his neighbour. Thereafter for three or four years I would send my work to him about every six or eight months, never failing to receive an encouraging but helpfully critical reply. Isolated as I was at that time — in the first two years especially — such letters from a man I so respected and admired were of inestimable value to me. (For years I kept them all safely throughout my many moves and travels; alas, it is now a long time since I have been able to find them — but I don't believe they are really lost: I expect to rediscover them some day.) And meanwhile poems of his — *Cranach* and *The Sorrows of Unicume* for instance — were working in me in deep, still unacknowledged ways. When my first book, *The Double*

11

Image, was published by Cresset Press, in 1946, I dedicated it to Herbert, to John Hayward (who had, as reader for Cresset, accepted the book for publication) and to Charles Wrey Gardiner (who was then editing *Poetry Quarterly*, the first magazine in which my work was printed). At some point in the 1940's I introduced Gardiner to Herbert's romance, *The Green Child*, which was then out of print, and suggested that his Grey Walls Press bring out a new edition of it. (Grey Walls Press being long since defunct, I suppose this edition also has now become rare.) This was the only opportunity I ever had to do something for Herbert in return for all his unfailing kindnesses to me — which included, in 1945, writing a reference for me to get a job in a bookstore (where, being incapable of making correct change, I was an abysmal failure) and, a decade later, recommending me for a Guggenheim Fellowship.

After I came to America in 1948 I saw Herbert occasionally on his visits here to read and lecture. He never forgot to have me invited to parties and receptions given for him in New York — and always on these loud, crowded occasions I was reminded of that moment of stumbling upon him hiding behind the hedge at Seer Green, for the guest of honour obviously shrank from being lionized and seemed to long to be invisible. On one such occasion he said to my husband that he believed he had made a crucial mistake at some point in his life, that he never should have let himself become a "public figure," that he would have been a great deal happier raising sheep in Yorkshire or even in Australia, writing more poetry and fiction and less criticism. The very last time I saw him, at Bill Bueno's house in Middletown, Connecticut, during one of his two or more long visits to Wesleyan University, I was deeply saddened by his evident weariness and illness and that sense he had, despite all his achievements, of unfulfilment as an artist. Yet his gentleness, and his enthusiasm and concern for the work of others, were untinged with bitterness. Here is the text of his very last letter to me; even though I feel some embarrassment at making public his praise of my poems, I want to show, in tribute to him, that gentleness of his, that integrity and simplicity so characteristic of him:

Stonegrave, York, 16.iv.67

Dear Denise:

Thank you very much for 'The Sorrow Dance' — I've told you again and again how much I like your poetry and this new volume does not disappoint me — indeed, it is better than ever. I like what I would call the objective poems better than the 'didactic' ones — how difficult it is to write about 'events' rather than perceptions. But most of your poems are visual in the sense I mean, the images so clearly seen. The 'Olga Poems' are very moving.

Your letter must have arrived near to the day (April 4) that Sophie had her second baby, here in Stonegrave. She is living in Liverpool now, where her husband Nick is studying architecture. Her first child, Eliza, is now an enchanting girl of eighteen months, very lively and intelligent.

I, alas, have been in and out of hospital and am still not quite better. I went to Portugal in search of sun and warmth, but it was just as cold as Yorkshire. It is lovely here now, thousands of daffodils and all the trees beginning to show their fresh green leaves.

Our second son, Piers, is coming to New York in September on a Harkness Fellowship and will be in the States for 2 years. He has decided to get married first and will bring his bride (18!) with him. He is to take Frank MacShane's course in Creative Writing at Columbia as a beginning. I hope you will see something of him. We all send our love —

> Herbert.

Finally, I would like to quote these words of his, copied into my notebook in 1942:

It is only an unintelligent and superficial realism that demands of the artist a mechanical reflection of the objects which lie in his field of vision, Nor is it much more intelligent to restrict the artist to what is called an interpretation of those objects — the running commentary of the impressionistic journalist. What history demands in its long run, is the object itself — the work of art which is itself a created reality, an addition to the sum of real objects in the world.

That definition — the work of art as an addition to the sum of real objects in the world — gave me, at eighteen, floundering in the beginnings of my life as an artist, a ground to stand on, a measure to try and fill. I think there was much experience that came to me later that I would not have been ready for if I had not then taken those words into my life.

Herbert Read was a wonderful friend to me for nearly 30 years. I shall miss him always.

Michael Hamburger

HERBERT READ:
INSTEAD OF AN ELEGY

"I LIKE YOUR LINES ABOUT HIM," Herbert
Read wrote to me on November 15, 1943, "but I think it is fright-
fully difficult to be successfully elegiac. I mean that the very consciousness of the attitude or expression is somehow false. I feel this
even about a poem like 'Adonais'." Herbert Read was commenting
on a poem I had written for Sidney Keyes, who had been reported
missing in North Africa and — as the same letter confirmed —
almost certainly killed. I took the indirect stricture to heart and
never published the poem.

Now that Herbert Read is dead I shall take his advice again,
though no elegy I might write for him could be quite as inadequate
as those early conventional lines, written for someone whom I liked
and respected as a poet but had known only briefly as a friend, for
a term or two at Oxford. For more than a quarter of a century
Herbert Read was a friend to me, and the words quoted are an
example of the special kind of friendship he was generous enough
to give a writer more than thirty years younger than himself. I don't
remember exactly how it came about that I got to know him when
I was only seventeen. His earliest letter to me, of December 1941,
suggests that I approached him at that time, sending him a poem.
Possibly we had already met, either at Oxford or in London. What
his letters bring home to me now is how much I owe to his advice
and criticism in those early years. It is characteristic of the man, and
of the role he adopted toward me, that his letters reveal more about
my preoccupations over the years than of his. Herbert Read was

shy, gentle and reticent; but he was also unassuming to the point of self-effacement. That is why he could take on young people like me without expecting any sort of allegiance, let alone idolatry or adulation. As he knew well enough, my supreme idol in those early years was T. S. Eliot, whose very remoteness as a person made him a better object of idolatry; but Herbert Read himself was devoted to Eliot and never tried to assert any kind of authority that might have counteracted the other. For the same reason there was never any need for me to revolt against Herbert Read's guidance, as I had to revolt against Eliot's authority before I could begin to be myself; and the simple human affection which I felt for Herbert Read from the first could grow without strain or disturbance.

Yet the record presented here instead of an elegy is a record of Herbert Read's unselfishness in a thankless task — almost inevitably thankless, because I was simply not able to help Herbert Read in the way he helped me; not, at least, until the last years of our friendship, and no letter records the meeting at which our roles, for once, were reversed, and Herbert Read broke his reticence to tell me about the harrowing stresses and frustrations in his life. It was then that I urged him to reduce his public and professional commitments before it was too late, and to return to the kind of work which I had always considered his true vocation — the work that included his poetry, his novel *The Green Child*, the autobiographical *Annals of Innocence and Experience*, essays on literature like those in his early book *The Sense of Glory*, and some of his writings on anarcho-syndicalism. Only his illness forced him into the partial retirement which he had desperately needed ever since his middle years, but thought he could not afford. It may have come too late, after all.

For a long time I took his kindness too much for granted; perhaps all the time, since it was the shock of his death that made me re-read his letters and discover the extent of his self-effacing further-ance of my work. If this sounds like conventional piety, as false as the elegiac sort, I must be specific here and confess a real sin of omission. It was Herbert Read who did more than anyone to bring about the publication of my *Hölderlin: Poems and Fragments*, a translation whose progress he had followed and encouraged since the beginning of our association. I cannot understand what made me dedicate the book not to him but to the memory of Arthur Waley, a man I had never met or corresponded with. Was it a ghostly residue of Eliot's "doctrine of impersonality" haunting me

15

still? A temporary absence of mind or heart? A perverse kind of tribute to the unselfishness of Herbert Read's motives? Whatever the cause, I was taking his help for granted, long after I had learnt that his readiness to be bothered has always been rare among writers, and is becoming still rarer than it used to be.

In his own quiet and uncomplaining way, Herbert Read was yet another victim of the philistinism that punishes British poets with more neglect and indifference than most of them can bear, while insidiously tempting each to become "somebody," which means almost anybody rather than a poet. Herbert Read preserved his innocence and his romanticism, but those very qualities proved detrimental to some of the activities — such as art criticism, sociology and psychology — into which he was led by genuine enthusiasms, only to find himself trapped in a variety of institutionalized functions. The elegy which I cannot and will not write was written by himself — in the form of a tribute to Hölderlin, the same poet who presided over our friendship, linking Herbert Read's first letters to his last. It is the poem *A Gift for Scardanelli*, from Herbert Read's *Moon Farm*:

> ... The clouds are unanchored: they might
> fall from the sky to cover you
> I have brought you a basket of figs
> and some fine linen
> but alas
> no white goat to slaughter
> and fingers have faltered
> that should have played the flute.

I wish I could be sure what poem I sent to Herbert Read in November or December 1941, but I should think it was the persona poem *Hölderlin*, which was also the first poem I ever published. Herbert Read wrote: "I like it very much. I would like to read it again & perhaps I could say something more critical about it when we meet." His letter was from his office at Routledge, but he gave me his home address in Buckinghamshire and suggested a meeting in London. Our earliest meetings were over tea at Yarners, near Broadcasting House, and I remember our being joined there on one occasion by George Orwell, whose gaunt appearance and forthright manner impressed me, though I scarcely knew his work at the time. During those war years, too, Herbert Read once came to my mother's house, where I was still living when on vacation from Oxford or on army leave, to look at a collection of ancient glass phials and jars — Phoenician, he said — that had belonged to my grandfather. The visit stands out not only because it was an instance of Herbert Read's extraordinary kindness — such glassware, it turned out, was fairly common and of little archeological interest to an expert — but because I recall only one later meeting on either's home ground, in the flat which the Reads occupied in London for a time. Most of our later meetings were over lunch at his London club — where he introduced me to tripe and onions, a plain demotic dish as incongruous with the menu of the Reform Club, even in war-time conditions, as Herbert Read himself with London club society. From time to time we met in other people's homes or in wholly public places like the Institute of Contemporary Arts. In 1964 I was to stay with Herbert Read in Yorkshire, but the lecture that was taking me to York was postponed, and the new date clashed with an engagement of his elsewhere. Of our meetings all I can say is that every one of them was a delight, since he bridged the thirty years' gap between us without effort or condescension. He never seemed bored or moody, though he had the habit of suddenly absenting himself inwardly from indifferent social gatherings. When there were silences between us, they were as congenial to me, and as relaxed, as our conversation.

Herbert Read's letters of 1942 are mainly concerned with my early Hölderlin versions, which he read in typescript but was unable to accept for Routledge, and with a surrealist fantasy by my friend John Symonds which I had also sent him. (John Symonds's *The Shaven Head* — a prose poem rather than a novel — was declined "chiefly because of its awkward length," and it has never been published. My Hölderlin versions were published in 1943 by Tambimuttu's Editions Poetry London.) In February of that year I invited Herbert Read to address the English Club at Oxford, but he replied: "I only manage to get through my work by a strict rationing of such obligations, & I am afraid I have more than enough for the next six months." I was too young and inexperienced to realize that he had more than enough for the next six years, or sixteen years; but the more I saw of him the better I understood that business and busy-ness were his chronic affliction. "I am really sorry to have missed you this time," he wrote in April, "but I have been so overwhelmed with work and business. I have to address two con-

17

ferences next week, & have had to prepare the lectures, in addition to my usual work. And all kinds of engagements in town.

"I am returning your Hölderlin translations, after reading them again. I like them very much — they don't read at all 'literally,' but at the same time they give such an exact rendering of the form and tone of the poems. I wish I could be more optimistic about publication, but I don't see much chance as long as the present conditions continue. But I think that when publication does become possible, you ought to make a substantial volume — a long introduction and *all* the best poems.... I hope you will write about Blake. I would like to see a fresh point of view on a poet I am so devoted to."

The really substantial volume had to wait another twenty-five years or so, and it was published by Routledge when Herbert Read had already left the firm. The long introduction, on the other hand, got written in time for the 1943 edition, packed with all my youthful pseudo-learning and miscellaneous references to almost any other writer who preoccupied me at the time, including Blake. That introduction had to be scrapped for later editions, and I was never able to replace it.

By October 1942 I must have begun to feel uneasy about burdening Herbert Read with my work and letters, but his answer was characteristically generous: "The apology should be mine, for neglecting your letter. But you know how busy I am, & you must never feel conscious-stricken if I seem indifferent. I am always glad to hear from you and wish I could find time to see more of you.

"I have read the poems with real interest, & do not find anything for definite criticism — But that rather implies, & it is true, that their virtues are rather negative. If only there were more lines like 'To the soft tyranny of drums,' — that gave me the authentic thrill. But mostly I find just the clever twist of rhetoric. It interests me, but it does not move me. The Hölderlin poem is surely the best.

"I am being honest with you, because that is my way of encouraging you. I don't want to dismiss you with conventional praise — I want you to press on, & to show me more of your work in the future ... "

No one could have done more for me than that. The "clever twist of rhetoric" was not to be expunged for a long time, because ideas remained more real to me than people, places and things. I could not act on Herbert Read's advice until that had changed — and it was a matter of learning to live, rather than to write. Yet at least I knew what was needed — thanks to that letter, and another, of April 15, 1943: "The relatively leisurely intervals of a conference at Oxford give me a chance to catch up with my correspondence. I have, since I got your letter, read the poems three or four times. 'Profane Dying' is an ambitious & on the whole successful effort. I think it is rhetorical rather than poetic — a distinction I am always in the habit of making. The images are apt, the expression forceful: but not essentially poetic. But this does not mean that it is not worth writing. Fine rhetoric, indeed, is an art we don't sufficiently practice these days & perhaps we have lost the tradition. It demands a high degree of technical 'finish' & in this respect I think your poem falls short. The rhythm is occasionally too staccato & there are awkward compressions and ellipses. But the force of the poem wins through."

It wasn't Herbert Read's fault that I took this response to be ultimately favourable. My principle in later years was to ignore all favourable comments on my work and make what use I could of the unfavourable. What I took to be his approval in this case made me publish that poem sequence — written at fever heat while I was waiting in London for my call-up, over several days and nights of such intense absorption that I refused to talk to anyone and had to have food brought up to my room — only to freeze with embarrassment every time I was confronted with the printed text. Yet the point about rhetoric did sink in, leaving an irritation that made me look for a remedy.

In November Herbert Read wrote again to praise the Hölderlin book and comment on the elegy for Sidney Keyes. By then I had almost finished my infantry training in the same regiment, the Royal West Kent, in which Keyes had served, and Herbert Read expressed the hope that I wasn't having too bad a time. We met again once or twice when I was on leave in London; but my first literary — too literary — phase was over, and for many years I struggled to come to terms with experiences that made all I had written seem worthless. I must have said or written as much to Herbert Read, who tried to reassure me in a letter of March 1945. That year a poem of mine was published as a pamphlet without my knowledge, with a mangled text and a largely fictitious "biographical" introduction. I was serving in Austria at the time and could do little about it. Herbert Read's advice helped me to get all but a few copies destroyed. In his letter of January 19, 1946, dealing with this matter, he mentioned that he hoped to see me, but would "probably be in USA from mid-March to mid-May." I doubt that I saw him again until after my demobilization and return to England in the summer of 1947.

The following year, on July 12, he wrote about a new batch of poems I had sent him, telling me that he had been travelling a great deal since receiving them ("USA and twice Paris"). Again he found a "lack of essentially poetic expression" in the poems, and I agree with him in retrospect, though I could not take his advice to try drama. "I feel you need a dramatic myth to give pregnancy to what you have to say," he commented; but after my early persona poems I was trying to get away from myths and fictions of every kind, reacting too strongly towards a prosy literalness. "I am glad you found the Adelphi article of interest," he added in one of his rare references to his own work. "Now that even Middleton Murry has given up pacifism, I feel very lonely."

My long absence from London and the anti-romanticism induced by my army life, or by the impact of what I saw in Italy and Austria, must have caused a temporary estrangement between us. I notice that in his letters of 1948 and 1950 he reverted to the address "Dear M.H.," after the "Dear Michael" of earlier letters. Something of the kind is also suggested by a note of January 24, 1948: "I am always glad to hear from you & I don't want to lose touch with you or your work. So please don't feel that you are being a nuisance. If I lived in London I would try to be more social, but my few days every week are taken up with 'business' of various kinds. I shall hope to see you occasionally & to hear what you are doing." We never lost touch, but I sent him no more poems for criticism. Though I was still far from being satisfied with my work I no longer believed that anyone else could help me to make it better. It was not a question of this word or that, this line or that, but of finding a modus vivendi between the poet and the anti-poet in myself.

In 1950 I added to Herbert Read's too many commitments once more by asking him to see a refugee German poet, Peter Höfler, who wrote under the name of Jesse Thoor. The desperate financial situation of this extraordinary poet, whose posthumous work I was to edit a decade later, was perpetuated by his absolute refusal to do anything only for money and by a state of mind close to paranoia. Höfler also went to see T. S. Eliot at Fabers to present him with a symbolic golden flower he had made and ask Eliot to provide him with a ship, so that he could spend the rest of his life at a healthy distance from the civilization he had come to loathe. He never managed to see Eliot. Herbert Read wrote on April 24: "I will see Peter Höfler, but I have not much hope of being able to help him. I see so many of these refugees & it is always the same hopeless outlook. If he is a good silversmith, it should be possible to make a position for himself. The Clerk to the Goldsmiths' Company might help . . . " I have forgotten whether the meeting took place. Even if it did, it can only have ended in a total misunderstanding. What Peter Höfler wanted was a gesture of recognition, not a recommendation to the Goldsmiths' Company or commissions which he would not have accepted in any case, preferring to live on horse meat and give away the jewels and ornaments which he made. The tragic irony of it was that Höfler, a self-educated visionary who had lived either as a vagrant or by his various manual skills, came as close as any poet alive at that time to embodying Herbert Read's ideas about "the grass roots of art" and his anarcho-syndicalist theories generally; and even outwardly he bore a striking resemblance to William Blake. Two years later, after a coronary thrombosis, Höfler bought a one-way ticket to Austria, climbed a mountain, collapsed and died. My elegy for Höfler, *A Wreath of Thistles*, appeared in a book of mine which Herbert Read accepted for Routledge. That was one elegy which I could not help writing, since it bore witness to an extreme and hidden agony.

By this time Herbert Read had moved from Broom House, near Beaconsfield, to Stonegrave House in Yorkshire. After 1952 our relations became cordial once more. In that year he advised the Bollingen Foundation on a project, their Hofmannsthal edition, in which I had some part as a translator at the time, together with Stephen Spender. After long delays and complications I took over the editing of the two projected volumes of poems and plays, to be published by Routledge in England. In 1955 Herbert Read was also instrumental in getting Routledge to accept a book of my essays and my third collection of poems. He had also tried to get them to publish an enlarged and revised edition of my Hölderlin translations, which another firm brought out in 1952. Most of our correspondence of those years was confined to those matters. In 1955 I reviewed Herbert Read's *Moon Farm*, showing a preference for those poems in which he presented images rather than arguments. He thanked me for the review and commented: "It is very perceptive, and I agree with you (and not the general public) in the estimate of the relative merit of the two kinds of verse which I write." He had probably forgotten that it was he who had made me wary of rhetoric and cogitation in verse.

On January 25, 1961 Herbert thanked me for sending him the Penguin *Hölderlin*: "I had been looking for it on the bookstalls. He is the one poet I return to again & again, and my German being so imperfect, I need just this kind of edition . . . I wish I could see you occasionally, but it is my fault for being so inaccessible." In September of the following year I wrote to tell him how much I liked his essay *What is the left to say?* in *Encounter*. The diffidence and vulnerability to criticism that beset him in his later years were distressingly evident in his reply: "I had been rather shy of the appearance of that Encounter article — they have had it for more than 12 months & I thought there must be something wrong with it. It is good to be reassured by you.

"I am glad that you like Ned O'G.'s poems. They have been badly received — very few reviews & not a single good one. I thought that there must be something wrong with the judgment of Kathleen Raine & myself, who recommended them to Hamish Hamilton. I have just returned from 5 weeks' absence & have to go to Washington on October 20 for the National Poetry Festival, at which I am 'the voice from abroad.' Not an easy assignment."

The same number of *Encounter* contained a contribution by me. Four days after that letter, on September 28, Herbert wrote again: "You must have thought (me) very self-centred not to have mentioned your article on Nietzsche when you had been so kind about my piece in *Encounter*. The truth is, I did not look into the magazine until last night, when I read and was quite absorbed by your essay. I was, as you know, a Nietzschean in my time, one of the circle around Orage. If only we had known how the Master had been betrayed by those nearest to him we might have remained more faithful!"

I never thought Herbert Read self-centred — and his accidental omission of the "me" in that context bears me out — but wished he had been more so, if that had meant more securely centred in himself. Yet his dependence on the judgments of others was inseparable from his fatalism and his humility. "My life has been guided by chance," he wrote in the same *Encounter* essay, "and that I accept as a natural condition. The people I tend to dislike are those who have successfully planned their careers: there is no conflict or contradiction in them because they have imposed a human ideal (of logic, of purpose, of consistency) on the divine irresponsibility." That is a poet's creed, a reaffirmation of Keats's "negative capability"; and in his best work Herbert Read was open to this "divine irresponsibility."

That year I had to find a new publisher for my next book of poems. Herbert Read wrote in July: "I am sorry about this. Routledge has a habit of dropping an author just at the moment he is about to make good. It has happened so many times that I have become cynical about it. But it does the author no harm . . . I could fight for your retention, but in such cases a victory leaves unhealing wounds. So you had better go, for your sake.

"But I should be glad if you could exclude the Hölderlin volume from any transfer of options. This is something I have worked on behind the scenes, as you know, and I would like to keep it under my wing . . . "

One way in which Herbert continued to work for it, even after leaving Routledge, was by sponsoring me for the Bollingen Foundation Fellowship which enabled me to complete what I hoped was my definitive selection and rendering. His wish was fulfilled, though his wing was no longer visibly over the book by the time it appeared — all the more reason for me to have acknowledged it by dedicating the book to him.

That same year I decided to try to live as a writer once more, after twelve years of university teaching. "I believe (or hope) you are wise to seek freedom," Herbert wrote on August 8. "I feel like a new man (at 70!) since I left Routledge. I wish now I had broken away long ago. As for London, I share your views and never want to go near the place again."

My projected visit to Stonegrave that autumn fell through. "I am spending the weekend with Henry Moore," Herbert wrote on October 1, "collecting information for a book on him (biography) which I have to write, & for various reasons I can't change the date. It is a great disappointment to me, and one more reason why I should dislike politics.

"I've been to Germany (Berlin, Kassel) for a fortnight — a congress of poets in Berlin, but no evidence of any poetry. Ingeborg Bachmann, whom I had hoped to meet, did not turn up. I met

23

Günter Grass & rather liked him — perhaps I will make another attempt to read his books, which hitherto have defeated me."

Our last meeting, over lunch at his London club, must have taken place before his retirement from Routledge, since it was then that I begged him to give up some of his many functions and commitments; but my unchronological memory tells me only that it began like earlier meetings, with Herbert as a quietly attentive adviser, before taking the turn I have mentioned. My only regret is that this did not happen sooner, and that we never met again. It had taken me too long to grow up and understand that being a father — literary or otherwise — is at least as hard as being a son.

In 1966, before leaving for America, I received this answer to a letter I had written Herbert about his recollections of T. S. Eliot: "Thank you for writing about my T.S.E. Memoir. I am glad Wesleyan sent you a copy & that you enjoyed it. I did not know you had been to Wesleyan — we enjoyed our two visits there very much. I went to Mount Holyoke once to give a lecture & it seemed a very pleasant college. You should be happy there . . .

"I come to London as little as possible. I find it very exhausting. But I would like to see you again & will let you know when there is an opportunity. I am very sorry I missed you when you came to York, but I hope you will come again & then you must stay with us. I see a little of the University & they were kind enough to give me one of their first honorary degrees.

"I always read your poems and reviews with pleasure when I come across them & hope you will always keep me in touch with your published work."

I did so, and he read it carefully enough to point out one of two technical errors in *Hölderlin: Poems and Fragments* so serious that part of the edition had to be withdrawn and reset. His wing was over me almost to the end, for it was in his letter of February 26, 1967 that he did me this service. On January 23 he had written: "An advance copy of your noble Hölderlin volume reached me this morning, & I rejoice to see the fruition of so many years of labour. I shall spend many happy hours with your book, especially in my present invalidish state, which has reduced my extravert activities to a minimum . . . "

Alarmed by this reference to his illness, of which I knew nothing, I wrote to ask him what it was. His reply gives precedence to the errors in the book. It continues: "You ask what is wrong with me, so I will tell you — cancer of the tongue. It is accessible & therefore can be effectively treated, but I have had three separate manifestations. But at the moment it seems to be under control & I feel well enough. I hope to go to Portugal for a holiday in about four weeks' time.

"I am sorry you have had such an exhausting time. I did too much at your age & can only advise moderation.

"If you come this way we would love to see you, at any time — there is always room for a guest or two.

Yours affectionately,

Herbert"

That was his last letter to me. If I wrote again, as I think I did, offering to take up his invitation, he did not reply; and I was half-reluctant, in any case, to intrude on him now that his illness had given him something like the leisure which he ought to have enjoyed throughout his active life. Yet I am sure that his illness did not change him, that he remained stoical and unselfish to the end. As late as 1962 he had written to me: "I no longer understand poetic standards in this country. But I did enjoy an article by an unknown (to me) person called Falck in *The Review* — do you know anything about him?" I was able to tell him something about Colin Falck, and he returned to this in a later letter.

Sketchy and faint though it is, this record may have the negative merit of not falsifying that side of Herbert Read which he chose to reveal in letters to one of many friends. His more essential self should be looked for in his works. For the greater part of his life Herbert Read was a neglected and misunderstood writer. His public honours were awarded to the public man he became out of a mixture of excessive modesty and a fatalism rooted in the trauma of his experiences in the First World War. The essential Herbert Read could have been honoured only by a realization of his vision, or at least by the kind of sympathy and concern with which he responded to the works of other men.

If I had presumed to write an elegy for him, it would have had to be as unassertive as the best of his own poems, with the quiet strength often concealed by his outward faltering; as unassertive, too, as the man whose tragedy was of the distinctly modern kind recognized long ago by Hölderlin, when he wrote in 1801: "For this is tragic among us, that we leave the realm of the living quite

25

calmly, packed into a container, not that devoured by flames we atone for the flame which we could not master." Hölderlin went on to write that this modern predicament was "less imposing, but deeper" than that of the ancient tragic heroes; and that noble souls confronted with it will "persevere in the teeth of exasperation." Herbert Read was often exasperated and often isolated; but the constancy of his affections is one instance of his power to persevere.

Walter Gropius

ON HERBERT READ

O<small>F THE MANY BOOKS</small> Herbert Read has written, his *Education Through Art* (Faber & Faber, London, 1943) has left the most lasting impressions on me. When I left Hitler Germany in 1934 and settled for a new life in London, I found in Read a kindred soul who was wide open to the problems of art and architecture which had occupied my life. My attempts to bring my longing for a reunification of the arts to a practical test in the Bauhaus had found his vital interest. He later told me that our exchange about the basic educational problems to be solved had fortified his decision to venture into a major study of creative education for children. He became deeply absorbed in a vast amount of literature on art education, psychology and other behavioral sciences, from Plato to Freud, the result of which was the thesis for his book, *That Art Should Be the Basis of Education*.

I have come to believe that this book is of fundamental importance for the future education of man and his relation to society. The evidence offered by Read for his thesis is overwhelming, of scientific weight and accuracy. In it he stands up with rare vigour and resoluteness to fight the inertia, "the universal sense of insensibility" of our society, charging that "the secret of our collective ills is to be traced to the suppression of spontaneous creative abilities in the individual." Overcoming his Puritan heritage and its frustrations which clip the wings of artistic impulses, Read envisages the possibility of a new way of life, of which "love is the tempering flame." He thinks that "art should so dominate our lives that we might say: there are no longer works of art but art only. For art is then the way of life."

27

He wonders why Plato's idea of the powerful influence of art has been misunderstood by generations and gives it a new convincing interpretation, namely, that Plato's aim had been: "to give the individual a concrete, sensuous awareness of the harmony and rhythm which enters into the constitution of all living bodies and plants, which is the formal basis of all works of art." With precise conceptual thinking, he then investigates the biological roots of human reactions and studies them in the child's uninhibited natural behaviour, being convinced that to do this is a fundamental necessity because "Society was no longer either ideally or practically based on natural law: its codes, stabilized from habits and conventions, became an end in themselves and the business of education was to subdue the untamed spirits, the 'unruliness' of young children, and to train them to conformity."

Instead, he felt that creative education must counter conformity and imitation, a thought which all too slowly is just beginning to penetrate into today's educational blueprints, for "in the occupation with art lie the powerful means to educate independence and strength of character." In all stages of education, therefore, occupation with art must not be treated anymore as a dispensable luxury or a status symbol at the margin of teaching programs only, but should be put right into the centre of any educational plan from the nursery on up. This is a precondition for the flowering of the arts as a mighty equal to science and the economics of affluence.

How to implement this idea for the most decisive part of human life, early childhood, has been painstakingly spelled out by Herbert Read, but first he states with passionate force what education should not be: "If we have no *a priori* notions of what art should be — if we realize that art is as various as human nature — then it is certain that a mode of aesthetic expression can be retained by every individual beyond the age of 11 and throughout and beyond the adolescent period in general — if we are prepared to sacrifice to some extent that exclusive devotion to the learning of logical modes of thought which characterizes our present system of education. The art of the child declines after the age of 11 because it is attacked from every direction — not merely squeezed out of the curriculum, but squeezed out of the mind by the logical activities which we call arithmetic and geometry, physics and chemistry, history and geography, and even literature as it is taught. The price we pay for this distortion of the adolescent mind is mounting up: a civilization of hideous objects and misshapen human beings, of sick minds and un-happy households, of divided societies and a world seized with de-structive madness. We feed these processes of dissolution with our knowledge and science, with our inventions and discoveries, and our educational system tries to keep pace with the holocaust; but the creative activities which could heal the mind and make beautiful our environment, unite man with nature and nation with nation — these we dismiss as idle, irrelevant and inane."

Read's own scope of a fundamental aesthetic education is marked out by these five points:

(i)   the preservation of the natural intensity of all modes of percep-tion and sensation;
(ii)   the co-ordination of the various modes of perception and sensa-tion with one another in relation to the environment;
(iii) the expression of feeling in communicable form;
(iv) the expression in communicable form of modes of mental ex-perience which would otherwise remain partially or wholly un-conscious.
(v)   the expression of thought in required form.

Proceeding in his treatise, Read subdivides the technique of aes-thetic education in distinctive aspects of visual, plastic, musical, ver-bal, and constructive education and elaborates on each. The system he proposes all throughout his book "has for its only object the integration of all biologically useful faculties in a single organic activity."

To the all-important teacher, Read gives this advice: "To confer the gift of drawing we must create an eye that sees, a hand that obeys, a soul that feels; and in this task the whole life must co-operate. In this sense life itself is the only preparation for drawing. ... Balance and symmetry, proportion and rhythm, are basic factors in experience: indeed, they are the only elements by means of which experience can be organized into persisting patterns, and it is of their nature that they imply grace, economy and efficiency. What *feels* right, *works* right; and the result, for the individual, is that heightening of the senses which is aesthetic enjoyment."

If a teacher wants to promote such fruitful learning, he needs humility in view of the wonder of the child's growth, a patient de-votion to generate a creative climate, "an atmosphere of spontaneity ... the main and perhaps the only secret of successful teaching." I have come to believe myself that for the whole range of education the capability of the teacher to stimulate the student is of paramount importance. A loving teacher who has the gift of motoric power to excite and stimulate his pupil can activate his initiative to explore and to discover. Then the student goes by himself into new ventures. I remember the story of a famed successful teacher in the Ecole des Beaux Arts in Paris. He mostly abstained from criticizing his pupils but was always present in a state of excitement, shouting to them with a challenging voice: "Continuez, continuez."

The learning process no doubt thrives better in laboratory-like surroundings than in the formal classroom. "It should always be remembered that the school is a workshop and not a museum, a center of creative activity and not an academy of learning."

This article can offer a very general outline only of Read's ideas on education, while it does not even touch on the many other facets of his creative life. I hope it will persuade the reader to go back to the original book, the lesson of which I agree with him must be brought to realization lest "civilization loses its balance and topples over into social and spiritual chaos."

In·his *Annals of Innocence and Experience* (1933), Read gives some lively glimpses into his childhood when he grew up happily on a farm but felt abysmally agonized when in school: "no wild animal from the Pampas imprisoned in a cage could have felt so hopelessly thwarted." Did his courageous fight for creative education subconsciously begin already here?

In 1954 Read finally succeeded in establishing under the auspices of UNESCO an "International Society for Education through Art," which now has many branches throughout the world. Still — in order to summarize again his credo in education — he published in 1966 *The Redemption of the Robot* with the subtitle "My Encounter with Education through Art" (Trident Press, New York). In it he states: "This volume ... constitutes my educational beliefs ... it represents my life's work and is as clear and forceful as I can make it."

The essence of this book is Read's most precious bequest.

HENRY MOORE: A TRIBUTE

I'VE KNOWN Herbert Read intimately for forty years. He was one of my oldest and very dearest friends. His death is a great sadness to me personally and a great loss to the world of literature and the world of art, not only in England but in countries all over the world where his books are read and his gentle influence felt. His work helped to change the whole situation for art in this country. For example his book *Education through Art* altered the whole balance of our educational system and showed younger people how important art should be in our lives. Indirectly it certainly helped to produce the larger number of gifted artists who have made England count in the international scene. But quite apart from the effect of his books, he gave his time unstintedly, both at an official level and to individual artists in whom he saw promise. At a time when English art life was beset by provincial attitudes and a narrow small mindedness, he consistently promoted a philosophical world view. Yet as a fellow Yorkshireman I never failed to find in his character, and in his actions, the authentic ring of our native county. Herbert Read had a great impact on the world of art, but I believe that his most lasting achievement will be found to lie in his own creative writing, in his *Collected Poems*, in his novel *The Green Child* and in the account of his childhood in Yorkshire, which he called *The Innocent Eye*; these words will live, but on this very day of his death, what I feel most strongly is that I have lost a wonderful friend and beautiful human being.

From a B.B.C. broadcast
June 12, 1968

Four Drawings

I   *Sculpture in Setting.* 1937. Coloured Chalk.
42½" x 14¾".

Collection: Mrs. Irina Moore.

II   *Five Figures in a Setting.* 1937. Chalk and
Watercolour. 14 5/8" x 21½".

Collection: Mrs. Irina Moore.

III   *Two Forms: Drawing for Sculpture.* 1937.
15" x 17½". Chalk and Watercolour.

Collection: Mrs. Irina Moore.

IV   *Square Forms: Drawing for Stone Sculpture.*
1936. 17½" x 11". Chalk and Watercolour.

Collection: Mrs. Irina Moore.

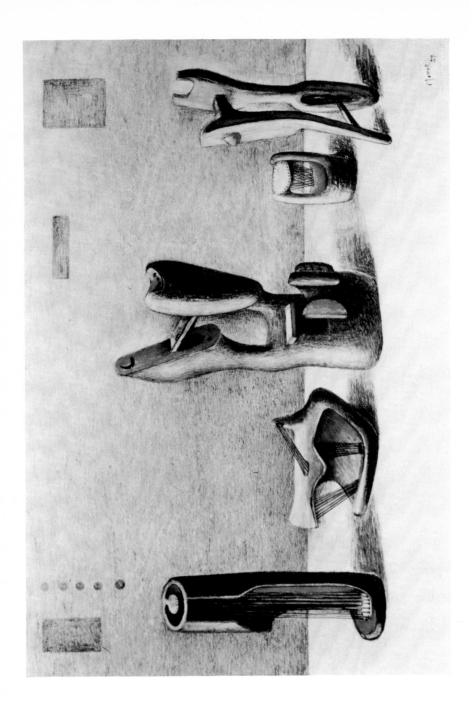

Herbert Read

THE LIMITS OF PERMISSIVENESS
IN ART

THIS ESSAY will be concerned with recent developments in modern art (including literature, but excluding music, which I do not feel competent to deal with) — developments that in my opinion are *excessive*, that in my opinion exceed the limits that define the very concept of art. My intention is not in any sense reactionary. The great experimental artists of the modern period — Picasso, Kandinsky, Klee, Mondrian in painting; Brancusi, Arp, Moore, Lipchitz in sculpture; Proust, Pound, Eliot and Joyce in literature — these remain great artists, pioneers who have established a new basis for the fine arts. We might call this basis super-realism to distinguish it, not only from the nineteenth century of realism, but also more decisively from those so-called neo-realists who have reacted against the experimentalism of the modern period and now attempt to re-establish the older conventions.

Modernism in art is a very complex phenomenon and our generalizations are more likely to obscure than illuminate it. But it must be affirmed that one principle, common to all the representative artists I have mentioned and to artists everywhere who are distinctively "modern," is fundamental and cannot be sacrificed without calling into question the whole movement. I would call this the principle of symbolism as distinct from the principle of realism. The modern artist claims that there is not one level of experience to be presented or re-presented in the work of art, but several, and that some of these levels are as important as, if not more important than, the imitation of phenomena from the outer world. Subjectivism is, of course, common to the whole romantic tradition in art; but what

37

has been discovered or reaffirmed in our own time is that subjective images have their own laws of being, and can be adequately represented only by symbols. The word "symbol," as an American philosopher of art, Richard Bernheimer, has remarked, "is admittedly one of the most protean in the language. But however it is defined ...it clearly suggests a mode of functioning different from that which we attribute to simple likenesses. Transcending the realm of mere visual similarities, all symbols tend to bring us into contact with realities otherwise partly or totally inaccessible."[1]

Such is the philosophic bedrock upon which the modern movement in art rests, and nothing that I am going to say will in any way call into question this basic principle.

Movements in modern art, such as the Cubist movement, the Surrealist movement, or the Constructivist movement, are usually regarded as attempts by a group of artists to organize themselves to further their common interests. Since the aims of a movement are not always formulated in words, the bond may be no more than the practice of a certain style. Sometimes the movement is first defined and made conscious of itself by critics; sometimes, as in the Futurist and Surrealist movements, a manifesto is drawn up by the leaders of the movement, and adherents are invited to sign the manifesto and follow its precepts. In the case of the Surrealist movement the discipline was strict, resignations and excommunications were the order of the day. Edicts were issued whenever the social or political situation seemed to demand an expression of the group's solidarity.

Movements in this strict sense did not survive the Second World War. In 1947 an attempt was made to reassemble the forces of Surrealism, but after one more manifestation it finally expired. The so-called movements that have followed — Action Painting in the United States, Pop Art and Op Art — have been pseudo movements, without stylistic unity, without manifestoes, without common action or association of any kind — the creation of journalists, anxious to find a label for phenomena they do not understand, even anxious to create an order where only confusion seems to exist.

If one looks at a survey of the present scene, such as *The Art of Our Time* edited by Will Grohmann in 1966, one notices in the first place that there is no attempt to classify contemporary art according to stylistic categories: the survey is made country by

[1] *The Nature of Representation: A Phenomenological Enquiry.* New York University Press, 1961, p. 4.

38

country, and within each country, artist by artist. If one then turns to the numerous and excellent illustrations in the volume, though these are again classified by country, no national characteristics can be detected. Instead there is a multiplicity of styles which cut across all frontiers, so that an extreme geometrical abstraction may be found in Great Britain, Venezuela, Italy or Japan and an extreme expressionistic abstraction in the United States, Spain, Germany and Argentina. But even these categories are meaningless, for there is nothing in common between the paintings in each category except a tendency towards one or other extreme of the formal spectrum.

We must next observe that the extremes are, like the North and South Pole, sparsely inhabited: a Ben Nicholson, a Jesús Soto at one extreme, a Karel Appel or a Vedova at the other extreme. I do not imply that there is any identity of style even between Nicholson and Soto; much less between Appel and Vedova. They merely represent extremes in a spectrum that consists of an infinite gradation of individualistic styles. Even the "pop" artists, Rauschenberg or Kitaj, when seen in a survey of this kind, cease to have any distinctive style — they merge imperceptibly into styles we have been accustomed to call surrealist or abstract.

The only quality all these painters of our time have in common is eccentricity, their apparently deliberate avoidance of stylistic unity. Each is an individual speaking a private language, and the total effect is a Babel. But the Babel is not cacophonous: the separate sounds merge into an overall harmony. Since this harmony is not stylistic we must seek some other definition of its total effect.

The only common quality left in contemporary art is perceptual coherence. That is to say, however extreme the permissive freedom enjoyed by the artist, an instinctive visual balance seems to assert itself in his work: the muscular action of the painter's hand as it moves over the canvas automatically conforms to laws of perception. This automatic nature of this control is confirmed by the paintings executed by a chimpanzee some years ago under the direction of Dr. Desmond Morris at the London Zoo. I possess two of these paintings and they do not differ in essential characteristics from typical examples of American action painting. This does not imply that the American painters are comparable in their general abilities to chimpanzees, but when they allow their brushes to be guided by instinctive gestures (and they proudly admit that this is what they do) then in that moment they gesticulate in the same manner as the chimpanzee. Of course, the chimpanzee cannot stretch and frame the canvas that has been presented to him: he cannot perform any of the ancillary activities that lead up to and follow the action of human painting. He cannot, for example, enter into a contract with an art dealer. But he can perform the gestures necessary to paint a picture of a certain kind, and the perceptual process ensures that this picture is organized into a significant pattern.

A significant pattern — there we have a phrase that may give us a clue to the unity underlying the diversity of the art of our time. That every work of art possesses a pattern — even in spite of the desperate efforts of some painters to avoid anything so commonplace — is evident from the illustrations in Professor Grohmann's book, or from any international exhibition of art such as the Venice Biennale. If we take two extremes illustrated in the same page of *The Art of Our Time*, such as those by Philip Guston and Barnett Newman or those by Obrégon and Soto, the extreme contrast of free and disciplined forms cannot disguise the fact that all four paintings are visually coherent — and this is true of colour as well as spatial values. It was long ago demonstrated by the Dada artists that the more deliberately the painter sets out to destroy the traditional conventions of art the more markedly he reveals his innate aesthetic sensibility. The work of Kurt Schwitters is the best demonstration of that paradox.

Is the good Gestalt good enough to constitute a work of art? I think it is, if by a work of art we mean what Matisse meant by a work of art — "an art of balance, of purity and serenity devoid of troubling or depressing subject-matter, an art which might be for every mental worker . . . like an appeasing influence, like a natal soother, something like a good armchair in which to rest from physical fatigue." Matisse's statement has never been very popular with critics of art: it seems to deprive them of their very function, which is to reveal spiritual or social or psychological profundities in art. No doubt such profundities exist, or have existed in the past. But the modern artist has proved that the artist can dispense with them. For him the good Gestalt is good enough, and though this looks suspiciously like the old doctrine of art for art's sake, the Gestalt psychologist will tell you that the intelligence itself, and our whole ability to order experience for conceptual apprehension and assessment, depends on this fundamental perceptual process. From this point of view the work of art becomes, not a reflection of experience, but the foundation of experience, the mental event from which all intellection proceeds. From infinite possibilities of form and colour the eye selects images that have visual significance, and though these images may not be matched in the world of appearance, nevertheless they become part of the world of appearance, in so far as man is given the power to create a visual order out of the confused material presented to his organs of perception.

The task of the critic remains, unaffected and perhaps clarified by this reduction of the work of art to its aesthetic nakedness. His duty is simply to assess the aesthetic effectiveness of any particular work of art, in relation to human faculties of feeling, emotion and prudence. This last word may cause you some surprise, but the work of art is always created in a social context, and it is legitimate to distinguish between aesthetic permissiveness, which in principle should be total and unrestricted, and a social permissiveness whose limits are determined by reason or discretion or consideration for the innocence and well-being of other people. There are many manifestations in the art of today which are vulgar and moronic, and there is no reason why, in the sacred name of liberty, we should condone them.

Perhaps I am only repeating the most important conclusion reached by Albert Camus in *L'homme révolté*, an idea which I emphasized in my introduction to the English translation of this book. It is the idea that excess either dies or creates its own "measure" or moderation. To quote Camus: "Moderation is not the opposite of rebellion. Rebellion in itself is moderation, and it demands, defends, and re-creates it throughout history and its eternal disturbances. The very origin of this value guarantees us that it can only be partially destroyed. Moderation, born of rebellion, can only live by rebellion. It is a perpetual conflict, continually created and mastered by intelligence. It does not triumph either in the impossible or in the abyss. It finds its equilibrium through them. Whatever we may do, excess will always keep its place in the heart of man, in the place where solitude is found. We all carry within us our places of exile, our crimes and our ravages. But our task is not to unleash them on the world; it is to fight them in ourselves and in others."[2]

Camus is writing of rebellion in its social or political context, but

[2] *The Rebel.* Trans. by Anthony Bower. London (Hamish Hamilton) 1953, p. 268.

41

his words are equally true in a cultural context. Here, too, we are in the presence of a paradox: the necessity, in order to establish an equilibrium, of constant revolt. But as Camus indicates, the problem is essentially one for the individual. We should not expose our private paranoia to the world, but seek to master it in art and through art. The alternative is an unrestrained exposure of mental conflicts or mental confusion that in terms of visual or poetic form is aesthetic nihilism.

I have, on another occasion,[3] dealt with the disintegration of form in modern art, but I would now like to be a little more specific, both in relation to literature and to the visual arts. Accepting perceptual coherence as the universal requirement in a work of art, at what point, in the history of modern art and literature, do we find this requirement set aside?

I will begin with literature and will briefly examine the later work of Joyce and Pound.

Joyce claimed that both *Ulysses* and *Finnegans Wake* were composed on a structural principle. *Ulysses* has strict correspondences with Homer's *Odyssey*: each incident is a reflection of a similar incident in Homer's poem. Ezra Pound, writing in French for the *Mercure de France* when *Ulysses* was first published, asserted that as a book it was more formal than the carefully wrought novels of Flaubert. "Not a line, not half-a-line, that does not have an intellectual intensity unparalleled in a book of such length." It has never seemed to me that *Ulysses* needed this kind of justification, and I suspect that Joyce used the *Odyssey*, not so much as a source of inspiration but rather as a structural prop for the images that welled up from his unconscious — a clothes-horse for his unwashed linen. At the same time a painter such as Giorgio di Chirico was using the classical structure of academic painting as a prop for the incoherent visual images that welled up from his unconscious. Any writer or painter knows that inspiration flows more freely if a ready-made channel is available.

At this point I should perhaps ask you to distinguish between the aesthetic and the social aspects of permissiveness in literature. *Ulysses* is a decisive document in this great debate, and as you know in 1934 an American court allowed the plea of aesthetic merit to prevail over the charge of obscenity. That such a distinction can be sus-

3 *The Origins of Form in Art*. London and New York, 1965, pp. 174-87.

42

tained is obvious to anyone with sufficient knowledge of the history of literature: literature, in this respect, is simply a faithful reflection of the behaviour of "the naked ape," as it is now fashionable to call man. If we want our literature to be decent, we must clothe the ape; that is to say, falsify the reality. What we are discussing now is not the nature of the reality reflected by art, but the manner in which the mirror distorts reflected images.

If Joyce's *Ulysses* had not been succeeded by *Finnegans Wake* we might exempt Joyce from the charge of formal incoherence, of lack of *mesure*. But in Joyce's own view, and obviously from any serious critical point of view, *Finnegans Wake* is a logical (or illogical) sequence to *Ulysses*. *Finnegans Wake*, too, has its prototype — *La Scienza Nuova* of Giambattista Vico, with its cyclical theory of history and its new conception of the relationship between history and imagination. Joyce, we are told, read this book in Trieste and used it centrally in *Finnegans Wake*.[4] But the structural parallel between these two works is not so close as it is in the case of *Ulysses* and the *Odyssey*. Joyce was inspired by Vico's structural ideas in relation to history, not in relation to the structure of the book he was writing. He took over a theory of history and applied it very loosely to the art of fiction.

Joyce's brother, Stanislaus, was a fearless and perceptive critic of both *Ulysses* and *Finnegans Wake*. James owed a lot to his brother — perhaps the very notion of using structural prototypes (Stanislaus had pointed out to him the resemblance between the "Bacchanals" of Euripides and Ibsen's "Ghosts").[5] Stanislaus was critical of many aspects of *Ulysses*, but accepted it for its realism, its stylistic energy and beauty. He took the talent for granted: "Dublin lies stretched out before the reader, the minute living incidents start out of the pages. Anybody who reads can hear the people talk and feel himself among them." But he went on to complain that at every turn of this, the longest day on record, there are things to give him pause. "There is many a laugh, but hardly one happy impression. Everything is undeniably as it is represented, yet the 'cumulative effect' as Grant Richards would say, makes him doubt truth to be a liar. You try to shift the burden of your melancholy to the reader's shoulders without being yourself relieved. To me you seem to have escaped from the toils of the priest and the king only to fall under the

4 Richard Ellmann: *Letters of James Joyce* (1966), Vol. III, p. 118 n.
5 Ellmann, *Ibid.*, p. 104.

oppression of a monstrous vision of life itself. There is no serenity or happiness anywhere in the whole book."[6]

These are shrewd thrusts, but for the most part they belong to the moralistic criticism I have put on one side. It is far otherwise, however, with Stanislaus's criticism of *Finnegans Wake*. The first instalment he read seemed to him to be "drivelling rigmarole," "or perhaps — a sadder supposition — it is the beginning of softening of the brain." He found it all "unspeakably wearisome," "the witless wandering of literature before its final extinction." These expressions are found in a letter to his brother, and there is no reason to suppose that they were inspired by jealousy: as he was later to show in *My Brother's Keeper*, Stanislaus was, in spite of latent antagonisms natural in the family situation, full of affection and admiration for James, and for this very reason he criticized his brother with "a startling lucidity of vision."[7]

At any rate, the witless wandering of literature before its final extinction is the phenomenon we are investigating. Though the wandering in *Finnegans Wake* may not be witless, it is certainly "inconsequent, desultory, heterogeneous" — words Stanislaus used to describe *Ulysses*. Thought, he added, might be anything you like, "but it must never be obscure to the thinker. . . . Bloom's woolgatherings as often as not leave the reader guessing."[7] But if this can be said "as often as not" about *Ulysses*, it must be said without qualification about *Finnegans Wake*. The whole work is designed on the principle of the Anglo-Saxon riddle: the more difficult to guess the meaning the better it is. I do not altogether discount the continuous musical phrasing of the writing, the humour, the latent fire of the embedded images. *Finnegans Wake* will survive as a curiosity of literature, the obsessive spinning of a word-master. It should rest at that. It is its influence that has been disastrous.

What in Joyce was a masterpiece of sick humour became in his imitators a simple failure to communicate any meaning but the meaninglessness of all forms of communication, and therefore the meaninglessness of social existence, indeed, the meaninglessness of life itself, individual or communal. Samuel Beckett has been the chief instigator in this permissive process — again a process with its moments of tragic or comic vision, but from a stylistic point of view leading to an apotheosis of futility. As one of his characters says:

6 *Ibid.*, p. 104.
7 *Letters*, III, 105.

44

"At no moment do I know what I am talking about, nor of whom, nor of where, nor how, nor why, but I could employ fifty wretches for this sinister operation and still be short of a fifty-first, to close the circuit, that I know, without knowing what it means. The essential is never to arrive anywhere, neither where Mahood is, nor where Worm is, nor where I am, it little matters to what dispensation. The essential is to go on squirming forever at the end of the line, as long as there are water and banks and ravening in heaven or sporting God to plague his creature. . . . I've swallowed three hooks and am still hungry. Hence the howls. What a joy to know where one is, and where one will stay, without being there. Nothing to do but stretch out comfortably on the rack, in the blissful knowledge you are nobody for all eternity."

This comes from page 341 of the Molloy trilogy[8] but it might have come from any of the 418 pages of this book, or any other book of the same author. Again I am teetering on the edge of a moral judgment, but a moral judgment is not my intention. A writer may express a philosophy of futility and still be a great writer: what I criticize in Beckett is a permissive logorrhoea that compels the reader to plunge into a sea of words with so little aesthetic reward. The trouble with works like *Finnegans Wake* and the Molloy trilogy (*Molloy, Malone Dies, The Unnamable*) is that they are superficially exciting but fundamentally boring. The underlying reason is a simple one: literature, from Homer to Henry James, has been essentially a dialogue, a dialogue between the author and the "dear reader." With the invention of the "interior monologue," literature became an uninterrupted stream of consciousness, uncontrolled by any intention or desire to communicate to an auditor. Now the stream of consciousness, whether in the related dream or in simulated narrative, is inevitably boring, simply because it lacks form, which is a device evolved by the tradition of art for the effective exchange of meaning. Without this dialogic structure, the auditor's attention wanders: he becomes indifferent to what is being said.

I would like to suggest that from this point of view an interesting comparison may be made between the style and structure of Beckett's prose and those linear designs which decorate the great illuminated manuscripts and jewellery of the seventh to ninth cen-

8 Calder (London), 1959.

turies in Ireland — the Book of Kells, for example, or the Gospel at St. Gall. The same phenomenon is found in early Nordic art generally. Here is a description of it by a German art historian (Lamprecht):

There are certain simple motives whose interweaving and commingling determines the character of this ornament. At first there is only the dot, the line, the ribbon; later the curve, the circle, the spiral, the zigzag, and an S-shaped decoration are employed. Truly, no great wealth of motives! But what variety is attained by the manner of their employment! Here they run parallel, then entwined, now latticed, now knotted, now plaited, then again brought through one another in a symmetrical checker of knotting and plaiting. Fantastically confused patterns are thus evolved, whose puzzle asks to be unravelled, whose convolutions seem alternately to seek and avoid each other, whose component parts, endowed as it were with sensibility, captivate sight and sense in passionately vital movement.

Wilhelm Worringer, who quotes this passage in his *Form in Gothic* (English translation, London, 1927, p. 41) notes that Lamprecht's words expressly bear witness to the impression of passionate movement and vitality, a questing, restless tumult in this confused medley of lines. "Since line is lacking in all organic timbre, its expression of life must, as an expression, be divorced from organic life ... The pathos of movement which lies in this vitalised geometry ... forces our sensibility to an effort unnatural to it. When once the natural barriers of organic movement have been overthrown, there is no more holding back: again and again the line is broken, again and again checked in the natural direction of its movement, again and again it is forcibly prevented from peacefully ending its course, again and again diverted into fresh complications of expression, so that, tempered by all these restraints, it exerts its energy of expression to the uttermost until at last, bereft of all possibilities of natural pacification, it ends in confused, spasmodic movements, breaks off unappeased into the void or flows senselessly back upon itself."[9]

These sentences, which eloquently and exactly describe the character of early northern ornament, seem to me to serve as an equally eloquent and exact description of Beckett's prose style in *Molloy* and later works. But while we can follow this linear movement with pleasure and even excitement when the medium is visual, the same method used verbally demands a concentration and tolerance to

9 *Op. cit.*, p. 42.

which we are not accustomed in literature, and in my opinion never can become accustomed. Celtic ornament was used to decorate the Gospels — a very simple narrative. In *Finnegans Wake, Molloy, How it is* and other works of this kind, the ornament has invaded the narrative, and the line of this fused expression "breaks off unappeased into the void or flows senselessly back upon itself."

I should perhaps at this point say something about "the new French school" of novelists that acknowledges the decisive influence of Beckett — the anti-novel of Alain Robbe-Grillet, Nathalie Sarraute and Marguerite Duras, but I shall refrain, partly because I have always found it difficult to read their works, but mainly because the criticisms I have made of Joyce and Beckett apply to them equally. Always a vital word-play, a glimmering imagery, a sense of despair or loneliness or futility, but no forward movement, no organic growth, no dramatic tension, no resolution of a tragic destiny such as we find in the great literature of the past. The creative imagination of the poet sinks in a sea of words.

I shall not deal with other examples of logorrhoea that have followed Joyce and Beckett as inevitably as the little fishes follow a receding tide, but instead say a few words about Ezra Pound in this same connection. Again I would not like to be misunderstood. Pound is a great poet, perhaps the greatest of our time. But his work, as Yeats already perceived in his Introduction to the *Oxford Book of Modern Verse*, in spite of its nobility — "at moments more style, more deliberate nobility and the means to convey it than in any contemporary poet known to me . . . is constantly interrupted, broken, twisted into nothing by its direct opposite, nervous obsession, nightmare, stammering confusion . . . " The words were written by Yeats in September 1936, at which time only the first 41 Cantos had been published. Since that year the stammering confusion has grown worse with every successive batch of cantos, until in the latest cantos the incoherence is absolute.

Stanislaus Joyce's "sadder supposition," a softening of the brain, is almost inescapable in Pound's as in Joyce's case, and one can only contemplate the spectacle with awe and compassion. But this stammering confusion is the characteristic of Pound's work that is now imitated by young poets who wish to be considered of his school. Of Pound's great qualities — his acute sense of musical cadence, his vivid imagery, his poetic vision and skill — these later poets show no trace. They mirror a great confusion and call it the modern style.

I must now turn to the visual arts, for the process of progressive disintegration is even more evident in painting and sculpture than in literature. Again we have a number of artists whose greatness cannot be questioned — at least, not by me. But their greatness lies in the past: either they are dead or they have reached an advanced age in which their work has become repetitive. The great creative period lasted from about 1905 to about 1955. In those fifty years all the major painters and sculptors of the modern movement had completed their characteristic work. I do not imply that the work done by artists such as Picasso, Miró or Henry Moore since 1955 is in any sense necessarily inferior to their earlier work: I am merely asserting that the peak of their creative achievement had been reached before mid-century and that what follows is an expansion or necessary development of their established styles.

The artists who have come to maturity since the end of the Second World War (1945) are desperately striving to escape from the influence of the masters of the modern movement, but the more original they try to be, the more they are compelled to deviate arbitrarily from the prototypes. There is no stylistic element in action-painting, in pop-art or in op-art, that was not present in some phase of cubism, dadaism, surrealism or expressionism. I must emphasize the word "stylistic," for it is easy to be original if one abandons the sensibility and discipline that constitute the essence of art. Art, in any meaningful sense of the word, must have three essential qualities: a formal correspondence to emotion or feeling, clarity (what that great contemporary critic Wilson Knight calls "a swift forward-flowing transparency"),[10] and a vital imagination, the struggle, as Coleridge defined it, "to idealize and to unify." The visual arts especially must exemplify this last quality, but it is the quality singularly lacking in the fragmented painting and sculpture of recent years.

Again we must discriminate. Kandinsky, who occupies in relation to modern painting an initiatory influence comparable to Joyce's in modern writing, has been grossly misunderstood. His principle that the work of art is an abstract expression of internal necessity has been applied without its corollary, which is, that what is necessary must also be significant to the spectator, must therefore be *composed* in a form that can be assimilated by the spectator. Kandinsky's final insistence is on composition — *melodic* composition and *symphonic*

10 In describing Swift's prose style: *Poets of Action*, London (Methuen), 1967, p. 164.

composition. Composition is defined as "an expression of a slowly formed inner feeling, tested and worked over repeatedly and almost pedantically," and he looks forward, in the final paragraph of his pioneer work, *Concerning the Spiritual in Art*, to "a time of reasoned and conscious composition, in which the painter will be proud to declare his work constructional — this in contrast to the claim of the impressionists that they could explain nothing, that their art came by inspiration."[11]

No convincing classification of the painting and sculpture that has proliferated in Western Europe, America and Japan since the end of the Second World War is possible. Terms such as abstract impressionism or abstract expressionism are not distinctive enough; terms such as "pop-art" or "op-art" are inexact and unhistorical. It is a confused situation in which one is conscious of new sources of imagery and content, and of an almost desperate attempt to be tough or ambiguous. An English critic whom I greatly respect, writing in 1964 of the "new generation" of British painters, uses these two words to explain the aesthetic aims and style of these artists, and defines toughness as "a desire to play it cool, be objective, unsentimental, detached and at the same time to pull no punches, be firm, decisive, hard." Ambiguity is defined as "a common enough element in all modern art, though not with the new value set on puns, puzzles, and double meanings. . . . The ambiguity goes beyond the sort of vision that anthropomorphized landscapes. It is not the metaphor that equates two known images, so much as a central uncertainty that leaves interpretation open. And beyond that, it suggests wit, or a puzzle, or a game, as the only terms on which interpretation can rest."[12]

The parallel with the later writings of Joyce and Beckett will be obvious. One of the artists in the exhibition which these remarks prefaced, Paul Huxley, is quoted as saying that "Paintings today should be about question-making, not story-telling ('it happened like this'), or recording ('I was there and it looked like this'). The sermon and the conducted tour have been dealt with and painting can only be enlightened by posing questions and making reconnaissance trips rather than by supplying answers. We become more wise by not knowing."

[11] *Concerning the Spiritual in Art*. New York (Wittenborn), 1947, p. 77.
[12] Catalogue of "The New Generation" Exhibition, Whitechapel Gallery, London, March-May, 1964, p. 8.

As a paradoxical, even a mystical saying, this is very interesting, but the alternatives implied — question-making or story-telling — evade the central issue in art, which is the creation of a form, the ability "to idealize and to unify." Clarity, which I suggested as another essential quality in the work of art, is deliberately sacrificed. Again it is not a question of upholding traditional values against revolutionary values: it is a question of communication, of a dialogue between artist and spectator. If instead of a symbol of feeling we are offered a symbol of nescience, of "not knowing," then we can only turn away in indifference.

In conclusion I return to my beginning, to Camus' plea for "mesure" or moderation, for the moderation created throughout history by rebellion. "Moderation, born of rebellion, can only live by rebellion." The artist, like any other citizen, must protest when political liberty is threatened or a censorship imposed on the freedom of thought. His moral behaviour is determined by the ancient precept: beauty is truth, truth beauty, though for "beauty" we might now substitute another concept, such as unity. Beauty is not necessarily the aim of the contemporary artist. But if he substitutes another principle, such as vitality, he must still accept this other necessity, which I have called unity. Contemporary nihilism in art is simply a denial of art itself, a rejection of its social function. The refusal to recognize the limits of art is the reason why as critics we must withhold our approval from all those manifestations of permissiveness characterized by incoherence, insensibility, brutality and ironic detachment. The exercise of such judgment calls for the utmost critical rectitude — for the maintenance of the supremacy of aesthetic criteria — if we are not to fall into old errors of judging art according to values that belong to another sphere of life — religious, moral, hedonistic or technological. What we seek is "a renaissance beyond the limits of nihilism." We cannot yet determine the outlines of such a renaissance, but we know that they must remain within the sphere of art.

BEN NICHOLSON: A TRIBUTE

HERBERT READ was one of those enlightened few whose creative spirit, whose gentleness and courage does not die and as I write I am very conscious of his thought and presence.

I met him first in the 30's and soon after this he came to live in The Mall, Belsize Park, nearly next door to Barbara Hepworth's and my studio. His immediate understanding of what Moore, Hepworth and I were working on was invaluable to us: among writers he and Geoffrey Grigson were the two who understood. His contribution as art-historian to the whole international art movement was also invaluable.

When during later years he was living in Yorkshire and I was living in Ticino our correspondence was lively and it was always a pleasure to see his handwriting and the clarity with which he wrote. Added to this was his annual visit to lecture at the Ascona "Eranos" cultural conference near here, and since he was always too much in demand there my wife, Felicitas Vogler, used to bring him up to our house where he could sleep or rest in a reclining chair in our quiet mountain garden overlooking Lago Maggiore.

Others can speak far better of his literary and philosophical contribution. But I can at least say that each year as he became older the expression in his face became more beautiful and the quality of his voice revealed more and more the depth of experience in his life. It had a special quality of great beauty which I can recall vividly at this moment and is a part of that enlightenment by which his spirit remains with us as something very much alive.

BEN NICHOLSON

Two Etchings and Two Drawings

I *Tweedledum & Tweedledee.* 1959.
Collection: Sarah and Alan Bowness.

II *Single Goblet.* Drawing. 1968.

III *Rafael.* 1967.

IV *Column, Tree, and Moon.* Etching. 1967.

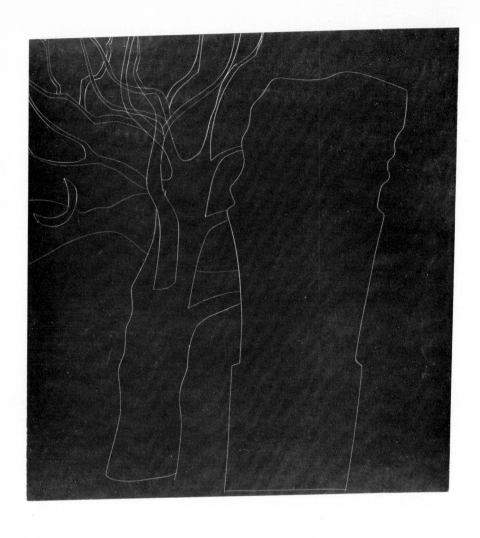

Sam Black

HERBERT READ: HIS CONTRIBUTION
TO ART EDUCATION AND
TO EDUCATION THROUGH ART

S IR HERBERT READ once recounted how he
found solace and inspiration in poetry while serving as an infantry
officer in the grim holocaust in Flanders in 1914-18. In those dark
days, when the Renaissance in Europe was ending in flames and
hatred, he found, through art, new hope for humanity not a mere
aid to temporary escape from his present and pressing anxieties and
their attendant doubts and fears. Some twenty years after World
War I when the second world war was emphatically underlining so
many of man's failures, hope was given to me by Sir Herbert Read's
Education Through Art. I carried, not poems in my knapsack, but
the inspiration of Sir Herbert Read's writing and his vision of a
better system of education for all — and his words sang as poetry
to me.

My bookmark was a portion of a German Iron Cross ribbon, a
souvenir picked up casually in a shattered, deserted gun emplace-
ment, somewhere along the torn, embattled coast of France. I have
it to this day. It was destined to have interesting significance for me
and a connection with Sir Herbert and his fundamental beliefs.

The ribbon had belonged to an enemy, nameless and separated
by the abyss of war, impersonal, unnatural and dehumanized by
propaganda. Not long after the war's end, 1951 to be exact, I par-
ticipated in the now famous U.N.E.S.C.O. Seminar on the visual
arts held in Bristol, England. Many former wartime enemies sat
down together, freely exchanging ideas and sharing a belief in the

57

value of the common language of art and the universal necessity for an Education through Art. So strong were the convictions of the seminar participants, at that assembly of nations, that they founded I.N.S.E.A. (The International Society for Education Through Art) and installed Sir Herbert Read as Honorary President.

Among the many lasting associations that were formed in Bristol, one person, who was to become an especially close friend, was the German representative — an artist and an art teacher, a man of humour, tolerance and understanding. Herbert Read's own words sum up the point of this anecdote: "Art is the name that we give to the only human activity that can establish a universal order in all we do and make, in thought and in imagination. Education through Art is education for peace."[1]

The aims of education have varied with the changing times, the needs and even the dictates of society. Circumstances have dictated specialties and man has imposed, sometimes accidentally but often deliberately, restrictions, limitations and retrograde diversions. The instinct for survival pressed man to cultivate self-development and acquire personal skills; later, as family and group mutuality increased the chances of survival, education was designed to strengthen this. The expansion of population and the growth of man's knowledge directed his efforts towards greater control and use of the powers and resources of nature, and an education to prepare and fit people for work, in large numbers, at the seemingly endless number of jobs being produced, as well as to mould them into useful, fairly uncomplaining citizens, grew to be the common practice.

Those were days of confidence. Educators, reflecting how pleased man was with himself and deluded into thinking they knew all there was to know, believed they could, simply by patient thorough teaching, impart, or by impatient and no less thorough strappings or canings, instil an adequate education in all for all life's needs.

Now we are not so sure. Thirty or forty years ago smug and satisfied physicists might have rejoiced in the comfort and completeness of their knowledge, but nuclear science has changed all that. In recent years developments in medicine, chemistry, electronics and communications have been phenomenal. The magnitude of the discoveries only serves to underline the paucity of our knowledge. We are beginning to realize that there is no such thing as the "last

[1] Sir Herbert Read, *The Redemption of the Robot*, 1966, p. 254.

58

word," at least as far as learning is concerned. The mechanical inventions of the Industrial Revolution, which provided more work, and gradually affected the behaviour and habits of man, also led him slowly towards an awareness of the impermanence of life's forms and to an acceptance of change. Today — and day after day, change is upon us. This time it is rapid, spreading, escalating change and man is powerless to stop, or even briefly halt, what is happening. The immense cybernetic developments, which provide more leisure than work; the promising yet fearful medical discoveries that assure longer life, as well as the swelling material progress and growth will go on proliferating and multiplying at increasing rates. The light winds of change issuing from the great knowledge explosion, which are already affecting society and our environment, steadily and inexorably will become like a powerful hurricane that could engulf and destroy or clear the way for an unprecedented richer age and vital creative life for mankind.

The rapid pace of developments sets up uncertainties in the minds of men and the magnitude of their possibilities, though felt by some, and sensed by many, are only comprehended by a few. Indeed even those involved most directly in affecting change, the scientists, are beginning to admit their uncertainties and are unable to give a sure answer about what is going to happen. Marshall McLuhan in *Understanding Media* states: "I think of Art, at its most significant, as a DEW line, a Distant Early Warning system that can always be relied on to tell the old culture what is beginning to happen to it."

Our technological civilization has come to stay and the urgent task before society is to prevent its own engulfment and self-destruction through lack of any controlling vision. Herbert Read believed that the traditional systems of education, with their emphasis on knowing and memory are disintegrative and productive of the present disordered state of civilization: "In our exclusive preoccupation with knowledge and science we have omitted to educate those human faculties which are concerned with the emotional and integrative aspects of human life. We have carefully nurtured inhuman monsters with certain organs of the intelligence gigantically enlarged, others completely atrophied."[2] He goes on to say that an Education through Art is the key to a true, balanced, integrative education that would produce individual serenity and social harmony. "The

[2] Sir Herbert Read, *The Grass Roots of Art* (London, 1955).

foundations of a civilization rest not in the mind but in the senses, and, unless we can use the senses, educate the senses, we shall never have the biological conditions for human survival, let alone human progress."[3]

Herbert Read clearly foresaw man's increasing dilemma — a scientific superman who, in spite of all his achievements and advances remains biologically and emotionally a poor simple primitive. There has been little evidence of change in his basic nature since the first recorded knowledge of him, and the Arts have but served as the surface trappings on the shallow veneer called civilization.

Twenty-five and more years ago Herbert Read was a prophet and far in advance of his time. Today his thoughts and vision are still ahead of these times and his message is even more important and more urgent because events and directions, barely guessed twenty-five years ago are bringing about a new and very different technological civilization whose existence can only be constructive and beneficial if rooted in an Education through Art, as Herbert Read has defined it — an education which gives predominant attention to the creative, poetic and aesthetic and which values perception, imagination and feeling — one aimed at "the progressive perfection of man as an individual," which will help him to help himself become progressively more human. To suggest the overthrow of the current system of education with its basis on memory training and the almost exclusive verbalization of experience and replace it with an aesthetic education in which the arts become the core and growing point for human development — is surely a revolutionary policy and is indeed advocating basic change in the very structure of society itself.

"Docility, apathy, insensibility — these are the achievements of education in our time, and they are achieved by the suppression of individuality, sensitivity, creativity. Social conformity or convention demands a general frustration of personal instincts, the surrender to herd instincts, which then carry the individual in the ebb and flow of their aggressive attitudes. For when the individual has been deprived of his creative functions, he is ready to take part in collective destruction. And then, if he can't have the real thing, which is war, he will indulge in fantasies of cruelty and murder, mass produced for one and all." These words of Herbert Read's are both a fearful

3 Sir Herbert Read, *The Grass Roots of Art* (London, 1955).

60

accusation and damning denunciation of a system by which society teaches, trains and influences its youth.

To suggest that education should be based on aesthetic theory, not on economic and political matters and expediency, may indeed be a new and revolutionary idea in the light of current educational practice, yet it is as old as Plato whose theories of aesthetic and moral education greatly influenced Herbert Read. Herbert Read's belief that education should be based on a training of the senses, human personality being largely formed by the aesthetic experiences of early childhood and adolescence, aesthetic experience being a vital and essential part of the fabric of life rather than a minor, even indispensable fringe, is drawn from Plato's theory of education. The popular reaction to the word "revolution" is to think of violence and negative behaviour. Herbert Read may use the word but would replace it with the word "Education" and would endeavour to effect change in society biologically rather than politically — on this point he has written: "it is only in so far as we can liberate the growing shoots of mankind, shoots not yet stunted by an environment of hatred and injustice, that we can expect to make any enduring change in society."[4]

Sir Herbert Read's influence on Education and Education through Art has produced no explosive, instant revolution. This however is no cause for dismay because a great deal has been happening quietly and unobtrusively. Other great thinkers have supported Herbert Read's views on the limitations of an education based on the verbalization of experience and discursive reasoning alone. Aldous Huxley speaks of the individual being, "the victim of the linguistic tradition," and Suzanne Langer adds, "Everybody knows that language is a very poor medium for expressing our emotional nature." An effective education must educate the whole man, not merely the conscious part of his mind. Similarly, as Herbert Read himself readily admitted, the visual arts cannot constitute the whole of education. In his inspiring address to the 1951 U.N.E.S.C.O. Seminar, Herbert Read said: "Education is the fostering of growth, but apart from physical maturation, growth is only made apparent in expression — audible or visual signs and symbols. Education may therefore be defined as the cultivation of modes of symbolic communication — it is teaching children and adults how to express themselves

4 Sir Herbert Read, *Anarchism, Past and Future*, Freedom Press (London, May 17, 1947), p. 6.

in sound, images, movements, tools and utensils. A man who can make such things well is a well educated man. If he can make good sounds, he is a good speaker, a good musician, a good poet; if he can make good images, he is a good painter or sculptor; if good movements, a good dancer or labourer; if good tools or utensils, a good craftsman. All faculties —of thought, logic, memory, sensibility and intellect — are eventually involved in such processes, and no aspect of education is excluded in such processes. And they are all processes of art, for art is nothing but the good making of sounds, images, etc. The aim of education is, therefore, the creation of artists — of people efficient in the various modes of expression and communication."

Herbert Read's theories have been, and are, far more widespread and his vision more influential in education, or perhaps in society, than many will understand or most may care to admit. Throughout the world art educators and teachers supporting Read's beliefs have steadily influenced growing youth over almost three decades, and have done so in spite of handicaps imposed by pseudo-art teachers whose aim has been the production of sentimental trash and trivial novelty. Insecure and insincere, their product-oriented teaching is revealed in their desire for "showy" results. Long ago, before current trends, the artist-teachers of the world demonstrated belief in the individualization of the educational process and experience and encouraged learning by discovery through personal involvement and activity. Art rooms long ago were the havens in schools where young people could associate with older mature, creative personalities who saw education not merely as a method of giving out knowledge, but rather a way of helping youth to realize and use what they already knew and so expand their individual capabilities. Art teachers believed with Read that young growing people learn not so much by cold, formal logic as by an education of the senses and a "creative communion with sounds and colours, textures and consistencies, a communion with nature in all its substantial variety."[5]

Art educators have deplored the lack of support or understanding demonstrated by those in authority who through the exercise of administrative power have controlled their destiny and relegated them, so often, to a second class position, and the public generally, who at best have paid lip-service to the "fringe" subjects, indicating

[5] Sir Herbert Read, *The Grass Roots of Art* (London, 1955), p. 156.

their true beliefs, however, by insisting on a job training education. But after all the countless, patient years during which Art Educators have been teaching, speaking and demonstrating their convictions and have been supported by the strength, scholarship and sensitivity of Herbert Read a great and, I believe, an irrevocable change is clearly under way. Society is now beginning to suspect that it, or its predecessors, perhaps chose the wrong kind of educational direction — at least it is very evident that the educational methods widely practiced are not adequate for the present changing times or the needs and aspirations of the new and stirring growing generation.

It would be a gross exaggeration to claim that the surging global movement for change, spearheaded by youth, can be attributed to the teachings of Herbert Read, although I am convinced that his theories and persuasion have indeed had global effect.

The multitudes striving to break down the barriers of alienation of self, alienation from others, alienation from nature and who seriously question the worth of an education which fragments experience, dulls sensibilities, cultivates distrust and scorns intuition and feeling may never have heard of Herbert Read, but that alone does not deny his possible widespread and quietly subtle influence. The young reformers would I'm sure subscribe to Herbert Read's belief that; "man, by his very nature and of his own accord strives toward self-realization . . . and cannot . . . develop his full human potentialities unless he is truthful to himself; unless he is active and productive; unless he relates himself to others, in a spirit of mutuality." And many would accept Read's list of aims of aesthetic education: "to preserve the natural intensity of all modes of perception and sensation; to co-ordinate the various modes of perception and sensation with one another and in relation to environment; to express feeling in communicable form." Based on this development of sensibility Read sees the final aim to be "to teach children how to express thought in required form," not however in the exact sense that this may be interpreted in relation to present practice. Read means (and his own words make his intention clear): "Education in constructive crafts, a practical craft like engineering, a conceptual craft like logic . . . however, constructive education only makes sense if it is firmly based on . . . visual, plastic, musical, kinetic, verbal and symbolic education."

The decay of civilization and the decomposition of human values in a world where materialism rules, where work becomes a relieving escape, and where playing a role is more profitable than personal integrity is seen and sensed by young people and they don't like what they see, and more than that they are saying so and endeavouring to practice a mode of living opposed to false values and of more human concern. Professor J. R. Seeley of the centre for the study of Democratic Institutions, Santa Barbara, California, writes: "They are everywhere, the drop-outs, disaffiliates and true and honorable rebels. For those who love facts I have it on reliable authority that for the first time in the history of the United States, the average I.Q., if you like to deal in such terms, of the dropouts is above the average I.Q. of the graduating classes. Their hero is the sage, not the master of anything. Their heaven is the 'high' . . . like everything else, passing . . . but, while lasting, and whether procured by drugs, contemplation, fatigue, music or discipline, that state in which the experience that is unitive of the self, unitive of the other selves, unitive to nature, and unitive to an All, is had. Their mode is childlike . . . not childish . . . renewedly capable of total absorption in the instant experience free of over-calculation, sensorily aware, experientially open and vulnerable, rapt, accepting, surrender-capable, and in grace and trust. They play, but they are not caught up in, or seek to disentangle themselves from games. They seek their 'thing,' each their 'thing,' and occasion and liberty to do it. Most delightedly so if it furthers the doing by others of their 'things.' They go gentle in the world, hoping that if they cannot be good, they may at least be harmless. And aimed at the conventional culture, hold no one as evil, believing that, good or bad, one should be effective. They make life move into theatre and theatre move into life. They would be and let be, trusting rather to the force of example than the force of persuasion or the persuasion of force, to win others into another way of life. They seek the honest, the authentic, the immediate. Getting the shit out of your head (as they say) is both the first and the never-ending task. They are present-oriented and discount, perhaps over-discount, past and future, though that is beginning rapidly to change also. They may well be the contemporary analogue of the little ragged band of eleven confused fishermen and others somewhere in Galilee, 2,000 years ago."[6]

The revolution is upon us; change is now a way of life. In man's

6 Professor J. R. Seeley, *The Person in the Process, Beyond Tinkering & Toying*, March 30, 1968.

search for reality and life-style values art and education are finding their roots once more in the lives of men, everywhere. A growing concern for the common humanity of all men is leading educators to discover why and how man everywhere, and from the beginning of recorded time, has made life meaningful through art — that art, by helping him to live more fully, more humanely, to see and feel more keenly helped him to know and understand himself and others better.

Herbert Read's words sum up succinctly the integrative qualities of art.

"I cannot regard art as something external which has to be imported into the sphere of education. Nor can I regard education as something which has an existence separate from art. In my view art is nothing less than a way of life. And since it is a way of life it must also be a way of education, for education is merely a prelude to life, the opening of the way, the pioneering and the pathfinding activity upon which we must all engage, individually and collectively."

As more and more men come to realize that Herbert Read, by an Education through Art, did not mean acquiring a narrow, specialized skill or set of skills, but believed that the most important art of any people is that which they create for themselves, through living their own lives, fully and creatively, here and now, both in and out of school, then perhaps we shall be able to claim that an Education through Art is an education for peace. And my threadbare Iron Cross ribbon will be but a reminder that the twentieth century by its present revolution is profoundly different from all previous centuries — not by reason of wars or vast and complicated technological inventions and achievements but by man's simple realization and expansion of his own powers, his greater knowledge and discovery of himself and the assertion and enjoyment of his humanness.

STEPHEN SPENDER

Four Sketches for Herbert Read

INNOCENCE

Farm house, green field. Stone
White in grey eyes.
The innocent gaze
Simplifies forms
To rectangle, circle.
The sun in the skull
Dissolves a world to light.

YOUNG OFFICER

Young officer, leaning
Against a bayonet hedge
Of blackthorn, its white
Blossom, your medals.
Your soldiers graze
Like sheep. You are their shepherd.
Mournful bugles
Engraved those lines
Either side your mouth.

CONFERENCIER

I took a pencil up
Idly at some conference,
Drew the lick of hair
Surround to your face,
The bow tie beneath
Made a question mark's dot.
In the hall of chairs
Fat platitudes sat.
You stood out like a question.

ANARCHIST

When you died, I was in France.
Supposing you were sad,
Listen. I saw the students
Tread the streets in dance.
Their heels struck fire.
Their hands uprooted pavements.
Their mouths sang the chant
Of a poet's final hour:
Imagination seizes power.

George Woodcock

THE PHILOSOPHER OF FREEDOM

"I HAVE NEVER BEEN an active politician, merely a sympathizing intellectual," said Herbert Read in 1940, and the statement is generally true of his whole career as a social and political philosopher. Yet I do not think the title "philosophic anarchist," which has so often been applied to him, is really justified. It suggests the detached thinker who conceives an ideal ungoverned commonwealth, but does not concern himself with the means by which that society might come into being. Read, as I shall show, was deeply concerned with the means by which, through art and education, men could be made receptive to the great political and social changes needed to create a libertarian world. He was also, on occasion, willing to take other action. But he certainly did not become involved in the day-to-day business of politics — even anarchist politics. This was mainly because he held strongly the anarchist idea that the struggle for freedom must be initiated by the worker within his own occupational group, and Read's vocation was that of poet and critic of art and literature. He believed the freedom of the arts was linked intimately with general freedom; he believed also that the artist had a function as mediator between the individual and society; these were the paths he mainly followed when he approached political terms. To stand as a representative of the workers, or even a preacher to them, would have seemed to him presumptuous. "Intellectuals writing for proletarians will not do," he wrote to me in 1949. "It is merely another form of la trahaison des clercs."

I knew Read for the last quarter of a century of his life, and during the 1940's, until I came to Canada at the end of the decade, I saw him often. As a publisher he brought out two of my books, one of verse and the other a biography of the anarchist Pierre-Joseph Proudhon. That combination marked the areas of our common interests in those days — literature and anarchism; not until a decade later did I also begin to write on the visual arts. But it was anarchism rather than literature that first brought us together, and, when I look over the letters Read wrote to me, I realize that it remained the subject we discussed more than any other until our last contact late in 1966. During the 1940's I observed directly the voluntary limitations of Read's engagement in anarchism, and his inclination to remain aloof, even among anarchists, from anything that resembled political organization. He did not aspire to be a leader. "Power corrupts even the intellect," he once said. But he had no intention, either, of being caught in the net of group orthodoxy.

I first met Read in 1942. I was then publishing in Cambridge a little magazine, *Now*, and, having come through pacifism to what still seems to me its logical end of non-violent anarchism, I asked Read for a contribution. He sent me "The Paradox of Anarchism," and a few weeks later he came to Cambridge. We met in a chintzy café on King's Parade, Read in the black pork-pie hat and bow-tie which in those years were almost a customary uniform, and I remember my slight bewilderment when I talked to him of the anarchist group which then ran Freedom Press and published *War Commentary*, and he replied vaguely. I thought then that he was an initiate being politic with a stranger; within a couple of months, when I myself had made contact with the movement in London, and became active in it, I realized that his vagueness was, on the contrary, due to his own very loose connection with the militants.

At that time the militant anarchists in Britain had a double organization. The Freedom Press group was a circle of intellectuals, some of them personal friends of Read, who operated openly and were concerned mainly with publication. It was part of a larger, secret organization, The Anarchist Federation of Great Britain, which balanced the grandiosity of its title by the thinness of its ranks. I was admitted to both groups, but Read did not belong to either, partly from his own choice, but partly also because, like Kropotkin before him, he supported Britain's participation in World War II, which the other British anarchists, except for a small Jewish group in the East End of London, opposed.

In 1943 or 1944 — I cannot now remember the exact date — the Anarchist Federation decided to come into the open, and, with the pressure of secrecy removed, immediately broke apart, the anarcho-syndicalist faction (which included a few real workers) retaining the title, a hollow victory, since the intellectuals retained the printing press, the stocks of literature, the paper license (vital in wartime) and the Freedom Press bookshop. A new organization of "pure" anarchists led by the intellectuals was formed in 1945, with a London Group and a Federation of Anarchist Groups, and Read took a close interest in the developments. He attended at least one of the organizational meetings, and in August he wrote me from a summer villa at Braemar ("a Victorian house with all its period equipment — amusing but exhausting, a relic of the slave age") "I am glad to hear that the London Group is taking shape. I would like to see a copy of the programme." I think he hoped it would be a true guild of anarchist intellectuals, which he could have joined, but the old pseudo-proletarian line prevailed, and he held aloof, as did Alex Comfort. I joined for a while, and withdrew in 1948; my reasons, discussed elsewhere, have no place in this essay.

If Read evaded involvement, he did not avoid action. As he wrote in one of his poems of this period:

> But even as you wait
> like Arjuna in his chariot
> the ancient wisdom whispers:
> Live in action.

He wrote pamphlets to be published by Freedom Press (*The Philosophy of Anarchism* and *Marxism, Existentialism and Anarchism*); he wrote occasionally for *Freedom*, the propagandist sheet that followed *War Commentary*, and more often for *Now*; he spoke at meetings commemorating the Spanish Civil War. When four members of the Freedom Press group were arrested in 1945 on charges under a wartime press law, he spent a great deal of time and energy in their defence. I remember drafting with him a letter which we persuaded a group of writers to sign, denouncing the arbitrariness of the government's action. Spender, Eliot and Forster were among them. Spender was censured by the Foreign Office, for which he was then working, and refused to sign any more protests. Forster insisted on altering a few words in the letter after Eliot had signed it. Eliot was angry that we had allowed Forster to change anything he had signed, but stood by the protest, a fact which I am always happy to quote against those who describe him as a reactionary. Read also became chairman of the committee which was set up to

18th April,1945

Dear Mr Russell,

          Thank you very much for your
letter of the 15th. I enclose a copy of "War
Commentray", the anarchist periodical, which
gives a detailed account of the police court
proceedings of March 9th when the four anarchists were charged, and details of the charges
brought against them. I also attach a copy of
the Circular Letter on which the prosecution
xxxx is apparently to be mainly based.

          From these documents I hope you will con-
clude that this is an outrageous interference
by the political police with the ordinary
rights of freedom of expression, and that you
will have no hesitation in allowing your name
to appear as a sponsor to our appeal. Personall
ly I hope you may be prepared to go even
farther. I remember the sympathetic account
which you gave of anarchism in "Roads to Freedom", and if you still feel as you did then,
you might be inclined to appear as a witness
when the case is tried at the Old Bailey next
week, before Mr Justice Birkett. The Attorney
General is prosecuting:our Counsel is Mr Maude
K.C.

          If you have the inclination and the time to
do this for us, I will at once ask Counsel to
communicate with you. What we should ask you
to establish is the philosophical integrity of
the views we anarchists hold, and our right to
propagate them freely.

                    Yours sincerely,

HERBERT READ: File carbon copy of letter to Bertrand Russell.
Collection: McPherson Library of the University of Victoria.

conduct the defence of the four anarchists, made speeches, wrote articles, raised money.

Later this committee was continued as a semi-permanent organization, the Freedom Defence Committee, to take up the cases of people arrested under the more oppressive wartime regulations, and to protest against police violations of civil rights. Read remained its chairman until the committee came to an end in 1949. Orwell was vice-chairman, Julian Symons a member of the working committee, and I the secretary. Read and Orwell, libertarians of different shades who shared the inability to live happily with organized political groups, were closer than their differing life styles and ways of writing might suggest. "His personality, which remains so vivid after all these years, often rises like some ghost to admonish me," Read wrote to me of Orwell in 1966. "I suppose I have felt nearer to him than to any other English writer of our time, and though there were some aspects of his character that irritated me — his proletarian pose in dress, &c., his insensibility to his physical environment, his comparatively narrow range of interests — yet who was, in general, nearer in ideals & even in eccentricities?"

To me, when I met Read in 1942, anarchism was new and dazzling. To Read, who held it as almost a life-time faith, it was already a familiar doctrine to which he had been converted in his own youth almost thirty years before. "Actually," he tells us in *The Contrary Experience*, "there was an unfailing continuity in my political interests and political opinions. I would not like to claim that they show an unfailing consistency, but the general principles which I found congenial as a young man are the basic principles of the only political philosophy I still find congenial."

The continuity was not quite as unbroken as Read suggests, for as a teenage bank clerk he followed the traditions of his class of Yorkshire farmers by becoming a fanatical Tory: "I worshipped my King with a blind emotional devotion, and even managed to make a hero out of Lord Salisbury." He also read all of Disraeli's novels, and these — with their doctrine of the two nations—appear to have disturbed rather than confirmed his conservatism, for as soon as he entered Leeds University, he began to read socialist writings, discovered Nietzsche and Sorel, and remained true to his ancestry by finding the opposing pole of peasant politics to Toryism — anarchism.

72

In spite of my intellectual pretensions, I am by birth and tradition a peasant. I remain essentially a peasant. I despise this foul industrial epoch — not only the plutocracy which it has raised to power, but also the industrial proletariat which it has drained from the land and proliferated in hovels of indifferent brick. The class in the community for which I feel a natural sympathy is the agricultural class, including the genuine remnants of a landed aristocracy. This perhaps explains my early attraction to Bakunin, Kropotkin and Tolstoy, who were also of the land, aristocrats and peasants.   (*Poetry and Anarchism*)

"Proudhon, Tolstoy and Kropotkin were the predilections of my youth," Read remarks elsewhere; add William Morris, Edward Carpenter and Sorel, and one has the central political influences over Read in the years of his early twenties after the Tory enthusiasm passed. Add Nietzsche on the individualist periphery, and Marx on the collectivist, and the pattern of shaping influences is complete. It was a pattern not unusual at the time among the literary young; Joyce in Dublin and Kafka in Prague were studying roughly the same writers at the same period. But Read remained permanently and profoundly under their influence; the others did not.

In his early thoughts, Marxist and Anarchist attitudes were intermingled, and he still believed — as he did not in later years — that nationalization of the means of production might be the prelude to the dissolution of the state. In a note written in 1914, and quoted in *The Contrary Experience*, he says:

... For the present, both Collectivism and Syndicalism have their respective duties. The role of Collectivism is the expropriation of Capital. This is to be brought about by the nationalization of industry. But Collectivists are wrong in regarding nationalization as an end in itself: it is only a means. For whilst the Collectivist state is evolving, Syndicalism will be playing its role — i.e. it will be developing the economic, industrial and educational functions of the Trade Unions. Trade Unions are, I am convinced, the units upon which the future society will be built. They must be organized and extended so as to be powerful enough to demand, and fit enough to undertake, the control of industry when it has been nationalized by the state. . . . By a devolution of power, a decentralization of control, and, above all, by a development in the social conscience of the nation, the ideals of today will become the realities of tomorrow.

Read was always to respect the doctrines of anarcho-syndicalism, and to regard the natural organization of society as one based on workers' control of industry; it was his trust in the state as a mechanism for achieving any social good that rapidly dissolved under the impact of his wartime experiences.

Read had been — as most socialists and anarchists were in 1914 — a theoretical pacifist, but at the same time he was a member of the O.T.C. at Leeds University. When he found himself thrust incontinently into the war, and realized that the international working class was unprepared to halt the militarists by a universal general strike, he made the Nietzschean best of a bad job, and set out to meet what he saw as a challenge. As late as May 1917, when he had reached the front but had not yet experienced war's full horrors, he could still write to a woman friend in England:

... I've no doubt about my position. If I were free today, I'm almost sure I should be compelled by every impulse within me to join this adventure. For I regard it as an adventure, and it is as an adventure that it appeals to me. I'll fight for Socialism when the day comes, and fight all the better for being an 'old soldier'. (*The Contrary Experience*)

Eight months later he had again become a pacifist, and this time with the conviction of experience. He remarked that "the means of war had become more portentous than the aim" and that among the soldiers there had been "an immense growth of pacifist opinion." And during 1917 and 1918, while he was writing articles for the *New Age* supporting both Syndicalism and Guild Socialism (variants of the doctrine of the control of production by producers) he was experiencing a cumulative revulsion against static social orders and the state in particular. In January 1917, he wrote to the same friend:

I've a theory that all the evil things in the world are static, passive and possessive; and that all good things are dynamic, creative. Life is dynamic: death is static. And as life is dynamic, passive remedies of society are false. Hence the folly of having cut and dried Utopias as ultimate aims: by the time you get to them, life has left them behind. Hence the folly of basing society on possessive institutions (such as property and marriage, as a rule). Our institutions should appeal to our creative impulses: what a man *does* and not what he *has*.

In April 1918:

I don't think I'm ready to discuss the change that is taking place in my 'political sentiment'. It is a revolt of the individual against the association which involves him in activities which do not interest him: a jumping to the ultimate anarchy which I have always seen as the ideal of all who value beauty and intensity of life. 'A beautiful anarchy' — that is my cry.

74

In May 1918:

But simply because we are united with a callous inhuman association called a State and because a State is ruled by politicians whose aim (and under the circumstances their duty) is to support the life and sovereignty of this monster, life and hope are denied and sacrificed.

In a positive as well as a negative way, Read's anarchist tendencies were intensified during the war, for he found — like Orwell during the Spanish Civil War — a comradeship in the trenches of a kind he had never before known, "a feeling of unanimity aroused by common stresses, common dangers," and so, in this unlikely setting, his convictions of the validity of the anarchist doctrine of mutual aid seemed justified.

Looking back in 1962 over the period after 1918, Read felt that "the no-man's-years between the wars" had been "largely futile, spent unprofitably by me and my kind," largely, he felt, because of forces outside their power to change — "blind forces of economic drift and political ineptitude with the walls of faith and reason turning to air behind us." At the same time, he adds that "in spite of a disillusion at once personal and universal, I persisted in a simple faith in the natural goodness of man," and it was towards the end of the inter-war period that he began to develop his theories of the inter-relationship of art and anarchism, and to write the series of essays and books that contain his socio-political arguments.

From 1919 to 1931 were in these respects years of enforced silence. There are points in Read's career when he surprises the observer — as he surprised many of his friends — by acting with an inconsistency that seems to exceed even the licence to impulsiveness which he allowed himself as a proclaimed romantic. A pacifist, he fought in World War I. After declaring in *Poetry and Anarchism* (1938) that "anarchism naturally implies pacifism," he came out in 1939 in support of Britain's participation in World War II. In 1953 he bent the knee to receive a knighthood, and set off an international storm among anarchists in which — so far as I remember — Augustus John and I were alone among his comrades in defending the right of a libertarian to make his own choices — even in his relations with the state. 1919 was another such time; after considering such strange careers for a professed anarchist as a permanent commission in the army and professional politics, Read finally elected for the Civil Service, in which he felt he would have more time and energy to devote to literature. He served for several years in the

Treasury, where he acquired a lifelong loathing for bureaucrats, and then moved to the Victoria and Albert Museum, where he gathered the knowledge on which he was to base his career as an art critic. In 1931 he was liberated when the University of Edinburgh offered him its Professorship of Fine Arts. For twelve years the rules of the Civil Service had prevented him from publishing anything expressing his political views, and even when he was set free, it was some years before, in 1938, he expounded his complete libertarian views in *Poetry and Anarchism*.

In the meantime, however, *The Green Child* (1935) was written with at least an oblique political intent. Read tells us that in this novel he "described symbolically" how "the realization of a rational blue-print leads to the death of a society." And if we look at *The Green Child* we see this process happening on two levels.

Olivero, the hero, became the ruler of Roncador, a mountainbound South American Republic — a minute, self-supporting, agrarian land. After establishing a democratic constitution based on the best theories of the Enlightenment, he discovers that the simple people of Roncador are willing to accept the good government he gives them, and he finds himself — with no effort of his own — established as a kind of philosopher-king, able to apply the "sense of order" which he regards as "the principle of government as well as of art." He constructs a self-contained world in which his people enjoy sufficiency, security and freedom from oppression. But it is almost an axiom of Read's political doctrines that the only healthy political order is a natural order, sustained by tensions between the individual and society. Olivero's imposed order merely produces stagnation:

In the absence of conflicts, of contending interests, of anguish and agitation, I had introduced into my environment a moral flaccidity, a fatness of living, an ease and a torpor which had now produced in me an inevitable ferment.

Olivero arranges his own fake assassination, to free Roncador from his good-intentioned but deadly rationalism, but he does not free himself; instead he enters the underground world of the green people, who have lost sense of time and space, who regard living flesh and the life-breath with disgust, and whose vision is bounded by the contemplation of crystalline forms and the mathematical structures of music, in preparation for death, when the green people themselves are turned into rational shapes of crystals in a world

76

growing even more narrow because of the encroaching multitude of the petrified dead who fill its caves. It is a narrative told in deceptively attractive prose; it must nevertheless be read, the author makes clear, as a minatory parable as well as a poetic fantasy.

The hopes generated by the Russian Revolution died hard and slowly during the 1930's even among many who were in no way orthodox Marxists.

From 1917 onwards and for as long as I could preserve the illusion [Read confesses in *Poetry and Anarchism*] communism as established in Russia seemed to promise the social liberty of my ideals. So long as Lenin and Stalin promised a definitive 'withering away of the State', I was prepared to stifle my doubts and prolong my faith. But when, five, ten, fifteen, and then twenty years passed, with the liberty of the individual receding at every stage, a break became inevitable.

The suicide in 1930 of the poet Mayakovsky, hounded by the Stalinist bureaucrats, began to stir Read's doubts, and in the Introduction to *Surrealism* (1936) he complained that "even Communism, the creed of liberty and fraternity, has made the exigencies of a transitional epoch the excuse for an unnecessary and stupid form of aesthetic intolerance." Two more or less simultaneous events in 1936 left Read with the conviction that he had no alternative but to break openly with Marxist communism and declare just as openly for anarchism. These were the Moscow Trials, and the outbreak of the Civil War in Spain, where anarchism emerged from the shadows Marxist had cast over it and attempted, in a land at conflict, to lay the foundations of a libertarian society.

Read wrote for *Spain and the World*, the anarchist paper of the time, addressed meetings, and wrote two of the best poems about the civil war, the compassionate and angry "Bombing Casualties in Spain" and "Song for the Spanish Anarchists," in which is condensed his whole vision of the organic strength of a free and natural society where the individual is defined by what he *does*, and where men *have* in common.

> The golden lemon is not made
>   but grows on a green tree:
> A strong man and his crystal eyes
>   is a man born free.
>
> The oxen pass under the yoke
>   and the blind are led at will:

But a man born free has a path of his own
and a house on the hill.

And men are men who till the land
and women are women who weave:
Fifty men own the lemon grove
and no man is a slave.

Read's socio-political writings, with minor exceptions, appeared between 1938 and 1954, and the most important had seen first publication by the end of 1943; one can perhaps fairly assume that Read's impulse to write on anarchism began to fail as the sense of glory associated with the early days of the Spanish civil war faded in his mind. There is a great deal of confusion in the publication history of these writings because of the various combinations in which Read issued and re-issued them. *Poetry and Anarchism* (1938), *The Philosophy of Anarchism* (1940), and *Existentialism, Marxism and Anarchism* (1950) all appeared first as separate volumes, or at least pamphlets, while "The Paradox of Anarchism," printed first in *Now* (1942) was later collected in *A Coat of Many Colours* (1945). All these eventually came together, with a new introductory essay, "Revolution and Reason," in *Anarchy and Order* (1954). "Chains of Freedom" appeared first in *Now* (1947), in an expanded version in *Existentialism, Marxism and Anarchism*, and in an even more expanded version in *Anarchy and Order*. *To Hell with Culture* appeared separately as a small pamphlet in 1941, and in 1943 was included as a chapter in *The Politics of the Unpolitical*, but a new volume in 1963, comprising most of *The Politics of the Unpolitical*, plus a few essays mainly concerning problems of the arts, was entitled *To Hell with Culture*. As I go on to discuss the leading themes of Read's socio-political philosophy, I shall do my best to avoid confusion by giving each book or pamphlet the title under which it was originally published.

The opening lines of "Song for the Spanish Anarchists" contain the image which most concisely expresses Read's view of the nature of a free society:

The golden lemon is not made
but grows on a green tree . . .

The free society cannot be developed according to a plan; it must grow according to nature; it is not Utopian, but organic.

The laws that govern its development may be according to reason, but they are not in the narrow sense rational, and perhaps it is from this distinction that one can begin the examination of Read's attitudes towards society and its political development. He calls himself a materialist; he declares that we must "admit the universalism of truth and submit our life to the rule of reason." The life of the reason he sees as "a practical ideal, extending to wider and wider circles of humanity, and promising an earthly paradise never to be attained only because each stage towards its realization creates its superior level." (*The Politics of the Unpolitical*) But he says also that reason is much more than rationality or mechanistic logic.

Reason should rather connote the widest evidence of the senses, and of all processes and instincts developed in the long history of man. It is the sum total of awareness, ordained and ordered to some specific end or object of attention.　　　　　(*Reason and Romanticism*)

In Read's view, a society that tried to exist on a purely rational basis "would probably die of a kind of communal accidie." We are involved inevitably in "certain intangible and imponderable elements which we call emotion and instinct," and while himself adhering to no religion, Read grants that "a religion is a necessary element in any organic society" and that a new religion might even develop out of anarchism. (*The Philosophy of Anarchism*) For "if ... religion is the life of contemplation, the fruit of pure meditation, spiritual joy, then it cannot help but prosper in a society free from poverty, pride and envy." (*Poetry and Anarchism*)

Freedom and anarchism are synonymous, but anarchism is not nihilism, and freedom is not license. It is, on the contrary, Read insists, part of natural law, and intimately linked with the phenomenon of evolution. "Freedom is not an essence only available to the sensibility of men; it is germinatively at work in all living beings as spontaneity and autoplasticity." (*Anarchy and Order*) But just as society gains life from its dialectical opposition to the individual, so freedom is made real by its dialectical opposition to existence.

And so with the individual and the community: complete freedom means inevitable decadence. The mind must feel an opposition — must be tamped with hard realities if it is to have any blasting power.
　　　　　(*Politics of the Unpolitical*)

Thus Max Stirner's egoism is rejected by Read in favour of the libertarianism of Kropotkin.

79

In all that concerns the planning of economic life, the building up of a rational mode of living in a social community, there can be no question of absolute liberty. For, so long as we live in a community, in all practical affairs the greatest good of the greatest number is also the greatest good of the individual.   (*Poetry and Anarchism*)

The "duty to create a world of freedom" is far removed from the "freedom to do as you like," which is the characteristic excuse of the capitalist and the imperialist. In opposition to such anti-social concepts of freedom Read is even willing to use that word shunned by most anarchists — *government* — though he quickly makes clear that he means some form of control quite different from the processes of the State we know.

Government — that is to say, control of the individual in the interests of the community, is inevitable if two or more men combine for a common purpose; government is the embodiment of that purpose. But government in this sense is far removed from the conception of an autonomous state.   (*Poetry and Anarchism*)

In choosing his political forms, Read rejects both authoritarianism (including Communist as well as fascist totalitarianism) and democracy as history has known it. A single passage of dismissal is enough to express his rejection of the authoritarians.

The authoritarian believes in discipline as a means; the libertarian in discipline as an end, as a state of mind. The authoritarian issues instructions; the libertarian encourages self-education. The one tolerates a subjective anarchy below the smooth surface of his rule; the other has no need of rule because he has achieved a subjective harmony reflected in personal integrity and social unity.   (*Anarchy and Order*)

There is of course no essential difference between ideal democracy and anarchy, since neither has in fact been tried. The democracy that has been tried has failed because it was tied to the notions of universal suffrage and majority rule. The theory of majority rule and the concentration of power in central parliaments have between them imposed on democracy the tendency to seek continually "some form of centralized control," and hence to increase the power of the state. As for universal suffrage, Read condemns it as emphatically as Proudhon did.

It is a myth, a quite illusory delegation of power . . . a fiction of consent where in fact no liberty of choice exists. (*Poetry and Anarchism*)

It is the myth of universal suffrage that allows even communists and fascists to claim that they are democrats: "They all obtain popular consent by the manipulation of mass psychology." What else, Read implies, do parliamentary politicians do?

The ideal democracy is another matter, and, as one sees by the three conditions which Read lays down for its fulfilment, it is, in his mind, not different essentially from anarchism.

The first condition is that *all production is for use, and not for profit.*
The second condition is that *each should give according to his ability and each receive according to his needs.*
The third condition is that *the workers in each industry should collectively own and control that industry.* (*Politics of the Unpolitical*)

These conditions represent Read's view of necessary organization as functional and economic rather than political and social, and of equality as dependent on community.

For the essential is not to make all incomes equal — the ideal of the average democratic socialist — but to abolish all incomes and *hold all things in common* . . .
It is essential to stress the radical nature of this distinction between equal partition, and community ownership. It is the distinction between false communism and true communism, between the totalitarian conception of the State as a controlled herd, and the libertarian conception of society as a brotherhood. Once this conception is fully realized, the ambiguities of the doctrine of equality disappear: the concept of equality is dissolved in the concept of community.
(*Anarchy of Order*)

This, of course, brings us to the classic anarchist position: the denunciation of the state, the proclamation that societies must be built, like houses, from the ground up. For a culture "grows out of the soil, out of the people, out of their daily life and work. It is a spontaneous expression of their joy in life, of their joy in work, and if this joy does not exist, the culture will not exist." (*Politics for the Unpolitical*)

Like all anarchists, Read is reluctant to create elaborate plans for the ideal society. Warnings against such presumptuousness are scattered through his writings. "The Utopia fades the moment we try to actualize it." Anarchism is planless, "a point on the horizon" towards which we progress. "It is foolish to indulge in anything but relatively short-term policies for the human race." "It is always a mistake to build *a priori* constitutions. The main thing is to establish your principles — the principles of equality, of individual freedom, of workers' control."

Decentralization and arbitration instead of normal legal procedures are the main additions that Read makes to these simple requirements on the rare occasions when he draws a sketch plan for the future, as in the early 1940's he did in *The Politics of the Unpolitical*. He listed as follows the features of his plan for a "natural society."

I   The liberty of the person.
II   The integrity of the family.
III   The reward of qualifications.
IV   The self-government of the guilds.
V   The abolition of parliament and centralized government.
VI   The institution of arbitrament.
VII   The delegation of authority.
VIII The humanization of industry.

Read differs from most anarchists other than Proudhon in the stress he laid on the family as the basic natural social unit. It is "the integral unit," "the most effective unit" because it is the smallest, and it is the basis on which can be built the next unit upwards, the parish, "the local association of men in contiguous dwellings."

Such local associations may form their courts, and these courts are sufficient to administer a common law based on common sense.
(*A Coat of Many Colours*)

Next in importance comes the guild, which anarchists with a different background from Read's early connection with *The New Age* might call the syndicate — "the association of men and women according to their calling or practical function." With "political power" distributed among families and parishes ("human tangible units"), with economic power vested in the guilds and workshops, with financial power "altogether excluded from society," with "productive labour" recognized as "the basic reality and honoured as such," the organizational shell of Read's vision of the free society is complete.

So far it is little different from other anarchist sketches of the future. One finds the same ideas more forcefully expressed by Proudhon and more elaborately by Kropotkin. What most distinguishes Read's anarchism from the anarchism of past theoreticians, and brings it closer to the socialism of William Morris, is the stress he

82

places on the role of the arts — on the artist as mediator, and on art itself as the vehicle of a revolutionary form of education. In my view this particular emphasis is much more important than the other novel feature of Read's anarchism, the wide introduction of psychoanalytical concepts and terminology, which mainly serve to replace the somewhat outdated scientism of Kropotkin and Reclus, who used evolutionary concepts in much the same way as Read uses psychoanalytical ones, to prove that anarchism was given support — and hence credibility — by the most contemporary scientific developments. I have always found Read's borrowings from Freud, Jung *et al* the least convincing features of his literary and artistic criticism, and I doubt if such borrowings have greatly strengthened his case for anarchism, though he has drawn out of them a few entertaining aphorisms, e.g. "I would define the anarchist as the man who, in his manhood, dares to resist the authority of the father" (a definition I am inclined to dispute, since I have known many anarchists with gentle fathers and domineering, hated mothers).

The place of art in Read's ideal society becomes clear as soon as we move away from his plans for its organizational functioning, and sense the kind of life he would like to see lived in that future. It is, needless to say, the rural world of a self-proclaimed peasant, rather like that of *News from Nowhere* without its earnest laboriousness, for Read, while at times he denounces the factory system, realizes that "industrialism must be endured," and goes beyond that to search for means by which the machine can not merely perform the unpleasant tasks, which Morris eventually allowed, but can also produce beautiful objects, which Morris would never admit. At the same time, Read is aware that no civilization or people can lose touch with things, can abandon organic processes, can forget the feel of wood and clay and metal worked with the hands, and still remain healthy. Therefore he wishes to use machinery to simplify existence, to bring more leisure, to end pointless labours, so that when men leave the cities they will find "a world of electric power and mechanical plenty where man can once more return to the land, not as a peasant, but as a lord."

In such a world play will resume its true place in human life, and

... it was *play* rather than work which enabled man to evolve his higher faculties — everything we mean by the word 'culture' ... Play is freedom, is disinterestedness, and it is only by virtue of disinterested free activity that man has created his cultural values. Perhaps it is this

theory of all work and no play that has made the Marxist such a very
dull boy.   (*Anarchy and Order*)

Of play, of course, art is the highest form, and Read sees for the
artist a high role in the free society, for he is

... the man who mediates between our individual consciousness and
the collective unconsciousness, and thus ensures social re-integration. It
is only in the degree that this mediation is successful that a true democracy is possible.   (*Poetry and Anarchism*)

Read wrote almost all his works on anarchism from the viewpoint
of the artist or poet; in this he resembled and may have been influenced by Oscar Wilde, whose *Soul of Man Under Socialism* also
envisaged a libertarian society as the best environment for the arts to
flourish. But Read did not express an élitist point of view. He might
intend artists to be, in Shelley's phrase which he quotes approvingly,
"the unacknowledged legislators of the world," but he does not see
them in this role as a minority, since what he hopes for, following
on the development of a free society, is the universalization of art,
in the sense that its standards will be applied to all human work
(factory-made or hand-made) and that by this token all men will
become artists. As the aim of work changes from profit to use, so
will the life-view of the workers change.

The worker has as much latent sensibility as any human being, but
that sensibility can only be awakened when meaning is restored to his
daily work and he is allowed to create his own culture.
                                        (*Politics of the Unpolitical*)

Then we shall realize that "every man is a special kind of artist,"
for "art is skill: a man does something so well that he is entitled to
be called an artist." So art is brought down from the isolation to
which bourgeois cultures have condemned it, and becomes a matter
of everyday activity. This does not mean that art itself has progressed, for it is impossible to see any pattern of qualitative evolution from the painters of prehistoric Lascaux to those of the School
of Paris. But it does mean that civilization has progressed because it
has admitted artistic impulses into its life and its relationships.

What applies to the man also applies to the child, who is a poten-
tial artist from the beginning, and in whom a system of education
through art can induce — in Read's view — inner harmonies which
will make him better prepared for social initiation. Undoubtedly

Read saw such a system of education as a potent agent of social liberation, but he also held, for long periods, to more orthodox views of change by physical means.

In a general sense Read regarded revolt as an inevitable and regenerative element in any human society. "Freedom is not a state of rest, of least resistance. It is a state of action, of projection, of self-realization." But this natural and spontaneous revolt was different from the specific kind of rebellion which Read deemed necessary in the unregenerate present. Poverty must be abolished, the classless society brought to an end, at the very least the more monstrous injustices of the social order must be ended, "and if we do not revolt ... we are either morally insensitive or criminally selfish." (*Anarchy and Order*)

During the late 1930's Read envisaged revolt in activist terms. "Naturally the abolition of poverty and the consequent establishment of a classless society is not going to be accomplished without a struggle," he said in *Poetry and Anarchism* (1938). "Certain people have to be dispossessed of their autocratic power and of their illegitimate profits." And two years later, in *The Philosophy of Anarchism*, he declared that "an insurrection is necessary for the simple reason that when it comes to the point, even your man of good will, if he is on the top, will not sacrifice his personal advantages to the general good."

Read did not however think in terms of violent action. He insisted that anarchist rebellion must be non-violent, that the example of Gandhi must be followed, and the only insurrectionary strategy he discussed at any length was the general strike, which he believed had never been used to its full effect. And, though he saw himself as a rebel, he did not admit to being, at least in the political sense, a revolutionary. As early as 1940 he accepted the validity of Max Stirner's distinction between *revolution* and *insurrection*, and later, when Camus made in *The Rebel* his even sharper distinction between *revolution* (a totalitarian act) and *rebellion* (a libertarian act), Read adopted it.

Revolutions, as has often been remarked, change nothing; or rather, they merely substitute one set of masters for another set. Social groups acquire new names, but retain their former inequality of status.

Rebellions or insurrections, on the other hand, being guided by instinct rather than reason, being passionate and spontaneous rather than cool and calculated, do act like shock therapy on the body of society, and there is a chance that they may change the chemical composition of the societal crystal . . . [Rebellion] eludes the world of power — that is the point, for it is always power that crystallizes into a structure of injustice.

It was, ironically, not until long after the period of his anarchist writings, not until the early 1960's (his own late sixties) that Read eventually moved into practical activism, and became involved in the passive resistance tactics of the Campaign for Nuclear Disarmament and the Committee of 100, sitting down in Whitehall not to usher in anarchy but to protest, with more conviction than hope, against the destructive aspects of the existing unfree society.

Read's later years were marked by a steady loss of hope of seeing a better world in his time or foreseeing one for his children. He seized comfort where he could, and sometimes in unlikely places, for I find a letter written in November 1959, with a postscript on his recent trip to China: "China — very exciting! The communes as near to our kind of anarchism as anything that is likely to happen." But soon he realized that even here his optimism had been misplaced, and it was with a flickering confidence in the world that he performed in 1962 the symbolic act of putting his autobiographical writings together in the final form of *The Contrary Experience*.

Nihilism — nothingness, despair, and the nervous hilarity that goes with them — remains the universal state of mind [he wrote then]. From such an abyss the soul of man does not rise in a decade or two. If a human world survives the atomic holocaust — and it is now difficult to see how such a holocaust is to be avoided — it will only be because man has first overcome his Nihilism. A few prophets have already pointed the way — Gandhi, Buber, Simone Weil, C. G. Jung — but the people are also few who pay heed to them. Spiritually the world is now one desert, and prophets are not honoured in it. But physically it still has a beautiful face, and if we could once more learn to live with nature, if we could return like prodigal children to the contemplation of its beauty, there might be an end to our alienation and fear, a return to those virtues of delight which Blake called Mercy, Pity, Peace and Love.

Resignation, with a little hope: a melancholy but not an unusual end for an anarchist. One cannot help contrasting the mood of this passage with that in which *The Philosophy of Anarchism* was brought to an end twenty-two years before.

Faith in the fundamental goodness of man; humility in the presence of natural law; reason and mutual aid — these are the qualities that can save us. But they must be unified and vitalized by an insurrectionary passion, a flame in which all virtues are tempered and clarified, and brought to their most effective strength.

It is such words that evoke for me the Read I knew. Though in many ways his life was curiously bourgeois, his anarchism had fostered — or perhaps merely refined — a limpidity of nature and outlook such as I have always imagined Kropotkin possessed. His periodical relapses into the Tory conformity of his youth one had to balance against the occasions when he took public stands, particularly in the defence of other people, that cost him a great deal materially and in terms of his career. One blamed at times his inconsistency, but never doubted his sincerity. I still do not know what romantic aberration leaping from a Yorkshire childhood induced him to become Sir Herbert, but I do know that Queen Elizabeth II never dubbed a gentler knight.

When one tries to sum up his achievements as a social and political writer, if one leaves out *The Green Child* and the poems of war and anarchism, they seem perhaps less than those in his other fields. He gave a new and attractive expression, a luminous clarification, to the few and simple truths that make up the anarchist doctrine. He investigated more thoroughly than any of his predecessors the relationship between freedom, art and the artist. He was largely responsible for the libertarian attitudes which dominated much English and American poetry during the 1940's. But one cannot say that in any of these fields — except in his work on education through art — he was a great originator. I believe his anarchist beliefs and writings attract and give most light when they are seen in the context of his entire achievement, in relation to his poetry, to his writings on education and revolutionary art, on industry and romantic poetry, for then one sees his world-view complete, with the love of freedom its moving spirit.

Four Drawings

I *Touchstone*. Oil and Pencil. 41″ x 18″. 1966.

Collection: Marlborough Fine Art
(London) Ltd.

II *Construction II*. Oil and Pencil. 40″ x 35″.
1966.

III *Equinox*. Oil and Pencil. 30 1/8″ x 24 1/8″.
1966.

Collection: Lady Debenham.

IV *Genesis III*. Oil and Pencil. 30″ x 40″. 1966.

Collection: Geoffrey Jellicoe, c.b.e.

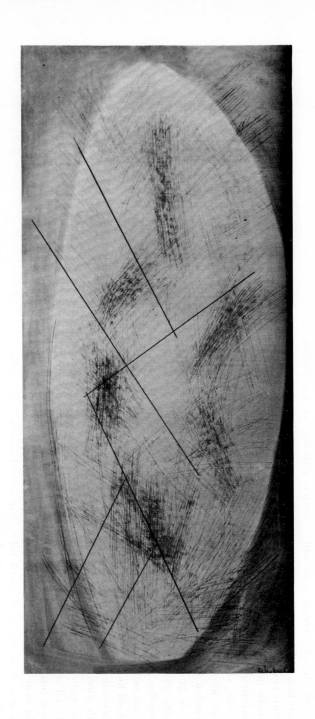

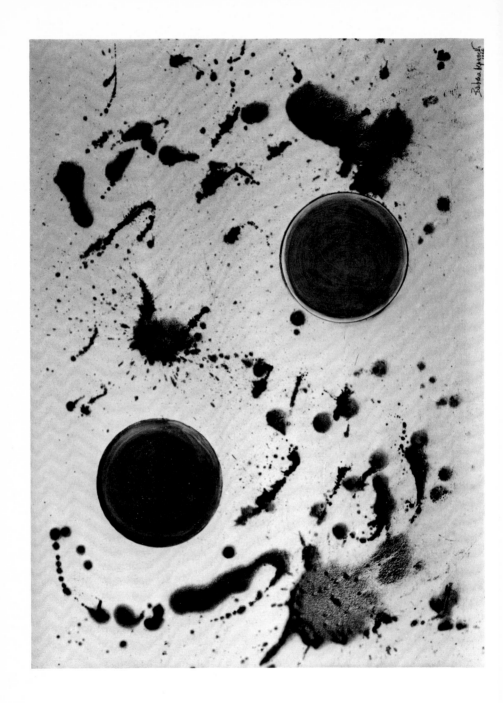

NORMAN NICHOLSON

The Borehole

A huddle of iron jammy-cranes[1]
Straddles the skear,   shanks
Rusty from salt rains,
Or halfway up their barnacled flanks
In the flood tide.   Paid-up pits
Lounge round the banks,
Turning out red pockets.
The cranking waders stand,
Necks down, bills grinding in their sockets,
Drilling the sand.
A steam-pipe whistles, the clanged iron bells;
Five hundred feet of limestone shudders and
Creaks down all its strata'd spine of ammonites and shells,
And a vertical worm of stone is worried
Out from the earth's core.
The daylight falls
Westward with the ebb, before
The night-shift buzzer calls:
But what is it sticks in the bird's gullet —
Rubble or crystal, dross or ore?

[1] Herons.

DENISE LEVERTOV

Craving

Wring the swan's neck, seeking
a little language of drops of blood.

How can we speak of blood, the sky
is drenched with it.

A little language
of dew, then.

It dries.

A language
of leaves underfoot.
Leaves on the tree, trembling
in speech. Poplars
          tremble and speak
if you draw near them.

Edward Dahlberg and Herbert Read

AN EXCHANGE OF LETTERS*

Edited by Reginald C. Terry

I am, as always, your socratic gadfly and friend,

EDWARD DAHLBERG

F OR TWENTY-THREE YEARS Herbert Read was
the most perceptive critic of Edward Dahlberg's work, his devoted
friend, and certainly the man who did most to introduce this unique
American writer to readers in England.

In a foreword to the English edition of Dahlberg's literary studies,
Sing O Barren, Read said:

There is not a page which lacks its vivid imagery, its memorable phrase.
It is not the slick prose of the smart journalist, nor the careful prose of
the timid intellectual, and least of all the intricate jewellery of the aes-
thete. It is the crystalline vein of the English Bible, of Shakespeare and
Sir Thomas Browne, running through the torpid substance of modern
life.[1]

*The letters of Herbert Read are part of the Edward Dahlberg Collection in
the University of Texas. Dahlberg's letters are among the Read papers and
mss. at the University of Victoria. Sir Herbert Read approved this brief selection shortly before his death. Mr. Dahlberg's letters were corrected by the
author when he was preparing material for *The Edward Dahlberg Reader*,
New Directions, 1967, when he made certain excisions of a personal nature.
Quotations in this introductory note are from the letters with dates given in
brackets where a text is indicated.

1 *Sing O Barren*, Routledge, 1947, p. vii, (first published in the United States
  as *Do These Bones Live*, 1941; reissued as *Can These Bones Live*, with illustrations by James Kearns, New Directions, N.Y., 1960.

95

Both writers share a concern for clear and correct expression. Read's is the style of a "lissomy deer" says Dahlberg in a typically vigorous metaphor. He finds *Annals of Innocence and Experience* a "faultless elegy." "I never quarrel with you as a remarkable stylist" (January 14, 1955). And the phrase he savours from Read's *English Prose Style* is "Word is act" (April 14, 1959). For it is the relation of style to the living experience and the quality of a culture which is the constant theme of the Read-Dahlberg letters.

He [Dahlberg] tells us ... that what our genius lacks most is being simple, and though he is as ever thinking of style, the style is not separable from the way of life ... [he] believes that bad writing shows a lack of love ... a poet concerned for style is likely to have a stronger sense of social values than the styleless sociologue ... his style is another name for his perception and his wisdom.[2]

Or, as Dahlberg affirms: "It is not possible to tell truth in ill assorted words." (January 14, 1955)

Both writers are dedicated to direct and vivid utterance of a simple truth, which in the broadest sense is Tolstoy's belief that men live by love. Their letters are an earnest and often acrimonious debate on two issues: the forces sundering man from his brother, and the way in which art, particularly literary art, may heal and inspire.

Literature is, in Dahlberg's phrase, "the sacred occupation of the heart (October 11, 1957) demanding a purity and asceticism that sets the teacher apart and condemns him to loneliness and exile. Ishmael is Edward Dahlberg's symbolic figure. As he says in *Sing O Barren*:

American Ishmaels are our artists, — "Call me Ishmael" prophetically utters Herman Melville in the first lines of *Moby Dick* — doomed to be cut away, afar from earthly mortal beginnings, the human vineyards, the beauteous Genesis of the protean and warming race-experience. We are brute giant pathfinders, without a remembrance of the past or tradition, discoverers of brand-new nostrums for sex, life, science, art, religion.[3]

Most of Dahlberg's poetic impulse is implicit here: the rejection of modern culture and the rediscovery of meaning in time past. By nature Dahlberg is thus a teller of parables; his work is surrounded by terms such as "vision," "prophet," "apocalyptic." To Paul Car-

---

[2] Foreword by Sir Herbert Read to *Alms For Oblivion, Essays by Edward Dahlberg*, University of Minnesota Press, 1964, pp. viii-ix.

[3] From "Can These Bones Live" in *Sing O Barren*.

roll he is "our one mythological poet."[4] As Dahlberg confesses to Read, "I have little patience with description, relying upon maxim, myth, and wit ... I am a coney-catcher of the past." (January 19, 1958). His work is a kind of diary of apothegms and epigrams from wide reading and meditation; thus his letters are always exciting, for they are the perfect medium for the confessional, anecdotal mind.

Style, dedication, learning are valued, but both writers also recognize their debt to nature. In the literal as well as the metaphorical sense "Writing is conscience, scruple, and the farming of our ancestors."[5] Relishing this phrase from Dahlberg's essay, "For Sale," Read continues to quote: "unless we return to the old handicrafts, to the wheat, stable, and horse village, to poems, houses, bricks, and tables, which are manual, we will become a nation of killers."[6] The letters are full of such thoughts. "Our separation from mountains, channels, rivers, and isthmus has left our intellects barren ... The sentence is void of the mountain, poplar, ash, the seas of Poseidon, the chanting bivalve." (February 3, 1955). Read's "cell of good living" (November 19, 1951) is intimately bound up with the land and rural community of his beloved York: "It is only so far as a culture keeps close to nature and the soil that it expresses any intensity of feeling or sensibility for beauty." (September 15, 1952). "Something has happened to our hands" laments Dahlberg in "Our Vanishing Cooperative Colonies."[7] Such thoughts provide the poetic symbols of his best work, the "knowledge before reason and science," (once again Read's extrapolation from the American writer's work), "a secret wisdom that is prior to logic — the vibrant god-telling PULSE,"[8] the equivalent of Read's own "true voice of feeling."

With such shared values it is not surprising that both reject the contemporary wasteland. Dahlberg unlocks a word-hoard against man's inventions, bourgeois values, American cities, modern art, grammarians; against Read himself for his concessions to the age and for his non-literary activities. Read calls him "a relentless scourge of all human frailties, especially those that threaten the in-

4 Introduction to *The Edward Dahlberg Reader*, New Directions, 1967, p. xvii.
5 Foreword to *Alms For Oblivion*, p. ix.
6 *ibid.*
7 *ibid.*, p. 92.
8 *Sing O Barren*, p. viii.

tegrity of the writer."[9] For Dahlberg is whole-hearted and uncompromising in his rejection of modern civilization. Moving restlessly around the world he preaches destruction on "the iron and macadam cities" (October 4, 1947). American dreams have produced a "nation of garage keepers and mechanics." (October 16, 1946). His first novel, *Bottom Dogs* (1930), for which another homeless spirit, D. H. Lawrence, wrote a preface, he describes as "a chronicle of a scrawny and unhallowed land." (December 19, 1946). America, he concludes, is "an iron-bowelled matriarchy." (March 29, 1962). Rejection of contemporary society includes its literature. He dismisses poetry: "Our modern verse is bullet and machine gun originality" (October 4, 1951); Sinclair Lewis writes "craven, newspaper prose" (March 1, 1955); Huxley is "the Hollywood mystagogue (March 1, 1955). One by one modern poets are assailed: "Joyce has annihilated a whole generation of values" (April 5, 1955); Eliot is "a sterile pedant" (October 9, 1957); and Pound is "a deranged Polonius of letters (March 5, 1960).

In their place he exalts the great writers of the past, among whom he mentions frequently the Greek philosophers, Shakespeare, Swift — "that dour and stony intellect" (April 14, 1959) — and Blake. "What is important to me," Dahlberg has written, "is honest workmanship, learning and human poetry."[10] If Read falls short of Dahlberg's exacting standards he is roundly abused, for it is the duty of a real friend to tell plain truth, according to the Socratic maxim "Truth is more sacred than friendship" (April 1, 1956), the title of their published exchange of letters on literary themes.[11] A constant aggravation is Read's neglect of his poetic vocation in order to spend time with "the exchequer gents of the arts" (November 15, 1951), to lecture and write books on art, and to "travel the world giving nosegays to painters" (March 5, 1954).

Read meets the lava flow of criticism calmly. It is the classic confrontation between the uncompromising dissenter and the moderate, pragmatic liberal. For Read there is no sense in reviling the world to the point at which men will cease to take any notice. Listen, persuade, is his counsel.

9 *Alms For Oblivion*, p. viii.
10 *Poetry*, vol. 78, no. 1, April 1951.
11 *Truth Is More Sacred*, Horizon Press, 1961.

What drives one out into the world is not the desire for fame (to which I am as indifferent as anyone could honestly and humanly be), nor the desire for lucre, ... but simply a missionary zeal, which may be vain in itself, but is surely not despicable. (February 13, 1949)

Remonstrating with Dahlberg for his Ishmaelism he urges "the capacity to compromise with life without sacrificing ... integrity as an artist." (March 6, 1949). Withdrawal and rejection logically lead to silence. The more positive doctrine is one of reconciliation, or, as he puts it in a characteristic phrase "to continue as a child; to preserve the innocent eye. I have pruning shears in my garden, but no thunderbolts." (November 19, 1951). "The mood the poet strives for, for himself, is serenity." (December 9, 1951). But serenity does not mean sloth, and reconciliation admits of no weakness: "there is no question of compromising with the prevailing vulgarism." (December 25, 1956). This is the crux:

But there is no audience for our belles lettres, so we must be content with whatever faith we have in the immortality of good writing, or we must make the necessary gestures to attract an audience. And to do this without losing our integrity! (December 25, 1956)

The qualities he urges on Dahlberg are those he has found in an essay on Henry James: "his [James's] vision, his harmony, his judgement, and above all his justice." (October 7, 1957)

While they share fundamentally the same beliefs in literary ideals, they are often in conflict because of their dissimilar temperaments. "You are a very quiet nature," writes Dahlberg, "and I am always an upboiling Vesuvius" (January 12, 1952). On one occasion Read called him "a boiling Diogenes" (April 18, 1956). But Dahlberg's anger is not that of the cynic but of the reformer — "a good primitive Jew of the Old Testament" (February 6, 1956) he calls himself — and the volume of his rage is equalled by the extent of his love: "Unless literature is for love it is a vice" (October 4, 1951). His best work, such as *The Sorrows Of Priapus* (New Directions, 1957) and the autobiography, *Because I Was Flesh* (New Directions, 1964), are ample proof of this. His "vexsome diatribes" and "constant admonitions" are no less instinct with love and respect: "You are the kindest Man in the world of Letters." (October 30, 1959)

Dear Herbert,

I am pained by your letter. Why should you believe evil in the mouths of others is in mine? What resentment have I toward you? I honor the quiddity of your identity, and tell you plainly when I believe you are departing from it. I risk your rancour, and for what profit? I am very alone, and can whisper to you what Christ asked Peter, "Will you go away?" and if you love the WORD, as I devoutly do, you will reply, "Whither shall I go?" Examine my heart as closely as I can, I do not know what I could say about you that could be regarded as coarse or base. Do you earnestly believe these rude, little anarchs, who do not respect you as I do, have the "Conscience of the ear" to have properly understood any remark I may have made about you? Are these unread men who feed and gander and spill their bile everywhere the troubled, enquiring hearts to whom you write a hundred letters a week? Then you have lived in an error.

I told you you had forsaken me, but that I have said to you and to nobody else. It is the ethical duty of a man of letters to prevent the WORD from dying in the earth; let the living word perish, and the seed, the plants, and the green, sticky leaves wither too. This is our burden. Were it not for me, [Charles] Olson whom you cite, would neither have written nor published the book [*Call Me Ishmael*] from which you cite. What I did for him I did at my disadvantage. When I was coeditor of *Twice a Year*, and had had not one jot of my soul on a page for six years and was as hungered as crusty Lazarus was for some morsel, I labored so ardently for his work that he was published instead of me.

You should not be angry with me for telling you that as a director of Routledge you *must* do something for literature, or in some chemic and baleful way you will mire upon your own spirit. It is more important to guard the vestal fires of a poet than to weep over the ruins of Germany. Had there been a half dozen soothsayers in that land the people would have been less predacious, and their earth not a cairn of asphalt and bitumen. People expire from their own decay, and it is very doubtful that any great nation has ever been destroyed by enemies from without. The weakness of Greece was in Demosthenes rather than in the might of the Persians.

Your allusion to my Ishmaelism is not just. You forget your own feeling of revulsion against America. Do you think you have more fortitude than Herman Melville who regarded himself as an Ishmael? But he was not a wanderer. For bread and the oil and blubber of the whale he had travelled to northerly boreal streams. But after his twenty-fifth year he spent some eighteen months in Pittsfield, Mass.; and with the exception of one brief and disenchanted pilgrimage to the Holy Land, he settled on Bleecker Street, and on 23rd, New York City, and remained in tenements here until his death.

You write that "Ishmaelism has none of the serenity of true resignation and retirement," but you admire a peripatetic Christ. If you mean that the wisdom of the Ishmaelite is bitter, pariah knowledge, you are right. But then you must set aside the parables of Christ, the anger of Jeremiah, Matthew and Luke who has the Nazarene cry out, "O I have overcome the world!" You make a snare for yourself when you bring fillets, rams, and the olive of Minerva to the world which Plato, Heraclitus and Nietzsche profoundly rejected. I do not believe you are discerning, speaking on the quick of your spirit, when you fleer at Melville's and my own feeling, "to live in the world without being of it" by adding, "Yes, but to live." But let us consider travel. Plato's Socrates says it is foolish to travel since you always take yourself with you. Christ, as I have written in "The Rational Tree" was a sick nature, wandering even after he was the Holy Ghost. There was no greater injury to the deceased among the ancients than to be deprived of quiet sepulchre which the migratory Holy Ghost was denied. Plato, in his desire to shape a martial Socrates, writes that he was at Potidaea and at Delium; Plato also states elsewhere that Socrates never left Athens. Thucydides makes no mention at all of Socrates as a soldier. Socrates was supposed to have stood in one place from one sunrise to the next solely to be quiet (Please see "The Rational Tree" and forgive the gimcrack pretence of an unpublished author). It is doubtful that Shakespeare ever left England. If you must travel, go then as Menelaus did to hear the oracles of Proteus in Egypt's Nile.

I wonder also whether you did not write the following in some haste, and would not, perhaps, after reflection, relinquish this: "You hate the world and because you revile it the world will not listen to you." It would be vain and repetitious to tell you that every sage and votary of the Muse has denounced the World. One of the three great curses, it is said in the Chester or the Miracle Plays, is the world. Heraclitus himself said that all the Ephesians should hang themselves. Democritus could not endure his countrymen, nor could Baudelaire, or Nietzsche, who was despised by the world which rejected him and heeds you. I cannot accept your acts as the palm branches and garlands to be laid at the altar of life. You cannot relinquish the forces to life and have enough strength for FORM.

I deeply appreciate your letter and have more tenderness for your GIFT than you appear to know; I beg you to guard it, and not to cast it to those who come to you for the five barley leaves and the two fishes. They pay the homage of a toady to your reputation, and would disregard you as much as they do me if you had none.

I know how fatigued you are; when I was with you last April I was dismayed. I work as an academic drudge for penury that I may write an occasional book which no one will publish, and give counsel to dear, good Herbert Read who will not heed me.

My tender affections to you, and my love to your children and to Ludo [Mrs. Herbert Read].

> March 6, 1949
> Beaconsfield,
> Buckinghamshire

Dear Edward,

We must not waste our correspondence on mutual recriminations. Such resentment as I did feel on the receipt of your letter about *Education for Peace* has long ago evaporated — but has left, perhaps, a clearer realisation of our different points of view. You attempt to impose on me some antithesis of Life and Form, or the World and Art, which fundamentally I don't accept. There is a certain sense in which form kills life, and my *Green Child* was written to demonstrate that fact. But it is life that must triumph — otherwise we are victims of that Death Wish which is the secret of so much corruption in German and Russian literature. Life is a continuous process of anamorphosis — of the *progressive* creation of form. It is the realisation of that fact which gives Goethe his greatness and makes him (and here I suspect we diverge) the representative modern man — the precursor of Nietzsche and still more viable than Nietzsche. What makes Goethe relevant, for my personal argument, is that he had the capacity to compromise with life without sacrificing his integrity as an artist. Instead of being overwhelmed by the busy-ness of life, he swept it all into the creative mould — he made the occasional the excuse for the immortal. "If you want to go into infinity," he said, "go within the finite in all directions." That, I suspect, is the fundamental wisdom, and I see it working in Shakespeare. The difficulty is a dynamic one — to have enough energy (spiritual and physical) and to expend it wisely. The curse of our modern age with its penny post and public telephones, mass publicity and swift communications, is that the impact of life, on any one individual, is almost unbearable. Goethe in Weimar is one thing — transport him to modern London or New York and I guess he would be as frustrated as any of us. Nevertheless, the complexity of modern life is no excuse for rejecting it. My desire to return to Yorkshire is a weakness unless I can be confident that I take life with me, stored in memorable experience. Melville in Bleecker Street surely had that confidence.

There is a patent paradox in rejecting the world and yet continuing to address it, even if only to revile it. Would not silence in such circumstances be more dignified? I cannot believe that the man who wrote the *Laws* at the age of seventy had hated the world and rejected it. Surely he loved it so much that he spent his life in a vain effort to reform it nearer to his heart's desire.

You often mention Dostoevsky with respect. Was there ever a man more cruelly caught in the sticky web of life — and yet doesn't his greatness emerge from that fact?

I am trying to extract your MS [*The Flea of Sodom*] from [Geoffrey] Grigson because I have found a young publisher who has expressed an interest in it. Do not be too premature in hope; but I believe that I have some conscience in the matter and always look for an opportunity to give your words currency.

Ben is not too well — the least cold or fever upsets his carefully controlled metabolism and it is a constant worry to keep him "balanced". The others are happy — it has snowed for the first time this winter and they have been busy building an igloo all day.

Our love to you all.

October 4, 1951
New York City

Dear Herbert,

Seeing you was that Balm of Gilead for which man no longer thirsts or hungers, for appetite has died, and Boredom is King. I would walk to Capernaum and to Sidon and return to this sooty nihilistic hole, New York, just to smell the first potherbs and nettles. I would yield up my poor, slain life to smell the First.

I abhor baring my poverty, for it is the only raiment I have left. None will let me teach, and very few will permit me to write. We hate the Buddha, a Socrates, and man no longer imitates them, for he wants above all to be original which is the source of modern spite and destruction. Look in vain for the milk of the Vedic heifer, or the curd of the Rig Veda in your poet. Our modern verse is bullet and machine gun originality, for to be new is to want to destroy the world.

You spoke of conventions; yes, they are good when uttered by Solon, or Jesus, or Samuel, and I have scant respect for those who overturn them. The present occidental Atlas does not hold the skies on his shoulders; he changes them, and when the weather of his soul is constant is wretched. You will pardon me if I was rather astounded, and wounded, when you wrote in one of your books such barren words.

Unless literature is for love it is a vice. I read your *Phases of English Poetry* with admiration, and I could only find fault with the amount of attention you give to pentameters, for I cannot see of what avail is that. When a man thirst for Rachel's Well, what can he drink that will not leave his throat more parched if he is offered iambics or other such grammar gruel? I want the Cana marriage wine, yes, I want the stones that have not been turned into bread or into Cain's rubble. The other is that though you ask for a communal prose, it seems to me that you will do little toward this end. If I say that the most accursed sin is to labor for one's self, for this is dropping one's seed alone, and that is what solitude has brought men, do I deceive anybody? I still think, Herbert, you have some belief in the cunning of the brain. I, of course, warmly believe in your grass roots in art, though I must own, that I suspect that art today is not the plain, simple illiteracy, and nihilism, but is the most sly and baffling illiteracy. It is a brush and typewriter brain pretending that he is using the reed that grows by the Chaldaic Tigris. Then you take a great deal of interest in inventions which I think is man's folly, for the more he invents, the greater is his inertia, and you cannot get two inert men either to trust or to love one another. For love is inward energy, and men who are concerned with the Cherubim, or with Daniel's Vision, do not make machines. In your

104

graceful little introduction to Klee you again lament that art and society are two, and yet how are we going to make them one? Man will always be divisible as long as he makes new and more machines, for the purpose of mechanical devices is not to ease the spirit, but to make him spiritless and altogether outward.

Maybe when Thales passed water he thought it was a first cause, and Cyrus, we know, had great concern for his own voiding, at least in a dream or a vision, and maybe we will have to go back to a naked, pissing Adam, for an Eden. I would rather know how to pass water straight than make the most cunning lines, for I am more afraid of the skilled mind than Erebus or death. You have gone to wise Plato to pasture your soul, and I see in your good, seemly face what I have always imagined Vergil to be, but why will you not come all the way through unto your own nature? Are we to be together by being apart? Are we to sow seeds on the page, but say it is not the age in which to be such a planter? All my life I have said that we must not sow in a book what we do not intend to reap in the life. I know you are a Good Man, and I tell you what the Angel said to Lot, Haste Thee from Sodom. For it is a kind of Gomorrah perversity to give two heads to one animal, the book and the life, for if we do we then give ourselves two faces too. I am, as you see, Herbert, sorely tried, but I am a learner, and would not presume to teach him from whom I would not seek instruction. I have thought of you a long time, and it is my belief, or am I wrong in this, that I was in some way responsible for your removal to York. Then I begged you not to waste your rich gifts going everywhere, and now I again beseech you not to fatten evil men whom you enlarge by your companionship . . . I have long ago perished, and even now at this instant I am still in my rags and in my grave. Who will give us the spittle to open our eyes, and is it our most evil paradox, that what man hates most today is poverty and human spittle, for both are so communal? We are all despised and on the ground. Please, remember, do not judge men by the way they praise you; ask them rather whether they despise Edward Dahlberg, reckon him hard and difficult. It is very easy to respect you, but only a man who has the old Pharoah's riddle in his soul, will bow to my obscurity and indigence. Charles Olson had said many years ago that the measure of a man was his ability to be my friend. He has since left me, and no book has come from his nature worthy of his first, the result of our great affections for each other, *Call Me Ishmael*. Do I brag? I do not think so, for it will matter little to the world whether I do or not.

I am sending you several manuscripts. There is the critical volume. It is not nearly as good as your *Coat of Many Colors*, nor as well written. I do not mind that it is not, or in saying so. It is honest and that at the present is enough. There is a part of a long Kansas City poem on my Mother, which may or may not entice you, and there is about twenty thousand words of a novel, some of which must be rewritten, and sharpened. What will you think of these? I do not know. I do not know how long it takes for a Lazarus to die and to be reborn between books. The bitterness of getting my bread has given me little quiet, and though I was born to be unquiet, I must have repose, for one must have some beast strength in him to save his will without which a book is very feeble and vicious.

I send you my love, as Hamlet gave it to Horatio. Had we love and trusting hearts our conventions would be savory, but when the loam, and the apple, and the goats have died, O Herbert, do not concern yourself with codes, but with the living waters between two people, and if they have perished, I then know that I am Lazarus in the grave, and not Lazarus reborn.

I am really happy about the Louis Zukofsky matter. I beg you to work for the publication of a collection of his poetry and prose after you have settled *The Test of Poetry*. Tell me, please, when you are to come down, and do not be vexed with my rebuke, for it comes from my heart. It is a part of what Pascal calls the desire to finish, and it is what we must speak to each other.

Remember, I reprehend the man to whom I am most indebted in this world, so I need not apologize.

November 19, 1951
Stonegrave, York

Dear Edward,

Your letter provokes a quick reaction! Not of anger — almost of amusement. Here you are again, insisting that my temperament should be like yours, my philosophy of life like yours, my social behaviour like yours. Or at least insisting that I should adopt some quixotic policy of anti-social isolation which, you assume, would give me some warm feeling of self-righteousness. Let me, once and for all, try to make myself clear on this issue.

What kind of anarchist am I? My own kind, no doubt. I do not

believe that I shall bring the anarchist ideal one step nearer by join-
ing an artificial commune, accepting the standard of life of savages,
or wearing a loin-cloth in a sub-arctic climate. I do not believe that
I shall bring that ideal any nearer realization by selling all I possess
and giving the proceeds to the poor. I believe that I can best serve
that ideal by cultivating my small-holding of seven acres, by establishing a sense of community in this village, by living at peace with
my neighbours, by creating what [Eric] Gill called a cell of good
living.

You accuse me of consorting with publicans and sinners — with
the bankers of art and letters. You do not go so far as suggesting
that I have been defiled by these contacts, but you obviously think
I am in that danger. In this waste land we inhabit I go where the
spirit calls me. I listen to those who would speak to me, and I help
those who cry for help — to the best of my ability. That ability depends on the confidence I have established with the people in high
places as well as the people in low places, and no one has yet
accused me of a lack of integrity in the office of mediation which I
have quite humbly assumed. In this sense I tried to help you, but
I failed. It was not for any lack of force in my application.

It was to these people that you now revile that you asked me to
appeal on your behalf. I am sorry I failed, but because I failed in
your case I cannot forego the possibility of doing some good in other
cases. Besides, I do not find these people so evil as you do. They are
dispensers of charity, and this was never an easy task. They make
mistakes, but so do we all. For the most part I find them decent
human people, perplexed but not sinister, foolish but not wicked.
I have no uneasy conscience when I sup with them. I will say something which will shock you even more: the most decent people I
have met in the world have been among the richest, and for a good
reason — they have been put beyond envy, spite and uncharitable-
ness. They have lived a life without anxiety or care — the life we
should all lead, the life of the citizen of an ideal republic. That a
millionaire should consort with an anarchist might seem to you
monstrous; it is merely the paradox of the infinite, where extremes
meet.

One more personal retort. If I am a money-changer of literature,
a Barabbas, a Pharisee, a Pilate and much else that is reprehensible,
remember that you too receive your mite from the same tainted
sources. *The Freeman* is not only subsidized by capitalists: it exists

to promote an extreme form of capitalistic ideology. I do not blame you for picking up these crumbs from the tables of the rich; on the contrary, I believe that we cannot individually contract out of the prevailing economy. A Gandhi attempted to do so, and though I admire him greatly, and think him possibly the greatest figure of our age, he was perversely wrong in some of his ideas (sex, for example), and his economic experiments were always disastrous. He was a fanatic (as perhaps you are), and had over-much policy. "He who tries to govern the kingdom by policy is only a scourge to it; while he who governs without it is a blessing." That is the *Tao te ching*, and from the same source I would quote a passage which is as near to my philosophy of life as anything:

"The wise man has no fixed opinions to call his own. He accommodates himself to the minds of others.

I would return good for good; I would also return good for evil. Virtue is good.

I would meet trust with trust; I would likewise meet suspicion with confidence.

Virtue is trustful.

The wise man lives in the world with modest restraint, and his heart goes out in sympathy to all men.

The people give him their confidence, and he regards them all as his children."

Not very different from the Sermon on the Mount perhaps; or from certain of Keats's letters.

You quote the Greeks, or the ancient prophets. I prefer the Chinese, for they had the virtue of simplicity. And if I must take a model I will not take him from a distant and unintelligible civilization (think of their attitude to women!), but from my own. Now you are going to be surprised, and shocked. For wisdom, serenity and achievement, I do not know anyone I so much admire as Goethe. A name that has never, so far as I remember, passed your lips. Of course he had his faults — he was all too human. He has been called a philistine, and I doubt if he was an anarchist! He supped with Grand Dukes and he too was a well-fed votary of Helicon. Mais, voilà un homme!

Why should I hate when there is no hatred in my soul? Why should I scourge and attack when it is not in my nature to kill a fly? "By restraining the passions and letting gentleness have sway it is possible to continue as a child." That is my deepest wish — to continue as a child; to preserve the innocent eye. I have pruning shears in my garden, but no thunderbolts.

What else is there to say? Nothing, except that I hope we can continue to respect one another, and love one another, and exclude these acrimonious bickerings over our irreconcilable natures. We should profit by our differences. "The apple tree never asks the beech how he shall grow; nor the lion, the horse, how he shall take his prey." An ambiguous proverb, perhaps, but you see its drift.

I am deeply sorry for your physical ills, and fear they are aggravated by your fretting spirit. When you left me at Idlewild the other day the following lines came into my mind — from where?

> Be calm, and strive all you can
> To live the life of natural man.

Perhaps I invented them for the occasion.

I shall hope for better news of your health. Please thank R'lene for her kind note. My love to you both.

January 12, 1952
New York City

Dear Herbert,

I have no reply to my last letter, and it may be that you are very vexed with me, and do not want to write. Whatever your reasons are I want you to know that I shall never be unmindful of your numerous kindnesses to me. If I cannot accept your encomia upon the rich, you cannot blame me. It also occurs to me that you would not care to print some of the remarks you made in anger. You could not reconcile anarchism with what appears to me to be a despisal of the poor. I do not think that you realize how needy we are. You imagine, perhaps, that people living in this Caliban's money sty must have goods and dollars. There is a great deal of poverty in America, with many sweating industries and much hopelessness.

I brought my unfiinished novel [*The Sorrows of Priapus*] to one publisher and he is very moved by it. He is also a great admirer of *The Flea of Sodom*. You, doubtless, imagine that I am a very arrogant man, and in some respects I am. However, I should tell you that I am always a learner and a very humble one. I never for an instant was irritated with you for rejecting the novel. Surely, there must be bad writing in it which I shall have to mend. What astonishes me is that no matter how long a man writes he is certain to write badly. I have a few lines here from the unfinished novel which

109

I wish to quote, and I hope you won't reckon it coarse to ask you to look at the lines again, for a great deal of this "bitter and bile book" is written in this manner: "We should have the deepest reverence for poverty, because we are New Testament ground, and every day I offer a sacrifice to the extinct buffalo, the horse and the savage Iroquois, who is our Muse of cereal, string beans and maize, and when somebody strokes my head, I walk to Mt. Shasta, to the Oregon apple orchards which are my epistles to the Corinthians."

The above may have to be reworded, but I don't think lines like that are hyssop. You recall you said that my writing is not art because it is bitter. Yet I must tell you that it was D. H. Lawrence who once said to me, "Always write with a great bitterness; that is your strength." I think he was right although at the time I did not understand him. You know that Mephistopheles is the denying spirit, and the learned Grote asserts that Socrates has a negative intellect, and since Socrates is Plato's hero, we must then grant that this same trait so admired by Plato was an essential of his nature.

I send you this epistle as another token of my thanks. I have a few astringent credoes, and never unsaying my thanks is one of them.

What you are doing for [Louis] Zukofsky is an act of goodness, and I hope earnestly that his *Test of Poetry* will have a sale so that you can publish a volume of his poetry.

I sent his Shakespeare essay to [James] Laughlin, [publisher of New Directions Books] quoting your fine praise of it.

You must remember, Herbert, you are a very quiet nature, and I am always an upboiling Vesuvius. We need both natures in the world. This morning I stepped into a bookshop and read a few lines out of Goethe's *Wilhelm Meister* that pierced my spirit. He speaks of the art of the living experience and it is a remarkable truth. But I have no Duke of Weimar as a patron. Heine, a great nature, did not have it either, for he was a Mephisto to the end, but he was a rare heart who mocked what he hated, and he derided much and with truth.

I have known so many thankless churls and I did not want you to think me a Nabal no matter what our differences are.

When the *Freeman* essay on you appears I shall send it to you. I do not know how long I shall last there, and besides I fervently hope that my novel may be taken so that I can go back to that, and it may be that by the time I have expunged what is dross in it, that you may find some pages to your liking.

Give my love to Benedict; maybe some day he will read *The Flea of Sodom*, and will not regard me as waspish as his father does. No matter, Horace says that the poet belongs to an irritable race of men.

September 15, 1952
Stonegrave, York

My dear Edward,

Again I have to apologise for a long gap in our correspondence, but I have had a very busy summer, and even now have not finished —I go to Venice again this week for another congress (UNESCO). But that, I hope, is the last of them for many months. When I get back I shall look forward to several months of relative peace.

I was very pleased to hear that you had found it possible to move to California. Delightful as you had made your little cell in Washington Square, I could not help feeling that the City was destroying you physically, and irritating your spirit. I feel sure that you will both feel better and write better in Topanga. Tell me a little of your new surroundings when you write.

I was very interested to read what you had written about Tolstoy, not only in the article from the *Freeman* but also in your letters. It is hardly true to say that I have a scant regard for his tract on art —on the contrary it is such a powerful polemic that it calls out all one's powers of resistance. One simply cannot ignore such massive arguments, but I still cannot accept it, nor your gloss on its arguments. If I have to choose between aesthetics and morality I should still choose aesthetics. Living in England I am too conscious of what I have called the "Puritan blackout". The moralists killed art in England — killed music, killed poetry, killed the theatre; they gave us only some good prose and perhaps some architecture.

Fundamentally, as I have argued in more than one book, only following in this matter your beloved Plato, I do not see any real necessity to oppose aesthetics and morality. I agree that aesthetics as interpreted by 19th century aesthetes is a thin and inhuman creed, but why should we accept such a limited conception of the nature and function of art? The moralists hide their sensibility. They inevitably become harsh authoritarians and reject not only Shakespeare and Beethoven, but everything that expresses a love of life — or as one might say the life of love.

I was reading [W. R.] Worringer's book on Egyptian art last night and he has a good sentence or two which are relevant. He says that they lacked "the dimensions of true metaphysical consciousness because creative Eros was wanting in their thin blooded severity". This I believe to be very true. It is only so far as a culture keeps close to nature and the soil that it expresses any intensity of feeling or sensibility for beauty. Morality is abstract, conceptual, the letter that killeth. I believe that you must agree with me about this, and that once again we are only quarrelling about words. The very fact that you are now turning your thoughts to a literature that is concerned with man's conquest of nature suggests that your morality is not written on tables of law.

I am glad to hear that Laughlin is publishing something by you in his new magazine *Perspectives*. He wrote to me about this project some months ago and was to have come to see me in London to discuss it, but he never turned up. I shall write again to the *New Republic*, and give them your new address and chide them for their neglect. Thank you for sending me R'lene's poems which I like very much.

The children have had a wonderful summer, and are all active and gay. Ben had one relapse, but after two or three days in hospital he is as well and happy as ever.

My warm love to you both and urgent hope for better news of your health.

April 10, 1956
Bornholm, Denmark

Dear Herbert,

I have written you several letters but have had no word from you. There is a transport strike, and what with the rain and fog few planes come to Bornholm. My epistles have been waspish though I have great affection for you. Let me not be unmindful of many kindnesses shown to me by you. Let me also not be covetous, and may I be plain in the diction of my soul to you regarding this point. I do not care whether you print three or four books a year though I do not think this is healthful for your spirit. It is bad medicine for the head to write too much; the more one writes the less one thinks.

I have admonished you many times over the years, and we are

still friends, and whether I was right or wrong, that is a great credit to you. Few people can endure any sort of a rebuke, and few who reproach others ever trouble to examine their own faults. We dearly love every vice we have, and gently stroke our sins. I may be the most self-loving worm in the earth, but I tremble with despair when I consider it, and try very hard to correct myself. I do not think I have succeeded very much. I say these things to you because it would be unjust otherwise to criticise you. I am an admirer of certain books of yours and hate some of my writings. I have told you before, and pardon me for repeating Tolstoy's wonderful remarks: "Many men write books, but very few are ashamed of them afterwards."

Now, my dear friend, you have given my work great praise, enough to give me ease and to relieve me to some extent of those gnawing doubts which well-nigh make nihilists of us. You may deem it the act of Narcissus when you tell me there are no voices in the occident, and I am sorely wounded, and my entrails pierced, write to you in return that you have called me a voice, nay, have compared me to Nietzsche, Blake and Landor. Am I wrong in crying out to you? Why do you name me a mountain, a strong torrent, a hundred rivers one day, and deny me altogether the next? Suppose that I write to you that nobody can write any more, will you not want to go at once, like the blind, the maimed, and the cripple, and wash in the pool of Bethesda?

Now, we come to the most crucial perplexity, the relation between art and literature. Can we go to painting, especially a modern canvas devoid of all legends, maxims, and lore and ritual of the past, and find therein definitions we can employ for our lives? Will an abstract drawing teach us how to be a friend, a lover, or enable us to walk more meditatively, be less busy with idle matters, and have more time for discerning human beings? Are we likely to be more just after looking at Picasso, or more tender when we have filled our eyes with the skill of a Dali? Do they increase our reverence for the Universe, and can any one compose one good day or act following a surrealist experience in paints? Ch'en Su-want once wrote, or was said to have done so: "The art of literary composition was originated by scholars, while the art of painting was originated by men of skill."

What does an abstract painting mean? Why is it that almost no one risks a human figure or face any longer, or that when we see a person done in oils today he looks as though he had been embowelled or bombed? Most of the abstractions resemble the carnage after a war or a plague.

Whether you assent or not, can we have a nobler commonwealth when painting takes the place of the Word? How much inertia has modern art produced? People seldom read because music and painting have made them very lazy. Even my own book [*The Sorrows of Priapus*], and this distresses me rather than delights me, will appear, whenever it does, as an art-book, which means that you cannot draw a reader to serious or important words except by enticing his eyes, or rather betraying them. I think our eyes and ears have become very perfidious and that they are consequently so indolent and froward that they prefer to gaze with the most undefined rapture at colors or lie down whenever Bach or Mozart are played? Is this good or baneful? I have not met a single lover of music who employed his higher faculties. I met a whole covey of artists in New York when I lived there; they were crude and unlearned, and I regarded their paintings, and with all the will to care for them, as the absolute perversion of design, form, and art. One ancient Chinese painter, though all of his work is lost, is still remembered as an astronomer. That is very good, and such a man is likely to be a benefit to a commonality.

Whatever you may think of yourself, you will be remembered as a most gracious stylist (which is internal) and a beneficient critic of literature. You will, however, be blamed for your writings on art; that is, every thoughtful person will turn away from them, just as the herd-reader at present neglects your literary volumes to look at the plates and reproductions of other men's drawings and oils in your books on art.

If literature is dying out, and who can deny it, why don't you give more of your energies to preserve the few who are laboring for those meanings, ideas, and learning which cannot be found in painting? You are a publisher as well as a very serious author, and you yourself know that what is best and most noble in you are your essays on writers. I would gladly relinquish every art-book you have ever done just to save your wonderful essay on Swift. You know, too, my deep yea on *Phases of English Poetry*, *A Coat of Many Colours*, and *Annals of Innocence and Experience*. Some of your later poems I care for a great deal. You, however, reprint everything you have done in the past, and you cannot hope to be as good in the past as you are when you are at your best now. I was sharp with you because you had put everything together in your *True Voice of Feeling*, and much of it was far beneath the way you think and pulse now. Still, even here, you show good sense, and you may have been annoyed when I said that your essay on Coleridge was exceedingly sensible. Here I was only following the dictum of La Bruyère; Johnson says the same and so does Coleridge himself. But if you are to give us savants in letters you must also present us with sages of the brush; otherwise, you do yourself much harm, neglect your companions in literature, and confuse many readers. I repeat, and I cannot say this too often to you, painting without the Word is barbaric, and is no more than a tool of the megalopolitan savage. You must, please, heed me when I say this to you. The artist now is the most passive vessel of all the mechanical filths which have dropped into our soul and made our cities wicked, dark, sooty, and hopeless. We have factory painters and authors, street-urchins of art and literature who curse and despise and demolish what they seem to practise. Most of the painters cannot draw a circle. When a messenger sent by the pope to see whether Giotto was the genius he was reputed to be, the latter to prove that he was took a piece of paper and drew a perfect circle which he asked the messenger to take back to his master as the evidence of his abilities.

I have not received your Epistle on [Henry] James; it distresses me deeply that with all your understanding you cannot see that James could not write. We do not read 20 novels to find a few lines when we can peruse one book by a gifted writer and learn as we read page after page. Why do you occupy yourself with so many dwarfs when you can fill your head with Erasmus, Longinus, Herodotus, Ovid, Virgil, Strabo, some of the early Christian Fathers, and countless other men who have disburdened so many of our days of tedium, sorrow, and hopeless disbelief?

I cannot blame you for writing for bread; Tolstoy did that, and he did not need a rye or black crust as much as you do, but let no one think that his work did not suffer and is not inglorious because he wrote for money and because he is so unlearned. But he had wondrous though sometimes gross energy, and he had a fierce passion which saved him from mediocrity. You despise *What Is Art?* I learn much from it though I violate many of his own canons, screeds, and even pure assertions of anger. But you must be vigilant and own that some of your work is for bread; it is as easy to forget that

115

as it is to ignore our worst turpitudes. We write for heaven and earth, for the intellect and the body, but shun one or the other, and you write only for the worst citizens of the world.

It is your duty first to heal the void in letters. If you fail to come to the rescue of one good author you must blame yourself and quite mercilessly for helping to increase illiteracy which will one day lead to apocalyptic violence. We are close to it now, and our books and paintings damage our nerves, sicken our hearts, and spoil our flesh, and the flowers and herbs thereof, and are more like machine guns, tractors, fierce implements of war than gentle, murmuring rivers, kind and loving glades, slopes, and trees which feed the hungry soul and the dry bones.

I beg you, as your friend and as your most affectionate companion in letters to listen to me.

You know, my dear Herbert, that *The Nation* is going to print some of our Letters. I am very happy about this; at first [Carey] McWilliams, [Editor of *The Nation*] wanted to do a page of my epigrams as he called them. I was not very content because I could not see what advantage readers could reap from perusing a page of wit. I have since asked him, if he could, to print two letters of yours and two of mine so that our values could be seen and weighed and understood. Whether he publishes more of you than of me is of no import, but that he is printing us pleases me deeply. Now, please, Herbert find a publisher for our volume [*Truth Is More Sacred*]. I have not been sluggish, though I have been sick, nor did I sit back and wait for you to act, and I do not have your influence in the world.

Your loving friend.

April 20, 1956
Stonegrave, York

Dear Edward,

Ruskin to his father, January 28, 1852: "I could not—or should not work at all — if I thought these things trifling. All my labour and all my writing are done under the conviction of pictures being of enormous importance, and of our neglect of them being Sin."

Ruskin was lucky in having a great artist — Turner — to write about. You do not think that the artists I write about — Picasso or Klee or Henry Moore or Ben Nicholson — are as great as Turner. You seize on one relatively obscure American painter, de Kooning, about whom I have never written a word, and impugn my activities in his name. I don't think that de Kooning can be dismissed with complete contempt, but I know little of his work and reserve judgement. But in general I know what I am writing about, I believe like Ruskin that it is of enormous importance, or otherwise I should not write at all.

Then you break in with your denunciations and accuse me of wasting my time, prostituting my talents, and so on. Is there any wonder that occasionally I get a little rattled, especially as I am always working under tremendous pressure, a fact you never seem to realize, and largely devoting myself to other people, with no thought of my own genius or my own fame. It would have been very agreeable to have conducted my life otherwise, writing poetry when the inspiration came to me, and spending the rest of my time criticising other poets. But somehow that always seemed a dilettante and self-indulgent mode of living. I don't claim any merit for the sacrifices I have made — they have been done by instinct, and in the belief that I had a duty to my family and even to the artists I write about, for I found myself in a situation (in this country) where I was the only person with the necessary energy and will to take on the defence of modern art. I would willingly have stood down and left the field to some other critic, but I belong to a generation that was decimated by war, and people who might have done this necessary task — men like T. E. Hulme — were killed in that war, and I found myself a solitary survivor in this field. I am not in any way ashamed of what I have written about art — I have not had the wealth and leisure of a Ruskin, and have always worked against time, and many things are hastily written, without the necessary grace. But the truth, as I see it, has prevailed, and that is all that matters.

You must forgive my irritation, and I am sorry to have to speak roughly to a man who is ill. But I wanted to stop the flow of your misunderstanding. I am sorry you do not think I have done enough for you: I have done what I can. It was I who suggested this way of publishing *The Sorrows* to Laughlin, and without my persistence and pleading he would not have done it. Only he can do it because he is not strictly speaking a commercial publisher and has a background of wealth. You cannot expect such actions from commercial publishers like Routledge or Faber, who have to balance their accounts and satisfy their auditors and shareholders. You demand patronage in an age when patronage is dead.

As for not writing about your books, one cannot praise a book in a preface and then praise it again in an article or essay. And where does one publish an essay on Edward Dahlberg? There are no literary reviews that you respect: they are all edited by men you have made your enemies.

I shall be proud to have *The Sorrows* dedicated to me, but if I then promise to review it in a magazine, the editor suspects a conspiracy.

I cannot go on with this acrimonious debate — it wearies me and I am overworked and tired. Cannot you forget your misfortunes for a while, and return to your disinterested love of letters? There would be solace in some quite objective activity.

I will send the James letter as soon as I have had time to re-type it — at the moment I am driven by endless tasks and duties. I would go mad but for the fact that I can walk every day on the hills and fill my mind with their peace.

Your loving friend.

December 12, 1956
Seville, Spain

Dear Herbert,

I am very glad to have your letter forwarded to me from Malaga.

What makes you think, Herbert, your judgments on James are *objective*, a foolish word bandied about by dust and flesh, and that mine are *personal*? Have you forgotten that in one of your Epistles you set aside his novels, but insisted that we owed him homage because he was heroic and wrote some few lines, very few, in his own letters? Do you imagine that Dr. Johnson's estimate of Swift was not personal? Do you think that Hazlitt was free from a plethora of prejudices, or that Addison or Steele wrote memorials on authors that were *scientific*? Look, I have read all the noble, dreary aesthetes, from Kant, Schopenhauer, Schiller to I. A. Richards, and am mostly bored, and seldom renewed or invigorated by their dingy, objective judgments. Dickens is an author for boys, but Homer can be read or misread at 20, and judged at 60. Do you imagine that as we grow older our feelings for masterpieces are doddering, fatuous and peevish, whereas we were cool and tranquil when we garbled their wondrous thoughts and lines when we were green and callow?

I don't care very much for Wordsworth, and though Coleridge admired him, some of his criticism of Wordsworth was very damaging. I read your own essay on Wordsworth with great delight despite my own prejudice against him. I think he was a mediocre poet. Is that personal, then no man can be otherwise, for when is one's idea sufficiently aloof and who can prove it? Your own remarkable essay on Swift would be thrown away by an adherent of the author of Gulliver. Who then would be right, you or he? Is my epistle on Joyce reckless or subjective, whilst yours is reposeful and olympian?

I have no faith in Aldington's criticism because I think a man who admires the best in Swinburne and yet defends Wilde and Pater and Hemingway has a meager intellectual faculty.

Please bear in mind that this is a didactic book [*Truth Is More Sacred*] written to furnish readers and the apprentices to literature a path toward understanding. I have not the least heart to hurt the ashes of Lawrence, but I am more concerned with his bad effect upon young authors. I am not a venal writer, and would publish our Letters without reward, even taking the abuse, because I think it is a deeply useful volume to people steeped in nihilism and the most hedonistic waywardness. I am not moral in the philistine sense. When I read Byron I do not care one way or another whether he lay with his half-sister, Augusta or not. There are some sexual sins that trouble me, but very few, and a good line by Rimbaud is still good whether he was a bugger or not. There are no good books that wither or stale in time; bad books were poorly written when they were made, and do not deteriorate because we have grown older. Nor have I lost my own energetic exuberance; I still kneel in my heart before Callimachus or Propertius or some reverence in Pausanias. Nor has *Don Quixote* dropped in my estimation because I am now 56 and not 26. I can still read the best of Flaubert and Stendhal with abundant delight, and understand them better than I did when I gave them my heart and devotion at 28.

Now, Herbert, I am not insensible of your labor for bread. You must have the loaves and the pair of gudgeons. But, please, recall that for my own work I receive sometimes by you tombstone encomium or nothing at all. I am very glad that you can earn money for your tribulations; but though no man will heed another until he has fallen down to the ground, and then he may curse you, I must remind you that you have to write at times solely because the Universe exacts truth and energy from you. As a stylist you are a lissome deer, and so I regard you, but you cannot write well, or think clearly in a hurry. You are trying to match your own rush, and objective judgments on books you have not read for many years with my very cautious, and personal remarks that come after the closest reading and scrutiny and meditation.

Now, my dear friend, will you kindly also remember that I have put a great deal of time into these Epistles, and that seems to be of no value to the world, and of the same worth to you. I cannot afford, and this is not a precautionary economic word, to pour my soul onto the ground after 14 months of reading, tedium, and anguish.

You have always been a hasty man, or much more so now than you were 15 years ago, and in those days I begged you to give more time to your own interior gifts. I have pleaded in vain, and this, too was a personal admonition? although I had in mind your life and bourne on this earth and not mine.

I am reading constantly, and it is my deepest hope that I shall begin writing in another two months or so. I cannot endure to be idle or not to write.

In your friendship with me, and in your relation to me concerning the book we are doing together, I beg you to be less personal and more considerate of my own pains and labors which I thought were ours together.

The paper from Stuttgart arrived too late for Christmas publication of the book [*The Sorrows of Priapus*] and I was very despondent for weeks because everything has been postponed. *The Nation* has neither printed our Epistles nor paid me a penny. Where is Justice, O my dear Objective Friend?

We both send you our devoted love, and I thank heaven that that is not impersonal, scientific or etiolated.

I have been rereading a good deal of Shakespeare, or had done so some months back. His miraculous lines I bow to, particularly to the Sonnets. But let me ask you, when I find horseplay in the Comedies, or some pun, which I cannot accept, is that petulant, and subjective, and when I read some of his best and august poems and weep over them is that mature, considered, and cool? Is Timon personal or not, and what of Lear? And are these criticisms or not?

Your friend, and again, as always with the warmest affections.

120

Dear Edward,

I had a card from Hull yesterday which tells me that you were to leave Seville on the 21st, so presumably by now you are in Ascona, where I hope you have found good accommodation. Hull promises to do what he can to help you — I think you will find a good friend in him.

I enclose a prospectus of an American school in nearby Minusio where it is conceivable that R'lene might find employment. Perhaps one enquiry might lead to another possibility. If [Erich] Remarque is in Ascona (Hull will tell you where he lives) he might have secretarial work for R'lene, and she could say that I recommended her to get in touch with him. But I think he spends a few months in the States at this time of year.

You react too violently to [Richard] Aldington. I do not mean that he has not provoked you beyond silent endurance, but you spend too much of your spirit on such personal affronts. I know how difficult it is to control one's resentment, and I am myself often touched to the quick by the malice of my critics. But resentment is a poison in one's veins, and destroys the peace of mind which is the only state of mind that is creative. I had a letter this morning from [Naum] Gabo, who is reduced to impotence because his brother (Pevsner) has given an interview to a Paris magazine in which he makes certain statements that Gabo considers untrue and unjust. False statements should be corrected, but that done, the mind should be indifferent to the motives that inspired them. A counsel of perfection, I know, and one which I do not necessarily follow myself.

Indeed, if the Epistles languish, it may be partly due to Aldington's poor opinion of them. One should never show half-finished work to anyone on whose sympathy one cannot rely. I am not blaming you for showing our work to Aldington — I should have done the same in your circumstances. And I don't agree with his criticism of them. But nevertheless it is a rebuff from which it takes time to recover.

The real reason is the one I always give — the complexity of my life, my inability to escape from the myriad cares that press me down. I have a box behind my table into which I throw the string from the many parcels that come in, string full of knots which then gets entangled with the heap, until to draw a length of free string from the tangled mass becomes impossible. That is the true image of my life.

I will make a new effort in the New Year. It seems that I must write another letter on James — the last one is admittedly not a good one. But then you must give a new turn to the correspondence. But a more positive turn. I do not believe that we should waste [time] on a fellow like [Robert] Graves. The big issues lie elsewhere — indeed outside the world of belles lettres. I see no future for poetry or the novel, or for drama, except in so far as these forms are embodied in the philosophy of a new humanism. We are at a stage of evolution at which we need philosophers and prophets, and these must be of a pattern adapted to our civilization. It is difficult to conceive a Socrates of the screen and there is no question of compromising with the prevailing vulgarism. But there is no audience for our belles lettres, so we must be content with whatever faith we have in the immortality of good writing, or we must make the necessary gestures to attract an audience. And to do this without losing our integrity!

This begins to sound like a sermon, and the house is stirring for the festivities. There are thirteen of us — the complete family, three guests, and two Italian maids.

I shall wait anxiously to hear how you get settled in Ascona, and shall hope for good news.

My love to you both.

October 30, 1959
New York City

Dear Herbert,

It is a great relief to hear that you are at home again after your journey to China. How good, too, to know that you are in such fine health. I cannot refrain from asking what you are going to do with your strength. Will you return to literature? I recall many years ago when you thought I was so overwhelmed by Tolstoy's hatred of art and letters that I should give over writing altogether. But, alas, it is you, my gifted Friend, who carry this Atlantean burden upon your heart. Or do you find it an easy load to bear?

I have not altered my own thoughts about communism. People everywhere pay the greatest price for their bread and miserable lodgings. An Eskimo gives less of his life for his lamp of moss, his knife wrought of the tusk of a walrus, and his food consisting of whale-blubber and seal, than we do for our mess, taken in a hurry, and our wretched wizened apartments for which we bleed most of the days of the sun. It does not matter much whether you give your flesh and your spirit for the State-cartel we title capitalism, or that corporation, known as a communistic society. And I don't think you can learn very much in a conducted tour in a land so alien to all that you know. I like oriental women, too, and have little doubt that it has been a tragedy to keep these people away from our country where the blood is anaemic if not dead.

I care little for greed or materials canonized by the soviets, or by western monopolists. I cannot see but that the Russians want what other people have, a refrigerated box, a subway, large, flagitious cities, automobiles. The Russians transport many coveys of ballet dancers to our shores, a few journalists and a composer or two, better than our own, but hardly men to compare with Bach or Handel or Monteverdi, and the American press swoons. It may be that they are in some respects not as demented as the occidental race of fools, but in other ways they are noddies too. I hear that the Russian teddy boys are utterly mad for rock and roll, and the vile debauched sounds we misname music here.

I am as weary as the worm of politics, and know no evil more devilish than a statesman, a man of the state. When you wrote your very fine Foreword to *The Flea of Sodom*, you said with great panic, and rightly so, that the Chinese were at the frontier of Tibet. Are you forgetting the tragedy of Hungary, Poland, Finland, the Latvian nations, and sundry other enslaved peoples?

Now, my dear Herbert, I spoke to Laughlin who just returned to America, and he is very interested in our Epistles, and I think we should make arrangements for their publication. You can get your work published far easier than I can, and I don't want to go on writing until I have assurance that some one will do the book. You know I am at the moment tormented by the autobiography, [*Because I was Flesh*] and am giving a lecture on Melville which is to be published, along with other lectures by authors. It took me a whole month to reread *Moby Dick* and it will take at least that time to gather notes, and take another look at *Mardi*, and his Poems, as well as compare his work with many volumes on voyages to the New World. *Moby Dick* belongs to that kind of writing rather than to the great store of human learning. Of course, I do not pretend that you are going to find some of his lines in Parry,

Pigafetta, Drake, Herrera, and so on, but the bulk of *Moby Dick* is for a man about to apprentice himself as a whaler.

I beg you, then, Herbert, to go ahead with arrangements with Laughlin who says he will write you, or if you prefer, with Mr. [Ben] Raeburn [of Horizon Press] whom I do not know. We could then complete the book [*Truth Is More Sacred*] without too much trouble, another five thousand words or so. You said we should write about Eliot, Pound, perhaps Yeats, I shall want to say something about [William Carlos] Williams, who, alas, never had a great development, but wrote one book, *In the American Grain*, and that grounded upon meager reading, but perhaps very good. I must reread it. I should like to add some words also on Wyndham Lewis, vastly overestimated, and essentially a newspaper mind. What he assailed was often right, but without much sense or culture of his own.

Your own very discerning Letter on Lawrence I read a couple of times, and give you my deepest thanks, dear Herbert, for your tribute. The heart is corrupt, Herbert, and I myself am often in an agony when I consider my own vanity. Who can utter his full vanity and not cower, or hide it, and not be speciously meek? You are the kindest Man in the World of Letters, and I owe you much, more than I can ever thank you for. You know that, and what is more important, I know it!

You once asked me about Zukofsky; I cannot continue a connection with a man who is so mercilessly uncritical of his own work, and who has so little gratitude in his heart. I cannot bear the unthanking biped, No-Man. Let it be. I am sorry that I was of use to him, not only through you, but I got many of his poems printed here.

I expect page-proofs of the second part of the autobiography, and will send you both magazines in which the memoirs appear. You won't care for the periodical [*Big Table*], but what can I do, save tell the truth in as strong a prose style as I know. Should I appear only in these places I regard clean, just and arcadian, I would be in no magazine.

Allen [Tate] has sent a marvelous statement to be used on the dust-jacket of *Can These Bones Live*, and so there will be your Introduction, his Yea, the drawings by James Kearns which please Laughlin and MacGregor deeply.

Of course, you know, dear Herbert, I shall, when I get to that parcel of the memoir dealing with literature pay you a great tribute as a formal essayist in the tradition of Hazlitt, Coleridge, and Dryden, and give you, I pray, that debt of gratitude I owe you for so much Human Goodness.

I have been ailing, and if this letter resembles lichen and scurvy grass rather than the savannas and meadowland please forgive me.

I have been culling much again from natural history, trying to find those equivalents of the mind, the heart, and the hands in an isthmus, the vegetable mould in the Arctic Circle, even the dung of the musk-oxen which provides those desolate and dreary grounds with the flowers that spring up from the sorriest shrubs.

R'lene has not been well either; since we returned from Spain we have not flourished. The summer here was noxious; any swamp might have been more salubrious than the month of October, terrifyingly humid, viscid, each night of sleep, with an electric fan blowing some false air on our faces, a going to and fro in the earth.

You have, as always my great admiration, and we both send you our warmest love.

Your devoted friend.

You did not imagine I wanted you to write a book on Ruskin simply to dedicate it to me. What a craven reason that would be. Of course, I was greatly elated, when you said that if you wrote such a chapbook you would give me that tribute. But I don't care to be more vulgar, ambitious, mean and sly than the vilest flesh is.

December 4, 1960
(my 67th birthday)
Stonegrave, York

Dear Edward,

The last epistle which I sent off some time ago has not been acknowledged either by you or Ben Raeburn: I hope it arrived safely and that it did not enrage you too much. If you feel you must have the last word, I have no objection, but I do not wish to prolong the correspondence and tried to give my last words an air of finality.

I did not yet receive a copy of the new edition of *Can These Bones Live*, but it may be on its way by surface mail. But I did receive *The Literary Review* with your reappraisal of Moby Dick. This is a wonderful essay, but how it will infuriate the American literary chauvinists! You are terribly convincing, and make clear to me why my children, to whom I have often recommended the book, could never persevere with it — I did not re-read it myself, and could not. I think possibly those few canorous lines you quote could be multiplied, and that there are whole paragraphs of eloquence buried in it. But your main contention is true: it is a suffocating blubber-room and no Homeric epic. I rejoice to hear that a collection of your critical essays is to be published. It should stir those vapid analysts, the New Critics, to envy or a belated acknowledgement of your integrity.

My days are full with futile busy-ness — I struggle like a drowning man for air. The world will not leave me alone, and if you say I should ignore its solicitations, I can only reply that the clamour would still distract me. I have created the fame that destroys me. You should sometimes be grateful for the neglect that gives you solitude. There is no even measure in this world of literature.

Those are fine lines of Allen's [Allen Tate] you quote in your Melville essay — I hope he has seen the essay and made some generous comment.

You mentioned Pascal in your last letter. I have recently gone back to him for a little spiritual refreshment and find his thoughts as wonderful as ever. If only we had his faith!

I hope you are feeling less lonely and have reasonable health. I enter my 68th year with a little arthritis but no other bodily ills, and for that I must be grateful. Please give R'lene my love when you see her.

Your devoted friend.

THOMAS KINSELLA

Drowsing Over the Arabian Nights

I nodded.   The books agree,
one hopes for too much.
It is ridiculous.
We are elaborate beasts.

If we concur, it is only
in our hunger;   the soiled gullet . . .
And sleep's airy nothing.
And the moist matter of lust

(— if the whole waste of women
could be gathered like one pit
under swarming Man . . .
then all might act together).

And 'the agonies' of death
— as we enter our endless nights
quickly, one by one, fire
darting up to the roots of our hair.

JOHN HOLLOWAY

Flower of the Mountain

I consider
    in this still and stony place
    between sea and mountain
Those who
    at one with the
    rupted, disrupted planet, its
    rent and torrent, quake,
    earthquake, core-tremor,
    tremendous chord of discord,
Those few
    at the fuse of now, the
    brunt of its
    troubled or flaring frontier
Still
    (as this green jet of a
    seaward country) run
    their springs through deep beds to
Issue gently. The all they do,
Humane and retiring.
    . . . fissured into
    a seep of sweetness.

And I
Hardly see this
        appraisal and raising nature as —
As anti-nature:
        for
        heavy with rightness, authentic,
        ancient in its seeming as the rocks of
        our west, our ledge where
        the wave bursts in greenness, in
        these last and modest pastures,
        is it not the
Second and
Heavenly nature?
        bedrock
        as this archaean
        erode and overthrust
        determining at once the
        angry outcrop and small
Flower of the Mountain?

G. Wilson Knight

HERBERT READ AND BYRON

IN THE BRITISH COUNCIL booklet on Sir Herbert Read, Francis Berry, discussing the *Collected Essays in Literary Criticism*, observes that, though its range is wide and "though there are frequent *en passant* references to Shakespeare and Chaucer, these are not substantial contributions in the way that his studies of Wordsworth, Coleridge, Shelley and Keats (and even Byron) are."

That bracket poses a problem central to both Byron and Read. Roughly, both may be called "romantic." Byron's romanticism is however only part of his contribution, since his literary valuations, and much of his practice, first in heroic diction and later in dramatic form, are Augustan. He bestrides two periods, as did Milton and Shakespeare before him. This is what Read did also, in his own way, within the context of twentieth-century letters.

He reverses the Byronic divisions. His literary and social philosophies support "organic" rather than established forms and "personality" in place of "character." But he was one of Eliot's circle, and a life-long friend. In literary practice his peculiarly reserved and unpretentious tone, or wavelength, corresponds; and may accordingly be called "classic."

In his British Council booklet on Byron, Read follows certain conventional views with which we can now, perhaps, part company; in calling Byron an "atheist" he is, simply, wrong. And yet the brief essay abounds in original comments that strike home. He accords the right priority to, and quotes in full, Byron's *Thirty-Sixth Year*; he finds Byron's to be "the wildest poetic energy in the whole range of post-Shakespearian poetry"; and he believes that Byron was "in some sense beyond good and evil, one of Nietzsche's 'free spirits'." When in the preface to my *Poets of Action* I referred to Read as "that fine Byronist," he wrote in reply, on December 10, 1967 that it was "a compliment I would like to deserve."

I had known him for some years. We met first in 1947 at the Present Question Conference at Birmingham, where I gave a lecture bearing the Nietzschean title "The Avenging Mind" (included in *Shakespeare and Religion*, 1967). He was generous in approval; as again, when I subsequently sent him my book *Christ and Nietzsche*. Later in London, in 1950, I showed him some photographs of dramatic poses, and he sent me a book by M. Feldenkrais, *Body and Mature Behaviour* (1949), which I used for the commentary on the pictures of the volume *Symbol of Man*, as yet unpublished. After that, in 1951, I sent him, as a director of Routledge & Kegan Paul, my *Lord Byron: Christian Virtues*, which was proving difficult to publish. It quickly won his, and the firm's, support. Read invited me to his club in London. He greatly liked my *Lord Byron's Marriage*; and on the publication of *Byron and Shakespeare* he sent me a reprint of his *Byron* booklet inscribed with a rating of my Byronic studies which manners forbid me to publicize.

That is the record of what Read did, selflessly, not only in support of a younger contemporary but, what is more important, for Byron. His actions were impelled by a creative, Byronic, generosity; and without him my three Byron volumes might not have appeared.

His interest in Byron was reflected in two recent publications. In *High Noon and Darkest Night* (Monday Evening Papers, 3; Center for Advanced Studies, Wesleyan University, 1964), an answer to José Ortega y Gasset's strictures on modernistic art, he quoted for his purpose various passages from Byron: "Perhaps it is Byron who gives the best expression to this romantic ideal of essential Night."

In 1953 there was a broadcast of Read's dialogue *Lord Byron at the Opera* (published by Philip Ward, 28 Parkfield Crescent, North Harrow, 1963). The main persons are Byron and Stendhal, and the setting a box of the opera at Milan, in 1816. The dialogue shows a delicate skill, with scholarship. In a preface defending Dialogue as a medium Read notes: "There is hardly a sentiment or even an expression in this dialogue for which chapter and verse could not be quoted."

The formal, even stilted, manner may be a true capturing of aristocratic, period, conversation; but it is rather strange that Read, so receptive to the tumultuous in Byron, could have so resisted all temptation to let the Byronic fire ignite.

True, this is a dialogue, not a drama. But when during the fifties Read sent me a typescript of a drama, *The Parliament of Women*, to comment on, I was aware of a similar limitation. The play is nevertheless fascinating. It dramatizes a French occupation of Greece in the thirteenth century, and the historical reading and creation of "atmosphere" are compelling. Against a background of imperial warring and political duplicity flowers a simple love-interest asserting the rights of the heart against convention. In 1960 the play was published, exquisitely produced and illustrated, in a limited edition of 100 copies by The Vine Press (Hemingford Grey, Huntingdon). I was honoured to receive a copy of it.

The Parliament of Women bears an interesting title. In the dramatic heritage of the West women, from ancient Greece to Shaw and O'Casey, regularly present a challenge to male warring and politics; and in this play, where women are left for a while in political control, Read had a theme which touched some of his most cherished tenets. The sexual balance is established and the points firmly made; sentences are finely chiselled and thought keen; and there are opportunities for sensitive production, in grouping and stately movement, to delight the eye. But there is less excitement than one expects; the whole is statically conceived, with little Dionysian thrust from the female party; and no strong dramatic conflict emerges.

Nor was that aimed at. Read contributes a preface on poetic drama, which includes a tribute to Byron's *The Two Foscari*. In his dramas Byron aimed at classic form and a lowering of dramatic tempo: "What I seek to show in *The Foscaris* is the *suppressed* passion, rather than the rant of the present day" (to John Murray, September 20, 1821). Read was following Byron. The play has exquisite verse interludes, one a messenger-speech and others of choric tone; in these the drama quietly takes wing into a more rarefied, clarified, philosophic, mode; but passions are not unleashed.

In rejecting what he regarded as the Shakespearian extravagance, Byron was only in part successful; there was so much dramatic power in him that his theories did no, or little, dramatic harm; but with Read, one feels that control came perhaps too easily. Drama was less instinctive to him than to Byron. Much of his life was given to the Apollonian arts of sculpture, painting and ceramics; though here too, as in literature, he was responsive to the darker energies, and a strong supporter of modern innovations. All this he could see, and know, and as a critic experience; but it was not quite natural to his own, more gentle, Apollonian, personality.

His was, the more one thinks of it, a baffling personality. A distinguished soldier, and decorated for his service, he became a pacifist; an anarchist by political tendency, he accepted, and did well to accept, in all humility, a knighthood.

To understand either a work of art or a personality one must search for the point where its contained opposites are blended; perhaps, if we are fortunate, found, if only for an instant, identical. The opposites in Read are (i) his respect to natural instinct; and (ii) his serene, perhaps "classic," manner. Similar oppositions are in Byron and Nietzsche too, but for them instincts were more unrestful, the struggle for serenity harder, and their life-works in consequence the more richly varied. Even so, in Byron the originating core, or impulse, was, as I showed, following Thomas Moore, in *Byron and Shakespeare* (VI, 194-5), a softness, a thwarted love; and probably it was so for Nietzsche too. Both these in their later works, in *Sardanapalus, Cain*, and *Thus Spake Zarathustra*, registered a victory in attunement to the softer powers; for we must remember that in Byron's *Cain* our first and archetypal murder is shown as motivated by horror of cruelty to animals. The ethical problem is not simple: original sin may be easier for us to place and handle than original virtue.

Now Read, a man, if ever there was one, of "original virtue," was by temperament peculiarly able to focus and express this very problem. Here, in *The Parliament of Women*, the opposites come together, are identified:

GEOFFREY: There are some things, that concern a man's heart, that he does not share with even his nearest friends.
WILLIAM: There I do not follow you. Guilt is the only feeling we do not willingly share.
GEOFFREY: No; there are innocent feelings that are shy of the light.
(III. ii)

That goes very deep into our human state. Our most terrible evils arouse a warm and congenial response; we are at home with them, and never more so than when we indulge in field-days of moral criticism. But what if such evils are all, in the manner of Cain's murder, reactions from some unconfessed, and feared, good; which,

133

if recognized, would strike greater terror than evil? As Nietzsche has it:

> So alien to your soul is the great that the Superman
> would seem to you *terrible* in his goodness.
>
> (*Thus Spake Zarathustra*; II. 21)

Some new assessment of the good-and-evil within us may be needed. Advance may be arduous, bringing not only dread but also, and perhaps worse, embarrassment; for we might have to ratify many an "innocent" feeling that dreads "the light."

Kathleen Raine

HERBERT READ AS A
LITERARY CRITIC

MY FIRST READING of Herbert Read's criticism and the beginning of an enduring friendship with him marked my own emergence into my generation, as an undergraduate in the late twenties. Indebted as I am in countless ways to their author, I cannot see those many articles and introductions, written to make known some new or still unvalued writer or painter, merely as "literary criticism." Much that Herbert Read wrote — and much of the best — must be seen as a mode of action on behalf of the living arts and living artists of his time. He was, above all, "engaged"; not in the sense of seeing literature and the other arts as so many auxiliary political weapons; rather he saw politics as the necessary field on which his battle for the unpolitical values must be won or lost. *The Politics of the Unpolitical* (1943) is not only one of his finest essays: it defines the ground of his own action in the field — the confused and stricken field — of the arts, from the mid-twenties to the time of his death in 1968. "The only taste is a contemporary taste," he believed; and "It is merely lack of intelligence to refuse the experience embodied in the poetry of the past; but it shows an even greater lack of intelligence to refuse the experience embodied in the present." "One has only to compare, for example, Saintsbury's essay on Pater with Eliot's essay on Pater and Arnold to see the difference between the literary gossip of a refugee from life and the criticism of a man for whom literature is an integral part of life; dealing with problems which cannot with any good conscience be isolated from life." Elsewhere, writing of Ruskin

135

(whom he admired as the greatest critic) he makes the observation, "I cannot think of any great critic ... — great as an artist in his own right — who has not found some good in the art of his own age."

The independent "man of letters" is ceasing to exist in modern society, greatly to our loss. From the interested motives of press and academe Herbert Read was free. What he once wrote of Walter Bagehot was true of himself: " ... varied interests gave to his mind a universality which is rare in literature but of incomparable value. It may seem, on a superficial view, that Bagehot dissipated his energies over too wide a field; that if he had concentrated on criticism, on politics, on economics, he might have attained the highest possible reputation in one of these narrower spheres. That would be to mistake the quality of the man and to misjudge the proper value of criticism: the opinion of such a man on one literary topic is worth the life-work of a solitary pedant."

It is strange to follow the stages of his progression from his Yorkshire boyhood to the rather bleak internationalism of "the modern movement"; in which he lived, I always felt, in an austere, self-imposed exile. A farmer's son, he was born into a natural world little changed since the Wordsworths and the Brontës, and a human world still regional, rooted, dignified. His life-long love of Wordsworth arose naturally from the similarity of their "formation"; and a nostalgia for regionalism haunts his writings. On Sterne he wrote: "It is almost possible to say that an epic needs for its creation the all-inclusive self-consciousness of a small community. The ideal conditions exist when you have a community large enough to employ all the capacities and exhibit all the passions of mankind, yet small enough to be within the knowledge of one man." And in *The Writer and his Region*: "It is this concentration of infinite time in a finite place that produces the intensities of great art. It is the finiteness of the region that makes the ethos that moulds the character that is copied by the dramatist or the novelist. As for the poet and the painter, the musician and the architect, they are in more direct contact with the same ethos — an epic, a folk-song, a lyric, even a house, these are emanations of the genius loci, which alone can give accent, colour and life to the universal prototypes of the mind." Wordsworth was the regional poet of a part of England no longer, in the human sense, a region, after the first world war, when Yeats could still, in Ireland, discover and create in some measure a "unity of culture" no longer possible in England; and Herbert Read was forced by the circumstances of his life into a field of action uncongenial to his natural sensibility, the no-man's-land of nomadic modern society. From the dales of the West Riding and the ruins of Rievaulx (the life of Aelred, abbot of Rievaulx, was one of his favourite books) to the Institute of Contemporary Arts, what a distance!

His contemporary Edwin Muir had travelled as far without severing some living link with his boyhood and his ancestors in the Orkneys which Herbert (although he returned in his later life to Yorkshire) somehow lost; perhaps because Muir (though he was one of the finest critics of his generation and made fewer mistakes in his judgments of new works and new authors than either Eliot or Read) never concerned himself with groups and movements. Herbert himself wrote that " ... the eternal works of art — those exempt from the morality of taste and fashion — are those which are based on individual sensibility to the exclusion of all conceptual or 'idealogical' motives. But this still leaves the individual at the mercy of those unconscious forces which we call taste or fashion, unless genius is precisely the capacity to evade these forces." As a poet Herbert Read was certainly not at the mercy of the *zeitgeist*; his own poems — which will, I believe, outlast most of his criticism — laconic, private utterances — are the creation of his own "true voice of feeling"; his concern with groups and movements a matter of principle, or the expression of another side of his character, to which, perhaps, he often sacrificed his poetic genius on behalf of talents of less value than his own.

Herbert Read's earliest critical writings, and those anthologies he made in collaboration with Bonamy Dobrée, seem nearer to his natural vein than what came later: *The Sense of Glory* (1929) and *English Prose Style*, with its fine sense of the native idiom of the English language. Curiously enough his best studies were nearly all of prose writers — Malory and Froissart, Swift, Smollett and Sterne, Berkeley, Hawthorne, James. The verse he liked was that nearest to prose: "free verse." He quotes, in *The True Voice of Feeling* from D. H. Lawrence's preface to the American edition of New Poems (1920): "In free verse we look for the insurgent naked throb of the instant moment. ... It is the instant; the quick; the very jetting source of all will-be and has-been." "Poetry of this instantaneous kind must necessarily be written in free verse" Read comments; but

137

he later seems to have reflected that it is prose which is most immediately responsive to "the instant moment," and in which "the pitch and interval of natural utterance" finds its freest expression. Herbert Read's after-thoughts were invariably perceptive; as on Lawrence: "I regard him as, all things considered, the most original English writer of the post-war period. He has enlarged or intensified our very consciousness of the world in which we are vitally involved. But 'direct utterance from the instant whole man' is prose; a prose that faithfully projects the man himself; and insofar as he projected himself, exposed his sensibilities and formulated his ideas, Lawrence made a unique contribution to our literature. But it was, in the technical sense, a prose contribution. Of the technique of free verse, as it was developing, under his eyes, he had, as Pound realized from the beginning, no grain of understanding."

Imagism, with its accompanying form of "free verse," was the first of the several movements with which Herbert Read was to associate himself. From the regionalism which inspired his first and enduring poetic loyalty to Wordsworth he moved, in post-war London, into the American expatriate *ethos* which, from Henry James to Ezra Pound and T. S. Eliot, introduced into English letters that internationalism which changed, perhaps permanently, the course of its native current. Eliot was to become his closest literary associate and lifelong friend; perhaps against his own natural bent he was caught up into the stronger current of the Imagist movement. T. E. Hulme's often-quoted lines

> I saw the ruddy moon lean over a hedge
> like a red-faced farmer

may be poor poetry, but they are good prose. Herbert Read's natural preference for the laconic, together with his adherence to Wordsworth's view that poetry should be a selection from the language of common men may have attracted him to a poem and a theory of poetry which does not, in retrospect, seem more than an incident, even an irrelevance, in the history of English poetry.

The word that Herbert Read most often uses of the kind of literature he believed in was "feeling." It was he who described *The Prelude* as "the epic of the man of feeling"; "poetry," he wrote (à propos Wordsworth) "is the culture of the feelings; not the cultivation of the feelings, but their education." He invokes Ruskin who had written that "the goodness of a man is a question of his sensibility; it is the goodness of his heart, not of his brain" and "the ennobling difference between one man and another ... is precisely in this, that one feels more than another. ... We are only human insofar as we are sensitive, and our honour is precisely in proportion to our passion." In his own declaration of *The Faith of a Critic* he writes: "at the basis is *pathos*. Sympathy and empathy, feeling *with* and feeling *into*." He saw Romanticism as "a sudden expansion of consciousness — an expansion into the realms of sensibility." What was revolutionary in its character was "the recognition of sensibility itself, as the raw material of literature and painting." In *The True Voice of Feeling* he takes as his examples Wordsworth, Keats, Hopkins, Whitman and Lawrence, T. E. Hulme and the Imagists, Pound and Eliot. What he means by "feeling" cannot be simply defined; it covers (in various contexts) a range of qualities from pure physical sensation to "sentiment," in the sense of the "refined and tender emotion" of Sterne and the late eighteenth century. At times the word seems to mean, or to include, flashes of intuition. Above all it is the quality of "life," D. H. Lawrence's "insurgent naked throb of the instant moment."

The fashion of scientific "objectivity" and the mistrust of all feeling as "sentimentality" which characterized the twenties notwithstanding, there was a logic in the transition from Wordsworth to Imagism. "It was with the school which Hulme started and Pound established that the revolution begun by Wordsworth was finally completed. Diction, rhythm and metre were finally emancipated from formal artifices and the poet was free to act creatively under laws of his own origination." Yet Herbert could always see the possible objections to those sweeping pronouncements which from time to time he felt obliged to make; for he adds, "It was not always understood that having cast off tyranny's obsolete laws, the poet was under the necessity of originating his own, and much of the free verse that had been practised since 1914 compromises the theory by its feebleness. Nevertheless the theory is right, and all true poetry of the past conforms to it; it is not the theory of a particular school; it is the theory of all essential English poetry."

The objections to free verse came, nevertheless, not from the upholders of "tyranny's obsolete laws" but from the poets. Yeats in his Introduction to the *Oxford Book of Modern Verse* finds Eliot "without apparent imagination" and criticizes him for working by a "rejection of all rhythms and metaphors of the more popular romantics rather than by the discovery of his own." Pound's "deliberate nobility" of style Yeats found "constantly interrupted, broken, twisted into nothing by its direct opposite, nervous obsession, nightmare, stammering confusion." Yeats's friend George Russell (AE) saw in free verse not the expression of liberated imagination but a failure of imagination: "the verse form is only natural when the soul speaks," he wrote; because "the heart in love, in imagination, in meditation, mounts at times to an ecstasy where its being becomes musical." Elsewhere he writes of free verse that "the angel who presides over hearing shakes its head and murmurs, 'No, it does not remind me of the music of the spheres'." Edwin Muir, Dylan Thomas and Vernon Watkins, precisely the most imaginative poets of the succeeding generation, give support to AE's traditional view of the "musical" character of the imagination. Herbert once confessed to me the difficulty he had in memorizing verse, even his own; a defectiveness of the inward ear which may in part have accounted for his bias.

He saw T. S. Eliot above all as an imagist; as in his earliest poems he was: " ... modern poetry — the poetry of Pound and Eliot — has recognized that the senses are the source of linguistic vitality." The image was to remain always his test of vital poetic experience. His Yale (1943) lecture on *The Image in Modern English Poetry* is one of Herbert Read's two or three best pieces of criticism. In it he defines in retrospect the Imagist position: "If the image could be identified as the only poetic force within the poem, why not proceed to identify form and image, as had been the common practise in China and Japan?" This involved a change of diction: " ... the image is most effective when conveyed in a minimum of words. It proved very difficult to reconcile this minimum with any regular metrical structure, for metre is basically aural and quite independent of image."

The incantatory character of verse is age-old and found in all languages, including the Chinese; but Herbert Read remained faithful to his early taste. In 1950 he wrote that "the Cantos constitute the longest and without hesitation I would say the greatest poetic achievement of our time. Technically the poem is the perfection of Pound's taut free verse, and there are passages of purest lyricism which in themselves, if extracted, would constitute a body of poetry for which there is no contemporary parallel." Perhaps too it was Pound's capacity for generous feeling, however violent, that held

Herbert Read's admiration; his honour in proportion to his passion.

It is notable that Read scarcely mentioned Yeats at any time. His earliest references were dismissive, and related to Ezra Pound, whom he regarded as the greater poet; "There is no doubt that Yeats was influenced, and influenced for the good, by the technique of some of his juniors, notably by Ezra Pound"; and "though one or two poems, such as *Byzantium*, seem to promise the necessary developments, Yeats remained to the end faithful to the spirit of another age." His analysis of *The Sorrow of Love* is an object-lesson in the limitations of the Imagist premises for the reading of a symbolist poem. The apparent discoveries of the avant-garde sometimes prove on examination to be failures to see the purpose of what they reject: "If I were asked to give the most distinctive quality of good writing I should express it in this one word: visual. Reduce the art of writing to its fundamentals and you come to this simple aim: to convey images by means of words." This may be one kind of good writing, but no symbolist poet could accept it; for the symbolist the visual image is not the end, but a word in the vocabulary of poetic discourse.

*　　*　　*

In his exposition of Imagism, Read developed a theory of poetry remote from, indeed opposed to, Eliot's own literary classicism, political royalism and religious traditionalism. Eliot was defended, as a poet, by his friend who claimed to be an atheist, a materialist, an anarchist in politics. He had early taken up a counter-position to Eliot's classicism and in 1938 in his Introduction to *The True Voice of Feeling* wrote that he "might accept a rehabilitation of romanticism" as an adequate description of his aims. It was rather to Wordsworth than to Coleridge, whose transcendentalism he rejected, that he turned for vindication of his own essentially materialist aesthetic theory. In his Clark Lectures (1929-30) he spoke of Wordsworth's philosophic debt to Locke and Hartley. Locke denied the Platonic doctrine of innate ideas and held all experience to come through impressions received from the external world: that is, from images. " . . . a lyric is simply a perception and all thought is based on primary perceptions. From the accumulation of selected perception expressed as lyrics, it is obvious that a general view of life may be constituted." "Hartley was almost what we should call a Behaviourist, and Wordsworth accepted his theories as infallible."

141

"The general effect of the growth of science has been to discredit transcendental reasoning altogether. Traditional criticism, therefore, insofar as it can claim to be fundamental, is a structure whose very foundations have perished, and if we are to save it from becoming the province of emotional dictators, we must hasten to relate it to those systems of knowledge which have to a great extent replaced transcendental philosophy." In the course of his literary life Herbert Read hastened to relate his criticism to system after system, most of them now themselves perished and replaced. Under the compulsive necessity always to have a theory, he was almost naively uncritical of ideas so long as they were new; and throughout his works is scattered a sequence of obscure names (most of them Germanic) of Freudian psychologists, Behaviourists and Heaven knows what, cited as infallible authorities in one book, forgotten in the next. The root of this continual theorizing was his refusal to accept the only final sanction there is for any qualitative view of the world. "Religious thinking always implies an act of faith — a belief in supernatural revelation. That kind of belief I do not profess. I am essentially a materialist. But as a materialist I find myself involved with certain intangible and imponderable elements which we call emotion and instinct . . . and finally all our other knowledge and judgment is referred back to such absolutes — absolutes of truth and beauty no less than of justice." "I think it will be found that the only universal quality in art is beauty," he wrote; and for beauty he sought to discover a materialist explanation, referring often to d'Arcy Thompson's *Growth and Form* and to Lancelot Law Whyte's laws of organic form: " . . . no aesthetic form exists save such as are in conformity with physical and mathematical law." The basis of beauty is formal: " . . . the world keeps returning to certain specific values. Those values are few, but they seem to be fundamental. I would mention as examples the geometrical proportions which are common for forms of organic life as well as forms of art — the so-called Divine Proportion — and those invariable qualities of harmony and serenity to which mankind returns after every period of storm and stress."

Wordsworth's atheism, which made William Blake turn pale, was acceptable to Read because in keeping with the atheist humanism of his own day. "Our attitude to Wordsworth's philosophy," he said in his Clark lectures, "must inevitably be our attitude towards humanism; it is the highest expression of humanism, even of scientific humanism, that the world has yet seen." Yet he saw the inherent flaw in Wordsworth's position, so understood: "the objection to humanism, and it seems to me to be a final one, is that it necessarily assumes this very infinity of the human mind which inspired Wordsworth. There is nothing in the history of humanity, nothing in our present experience, to justify such a belief. . . . the choice can only lie between an extreme scepticism and an un-compromising supernaturalism. . . . There is no compromise between these alternatives. But Wordsworth pretended there was, and his whole philosophy is vitiated by this inherent inconsistency. Wordsworth knew this, and the last phase of his life shows him vainly endeavouring to hide the disastrous significance of his philosophy of nature under a screen of orthodox beliefs."

Elsewhere he writes of the "convictions" with which Wordsworth sought to "oppose the nihilism that already, at the opening of the nineteenth century threatened European thought"; the hidden conclusion the atheist humanist must dodge, and Herbert Read himself with the rest. Having rejected the transcendental, he was committed to that relative absolute, the vital principle; D. H. Lawrence's belief that "*life* is the great reality, that true living fills us with vivid life, 'the heavenly bread' " — a definition that begs many questions.

In this vitalism lies the consistency which runs through all the apparent inconsistencies of Herbert Read's thought, his changes of theoretical ground in justification of an idea essentially simple. The *zeitgeist* is involved in a process of perpetual transformation; and if he adopted and abandoned a succession of points of view, from Behaviourism and Freudianism to the structuralism of Cassirer and Suzanne Langer, Jung's view of the Collective Unconscious, and Existentialism, he was (to use Blake's term) "exploring the States": every belief possible to man is an experience of protean life; and no knowledge can in its nature be more. No period ever underwent so many decampments or set up edifices of ideology so impermanent as the period to whose every significant experience Herbert Read in turn subjected himself. "Stability, which we foolishly yearn for, is but another name for stagnation, and stagnation is death. The ideal condition of society is the same as the ideal condition of any living body — a state of dynamic tension. . . . Only on condition that the artist is allowed to function freely can society embody those ideals of liberty and intellectual development which to most of us seem the only worthy sanctions of life." Liberty, for him, seems to have signified a condition of perpetual revolt. The Romantic movement, he wrote, "was more than a change of style: it was a sudden expansion into realms of sensibility not previously accessible to the human imagination. I believe the way then opened still presents itself as a challenge to the human mind. Our duty at the moment, as creative writers and as critics, is to maintain the impetus of that revolution."

In this context of perpetually evolving consciousness he saw the arts: "This new world would never have been discovered but for the invention of new vessels of exploration—new forms of literature like the novel and the short story, new techniques like free verse and the interior monologue. Even now further progress awaits new inventions."

At his best no-one could be more sensitive in his response to the living "now." In the circumstances of the present, so lacking in solidity and permanence, he wrote, "the poet has no alternative but to rely on 'a certain inward perspective', a coherence of the personality based on the widest evidence of the senses."

The weakness of such a position is of course that, in making the relative itself the only measure, all other distinctions are abolished, and an expression of ignorance is of equal value with an expression of knowledge — if indeed the terms any longer mean anything: "The new images presented by the younger artists are not indistinct for lack of focus: they are authentic symbols of chaos itself, of mind at the end of its tether, gazing into the pit at the other side of consciousness." In moments of detachment he could see the inadequacy of avant-gardism; in a late essay, *The Problem of the Zeitgeist*, he wrote: "a given age always looks at its contemporary art with contemporary prejudices. When ... these prejudices disappear, the art of that given age is revalued once again with contemporary prejudices — the prejudices of a new age." All knowledge, it is implied, is relative; perhaps the worst of the contemporary prejudices in which Herbert himself was involved. Yet he could forget, with fatal consequences, that the zeitgeist spares no avant-garde, and write of some ephemeral ideology as if it were an absolute: "It is only now, with the aid of modern dialectics and modern psychology in the name of Marx and Freud that they [the poets] have found themselves in a position to put their beliefs and practises on a scientific basis, thereby initiating a continuous and deliberate creative activity whose only laws are the laws of its own dynamics." — Herbert at his worst.

*　　*　　*

It was inevitable that, seeking to find for the Romantic view of the imagination a materialist basis he should have sought to discover in the atheist psychology of Freud a ground for the mysterious creative processes of poetic inspiration. "Since the eighteenth century, inspiration has lost its religious significance and become almost exclusively an aesthetic form. . . . But whilst hitherto romanticism has had to rely on subjective convictions [he is thinking perhaps of Wordsworth] and has earned a certain critical disrepute in philosophy and the science of art, it can now claim a scientific basis in the findings of psychoanalysis." "Physics, demanding as it does such impressive modifications of aspect and attitude, provides the most general background for all subsidiary efforts, but for the literary critic psychology gains an intimate importance because it is so directly concerned with the material origins of art." In 1938 he wrote, "my increasing tendency, step by step with my increasing knowledge of modern psychology, has been to give literary criticism a psychological direction"; and, *à propos* Shelley, he wrote that the "only type of criticism which is basic is ontogenetic criticism, by which I mean criticism which traces the origins of the work of art in the psychology of the individual and in the economic structure of society."

In retrospect, Herbert Read's, together with many less distinguished applications of Freudian dogma to works of literature and the arts, seems crude. To be just, he formulated, but never applied, the worst Freudian absurdities: "The essential point to notice is that psycho-analysis seems to show that the artist is initially and by tendency a neurotic, but that in becoming an artist he as it were escapes the ultimate fate of his tendency and through art finds his way back to reality." He goes on to quote (without irony) Freud's even more excessive notion "that the aesthetic pleasure produced in us by the creative artist has a preliminary character, and that the real enjoyment of a work of art is due to the ease it gives to certain psychic tensions." Were this so the value of any work must obviously be in proportion to the force of the neurosis it liberates, and its shared experience a sharing of our collective urge to violence, repressed sexuality and every other form of anti-social perversion and mania; a view of art which, however false, has, with or without the help of Herbert Read, produced works in abundance, according to its kind, within the phantasmagoria of the Modern Movement.

More extraordinary still was Herbert's willingness to accept the crudities of Behaviourist explanations of experience: "McDougall

145

has shown that physiology may yet identify and classify the various glandular excretions and their appropriate lyrical responses." Such extravagances were of course abandoned as both Herbert himself and the science of psychology improved their knowledge; and he was the first, so far as I know, to point to Jung as possibly more relevant than Freud to any consideration of the imagination. Towards the end of his life Herbert had adopted a great deal of Jung's thought on the nature of the psyche, and the collective unconscious, and even much earlier there was a point of credulity beyond which he refused to be led. Quoting the Freudian Ernest Jones who seeks to explain the mentality of the artist by "the reaction of the young child against its original excremental interests" Herbert comments that "the repression of such interests may indeed contribute to the details of aesthetic activity but this particular hypothesis seems too limited in conception." Such fantasies are no longer in need of refutation, having gone with the Zeitgeist which brought them; but are worth recalling as typical of their period.

The Clark lectures on Wordsworth (1932) were a moderate enough experiment in psychological criticism, though at the time they outraged survivors of the cult of Wordsworth as a religion for the irreligious. Basically he was right in drawing attention to the importance of erotic love (Wordsworth's illicit love-affair in France) as the prime agent of imaginative inspiration; perhaps Freud's most enduring contribution to the understanding of the life and art. Yet it was a pity that so sensitive a reader of the text of prose or verse should have sacrificed his best gift to any theory outside the real terms of literature. Of his *In Defence of Shelley* I find it hard to say any good. It was this essay which gave currency to the theory of Shelley's "homosexuality"; a mare's nest typical of the mentality of the thirties. The argument is a fine example of the Freudian logic: Shelley was, from adolescence, always involved in some love-affair with young and pretty women; in the first draft of *Laon and Cythna* the lovers, brother and sister, were an incestuous pair; *The Cenci* also treats the incest theme, of father and daughter: therefore Shelley was clearly a *repressed* homosexual. A generation who could accept such an argument was certainly liberated from the tyranny of the rational.

There are of course — for Herbert Read was after all a critic of high distinction — excellent incidental perceptions in both essays; nor was his motive the journalist's vulgar interest in scandal. On the

146

contrary, Herbert was making an attempt to discover the roots of the poetry: "A poet's poems are facts far more essential in his life than his sexual adventures or his financial difficulties, and the biography of a poet should therefore be primarily an account of his creative activity, *the life of the muse*, and the other facts are only important in so far as they contribute to an understanding of this process." It all turns upon what is relevant or irrelevant knowledge; and the fashion of psychoanalyzing the poets has been one of the most disastrous. Many years later, reviewing Carl Grabo's *The Magic Plant*, he virtually admitted the inadequacy, or irrelevance, of the psychological approach to Shelley: "I myself, who have never been inclined to depreciate the quality of Shelley's philosophy, had no conception of its range, depth and coherence until I had read this Chicago professor's patient exposition of the ideas underlying Shelley's poems."

*   *   *

It was inevitable that Herbert Read should have become involved in the Surrealist movement, whose "pure psychic automatism" gave a greater scope (within the materialist hypothesis) to the imagination than does Locke's theory of the mind as a blank page on which perceptions are impressed, or the Behaviourist theory which is but a modern amplification of that view. In retrospect it is easy to see that Surrealism was less an exploration of the psyche than a doctrinaire application of Freudian theory; no structure of the mind is presumed, but pure expression of "the irrational." Of Coleridge's poetry Herbert Read wrote at this time, that "its poetic worth is in inverse ratio to its logical sense, reaching its greatest intensity in the incoherent imagery of Kubla-Khan" — already a notable departure from the view that the function of poetry is visual. But *In Myth, Dream and Poem* (written before 1938) we feel that he is already feeling beyond the Freudian and Surrealist conception of the irrational to some kind of ordering principle which would explain the universality of certain themes; a Jungian rather than a Freudian concept. "The works of art which survive," he wrote, "are those which most nearly approach to the illogical order of the dream. . . . These works of art are irrational and dreamlike — legendary myths and folk-tales and the poems which embody them — these survive all economic and political change. . . . They are retold in every age and every climate, and though modified in detail, are always essentially the same, irrational and superreal." There are other possible views of myths, which within those traditions to which they respectively belong are vehicles of religious and metaphysical meaning of an exact, though certainly not of a logical and rational kind. From this point of view Surrealism is a misreading of symbol, even of dream symbols other than those belonging simply to the Freudian "personal unconscious," the confused re-presentation of physical impressions, reshaped according to our night-thoughts. The particular brand of irrational images in which the Surrealists trafficked were produced, besides, *au service de la révolution*; for the Surrealist movement was a thinly disguised political movement of the extreme Left (even though the Russian Marxists would have none of it) subversive and "engaged." The anti-social and nihilistic images were acceptable to Herbert Read, who like the Surrealists believed that our present society is rotten. His own understanding of anarchy was Utopian rather than subversive; but there was enough in common to blind him to the fact, obvious enough in retrospect, that Dada and Surrealism had more in common with Nazism (another manifestation of "the irrational") than with Marxism. The blind faith of the avant-garde of the thirties in whatever emerged from the Unconscious through "pure psychic automatism" seems in retrospect altogether too simple. There are many spirits, and those who come are those we invoke, whether from heaven, hell, or "the unconscious"; where also both devils and angels inhabit. Odin and his host would never have been allowed to pass the Surrealist censor; but neither would Yeats's woman of numinous beauty shooting an arrow at a star; or Edwin Muir's cosmic vision of creation; still less the angels of Mons or Our Lady of Fatima.

At the time neither Herbert Read nor anyone else infected by the excitement of the Surrealist movement stopped to ask whether those who opposed it might have motives other than ignorant prejudice, reactionary obstructivism, and so on. The intoxication of Surrealism could not, obviously, infect believers in a spiritual order, whether Christian or theosophist, for whom the "irrational" hierarchies of heaven and hell were in any case real, and more clearly conceived then by these newcomers from Behaviourism, Freud, French anticlerical rationalism and what-not. It seemed easy to make light of the criticisms of so popular a writer as J. B. Priestley, who had strongly attacked the movement on the self-evident grounds that "the Surrealists stand for violence and neurotic unreason," and that "you catch a glimpse behind them of the deepening twilight of barbarism that may soon blot out our sky, until humanity finds itself in another long night." C. S. Lewis, scholar and Christian theologian, was another opponent. Yeats, who had been studying "the irrational" ever since the eighteen-eighties, and who could have told not only Herbert Read and the Surrealists but Freud and Jung themselves a great deal about the *memoria* and the *hodos chameleontos* which is only now beginning to be understood, reached Priestley's conclusion; "After us the savage god," he wrote, after seeing in Paris the first performance of Jarry's *Ubu Roi*.

In retrospect Herbert himself related the movement to "a state of religious unbelief, of psychological imbalance, and social unrest ... mental insecurity, social insecurity, metaphysical insecurity" — a fair description, one might think, of the blind leading the blind.

This however was not how Herbert saw it: the function of the artist is to express the Zeitgeist; and his ignorance is neither here nor there. "Just as superrealism makes use of, or rather proceeds on the assumption of the knowledge embodied in psychoanalysis, so abstract art makes use of, or proceeds on the basis of, the abstract concepts of physics and dynamics, geometry and mathematics. It is not necessary for the abstract artist to have knowledge of these sciences (nor is it necessary for the super-realists to have knowledge of psychoanalysis); such concepts are part of our mental ambience, and the artist is precisely the individual who can make this ambience actual." I am reminded of a remark made to me long ago by T. S. Eliot: that there are two kinds of borrowing, conscious and unconscious; and of the two unconscious borrowing is far the worse.

"The mischief began at the end of the seventeenth century when man became passive before a mechanized nature," Yeats wrote in his *Introduction* to the *Oxford Book of Modern Verse*; and it would be a fair criticism of Herbert Read that, grounded as he was in Locke and Behaviourism, his view of art was a passive one: art must "make this ambience actual." The intoxicating sense of powerful originality which possessed the "Modern Movement" was in fact a passive possession of this kind. The creative genius who strives to change that ambience has none of this sense of "possession," of going with the stream. Herbert Read was himself — as all who knew him will testify — a man of supreme natural goodness; and for that very reason could not easily discern evil. But to deny the reality of evil may be to give power to principalities and powers of the collective mind, and to "rulers of the darkness of this world." Herbert Read lacked what in Christian theological terms is called "the discernment of spirits"; or was he at times carried away by some theory into supporting movements uncongenial to his natural sensibility?

During the war he admitted the destructive character of Surrealism while not on this account condemning it: "As for surrealism, when it has finally accomplished its *destructive* work (and the war is rapidly doing that for it) and begins to concentrate on the problems which have been raised by the discovery of the unconscious, then it may evolve something in the nature of a collective idiom." Under the growing and salutary influence of Jung he went further; "In *The Integration of the Personality*, Jung has suggested that the modern world is suffering from the consequences of iconoclasm, from the lack of any archetypal symbols to act as safety-valves for the suppressed forces of what he calls the collective unconscious. The artist from the prehistoric times down to the Middle Ages was the agent who created these symbols for society, and he has now to recover that public function."

He was always careful to say that not all surrealism was, as he would understand the word, art; all the same, there was already in the concept of surrealism the beginning of the confusion that has since threatened to submerge any such distinction. There has never been any precedent, in the art of the past, for the notion that the function of art can ever be "destructive"; but once art and literature are conceived of as expressions of the zeitgeist, and that zeitgeist itself at the service of a nihilism (as Herbert himself knew very well) the only possible term can be the destruction of art itself. This the surrealists themselves were the first to proclaim, at a time when few could have foreseen the triumph of the principle of destruction they deliberately introduced into the arts.

He also came to question the alleged therapeutic value of giving expression, in literature, to the suppressed destructive impulses. Writing on *Realism and Superrealism* he admits that "since our age is one of increasing savagery, it is only natural that our artists should revert to a savage type of art. But that is not quite the line of my argument. I would rather say that there is a savage in every human being, and always has been; and that our savage instincts find sublimation in art. But that too is not an altogether satisfactory argument — it suggests that art is a sort of medicine to make us mentally healthy." In *On the Failure of War Books* he reflects on his own poem, *The Happy Warrior*: "the suspicion now grows upon me that such writing was fuel to the inner flames of the war spirit. If we human beings have an irresistible urge to self-destruction, then the imagination will feed ravenously on any vivid description of the process of destruction."

The revolution in the teaching of art and poetry in English schools worked through Herbert Read's lifelong work in the cause of "education through art" is a matter of history. Again and again he affirmed his belief that the creative expression of the imagination is life itself. But the point at which he always stopped short was the admission of any metaphysical ground in which the imagination is rooted; nor could he admit that the "isolation and insecurity" of the modern attitude which he so clearly saw is basically an alienation from that ground; and in consequence a sickness of the imagination itself. By what possible stretch of credulity could the products of "pure psychic automatism" or the later productions of "action painters" and the like be attributed to the Spirit that "knoweth all things," Coleridge's "repetition in the finite mind of the eternal act of creation in the infinite I AM"? The absence of that informing principle is all such work communicates.

*   *   *

The great confrontation for Herbert Read was with tradition. "Without contraries there is no progress"; Herbert had seen a truth, and his affirmation of a vital imaginative principle throughout a protean sequence of changes of theoretical ground, was his great contribution to his time and the future. In reading his early criticism we often feel that Herbert is talking to T. S. Eliot; and especially so on the issue of tradition. On Eliot's *Tradition and the Individual Talent* he wrote, in *The Poetic Experience*, "there is not one literary tradition but many traditions; there is certainly a romantic tradition as well as a classical tradition, and, if anything, the romantic tradition has the longer history" and he quotes a famous passage from the *Ion* on poetic inspiration. His temperamental affinity with Wordsworth notwithstanding he was continually drawn back to Coleridge; and in this too his afterthoughts were best. In his lecture on *Coleridge as Critic* (John Hopkins University, 1949) he reverses his earlier adherence to Locke and Hartley and (by implication)

Behaviourism: "There are in our world currents of thought that are central and others that are merely contributaries and wander off into the bogs and deserts of philosophy: that stream which first became defined in Kant's philosophy and continued to flow however irregularly through the minds of Schelling, Coleridge, Kierkegaard, Hegel, Nietzsche, Husserl, Heidegger, divided by a watershed from the contrary stream to which we can attach the names of Locke, Condillac, Hartley, Bentham, Marx and Lenin — that first stream to which we give the fashionable name of Existentialism but which is really the main tradition of philosophy itself — in that stream Wordsworth is confidently carried."

The ground of his difference with Eliot was of course the religious one. It is perhaps a pity that it is in Eliot's historical terms that the question is discussed. In a review of *Notes Towards a Definition of Culture* (1948) he states his objections to Eliot's view in the reasoned terms which a controversy with his friend imposed. "I agree with Mr. Eliot on so many essential points that it is only with a feeling of hopeless bafflement that I find myself being skeptical on the issue which he obviously regards as most important of all"; and he states his case: " . . . the fact that societies have in historical times evolved from primitive to more elaborate or 'civilized' patterns, taken together with the assertion that culture is the incarnation of a religion, implies that religion itself has also evolved. But once we admit a principle of evolution in religion we are committed (as sociologists) to the prospect of further steps in the evolution of religion. But that is not the underlying assumption of Mr. Eliot's thesis. If I do not misunderstand him he assumes that our European destiny is to work out a pattern of culture ordained nearly two thousand years ago. I have always assumed that Christian culture reached its perfection in the Middle Ages. . . . " Teilhard de Chardin (whose writings Herbert admired) was indeed to introduce the evolutionary principle into Christianity itself. But the great aesthetician of tradition, Ananda Coomaraswamy, starts from a different ground altogether; not history but metaphysical reality, St. Augustine's "wisdom that was not made, but is now what it always was and ever shall be." Such a definition raises quite other questions, for it rejects Herbert Read's relativism outright: the Zeitgeist is no longer the test of truth. "From the Stone Age until now, what a decline!" Coomaraswamy somewhere says; he meant of course "a decline in intellectuality, not in comfort. It should be one of the functions of

a well organized Museum to deflate the idea of progress." This calls
in question Herbert Read's avant-gardism precisely at its most vulnerable point; for he could see as well as Coomaraswamy that the
"evolution" of European art from, say, the eleventh century (the
perfection of Christian art) to Jackson Pollock could be read in
Coomaraswamy's sense. The evolutionary optimism of atheist humanism is (given the atheist's denial of a metaphysical principle or
a divine purpose) mere wanton self-deception. According to Coomaraswamy "progress" is a meaningless word, for art is to be meas-
ured only by its nearness to or distance from enduring standards of
perfection, determined by "unageing intellect" — Yeats's phrase,
who was himself a lifelong student of the perennial philosophy, basis
of traditional aesthetics. But according to Herbert Read, "To accept
the view that the purpose of art is 'primarily to communicate a
gnosis' is to acquiesce in a petrifaction of life — the supersession of
human relations by abstract doctrines . . . the power of art is to communicate . . . let us leave it at that. That art is the power to communicate, and this power depends without any doubt on a vitality
of the senses which are used by the artist in the process of giving
form to anything — be it a religious symbol or a chair to sit on or
a poem or an aeroplane." So he wrote in a review of Coomaraswamy's *Why Exhibit Works of Art* (1941). So he evades the
argument that the means of art must serve its end; a little disin-
genuously, we may say; for he had supported in very different terms
surréalisme au service de la révolution. We must conclude that it is
those ends themselves which Coomaraswamy is indicating as the
traditional ground of art that he cannot accept. "The vitality of the
senses" is, besides, begging the vital question — one which Blake
answered when he said that he saw "not with but through the eye,"
and "a fool sees not the same tree as a wise man sees." Blake might
have included the Surrealists and many since among those who see
nature as "all ridicule and deformity." Nor is "a chair to sit on"
merely a sense impression; it is, according to another of Herbert's
friends, David Jones, a focus of many memories and associations.
"If the painter makes visual forms, the content of which is chairs,
or chair-ishness, what are the chances that these who regard his
painting will run to meet him with the notions of 'seat,' 'throne,'
'session,' *'cathedra,'* 'Scone,' 'on-the-right-hand-of-the-Father' in
mind. If this haphazard list is, in some of its accidents, yours and
mine, it nevertheless serves, *mutatis mutandis*, for Peloponnesians

and for Polynesians too." Proust, whose criticism Herbert admired, had argued in similar terms against Zola and the French Realists years before. There can no more be "pure sensations" than there can be "pure psychic automatism." Our perceptions are determined by what we are, and that includes a great deal besides the sum of our sense impressions; "As a man is, So he Sees". Blake too had his answer to Locke.

Herbert was essentially a humanist; and in this, though not in his atheism, he has the Christians with him, in at least one of his objections to Coomaraswamy (in the same review) : "The art we call humanistic, restricted to the expression of individualistic feelings and concepts, must seem almost meaningless to the Indian artist." This is perhaps true; and to dismiss the humanistic is to dismiss virtually the whole of Western Christian culture in what David Jones calls its "incarnationalism." I remember Herbert describing to me his impression of India, and saying how infinitely he preferred Christian to Indian mediaeval art because of this very difference; the "incarnational" aspect being eliminated from Buddhist, and dissolved in Hindu art. There is at stake a basic difference of point of view, and one which Coomaraswamy himself discusses in the book Herbert Read is here reviewing; he shows, for example, a naturalistic drawing of a Maori chieftain by a European; and an abstract mask of the same chieftain in which personal features are eliminated in order to communicate a hieratic concept of "kingship." Truth to say Herbert himself would have preferred the abstract mask also, but on different grounds; the fashion for "primitive" art characteristic of "the Modern Movement" was on purely aesthetic grounds. The choice of "tribal" rather than Christian, Buddhist or Islamic art was rather to evade metaphysical implications than to illustrate them, and Coomaraswamy's reminder that the motives involved in the creation of such works were of another kind was no more welcome than was his insistence on other aspects of the implications of the traditional *gnosis*.

Once I spoke with Herbert of Coomaraswamy, to whom I owned myself indebted. I was surprised at the bitterness of his retort: "He is *dead, dead.*" I had not found it so; on the contrary it was the Modern Movement I found "dead"; for in retrospect that movement can be seen as essentially an expression of the progress of atheist humanism towards that implicit nihil from which, according to Herbert, Wordsworth himself had recoiled in vain. Not all poetry of this century has been an expression of this mentality. Eliot, David Jones, Edith Sitwell, Edwin Muir; in Wales, Dylan Thomas implicitly, Vernon Watkins and R. S. Thomas explicitly, are all Christians. The Irish renaissance was grounded in theosophy, Platonism, and the Western Esoteric tradition; Joyce, though a rebel, on Catholicism. Ezra Pound is a follower of Confucius.

Even on tradition Herbert had wise afterthoughts; he never closed his mind, and in *The Modern Epoch in Art* (1949) he reflects upon the only possible alternatives in face of the present crisis; "To renew one's sensibility towards one's environment — that is the method both of the traditionalist and the revolutionary." Either "the artist retraces the historical development of his art and resumes contact with the authentic tradition" or "resolves the crisis by a leap forward into a new and original state of sensibility — he revolts against existing conventions in order to create a new convention more in accordance with a contemporary consciousness." But revolt and rejection and destruction are not themselves a creation of anything except chaos; and what happens when revolution and rejection have become the only convention?

In his criticism of the present he is at one with Coomaraswamy: "There is no spiritual integrity in our life, and no artist of any worth will put his skill and sensibility at the service of any less worthy cause. An artist will serve either the light within him, or the light of humanity embodied in a superhuman concept of reality which is valid in the modern world, and therefore an artist like Hélion must remain true to the only reality of which he has knowledge — the subjective reality of his own vision. . . . For we are, in our baffled way, all compelled to construct a personal vision." Yeats, and David Jones too, would have seen the force of Herbert Read's desperation in face of the absence of any "unity of culture" in our society to which the modern poet can relate his life or his work. What Herbert Read never could admit was that tradition and the imagination affirm the same truth; that, in Coomaraswamy's words, "we are considering a catholic or universal doctrine, with which the humanistic philosophies of art can neither be compared nor reconciled, but only contrasted."

Another afterthought on Coomaraswamy may well be reflected in an article on *Modern Chinese Painting*, in which he admits that " . . . a tradition that has survived the vicissitudes of thirteen centuries is likely to possess some principle of vitality unknown to the short-term policies of European art . . . that tradition is partly technical, partly philosophical. But the philosophical aspect is the primary one, the technical one being fixed because it is best adapted to express the philosophical aim." (This is almost a paraphrase of some of Coomaraswamy's arguments in *Why Exhibit Works of Art*). And he adds, "the traditions that die are the impersonal abstractions that have no roots in the self, and in the eternal need of the self to be objectivized. Chinese painting is a technique for self-expression; by keeping to this standard of self-expression, it bases itself on the eternal verities of the human mind and sensibility which, through all the stress of religions and philosophies, remain in direct communication with the physical phenomena of the world. But to the Chinese these phenomena are not disconnected and discordant events; they are part of a universal harmony." — and so back to Wordsworth, his first master. This may still be an atheism, of a sort; but of a very different sort from the perpetual revolution of the Modern Movement. Perhaps Herbert had in mind a sentence of Coomaraswamy's with which he would probably have agreed: "An integrated society of this sort can function harmoniously for millennia, in the absence of external interference. On the other hand, the contentment of innumerable peoples can be destroyed in a generation by the withering touch of our civilization."

He comes nearer, in some respects, than Eliot, to the metaphysical view of tradition in a passage in *Realism and Superrealism*, written about 1944; "Surely these people, who inherit their culture and preserve it unchanged, are not the true traditionalists. Tradition is not a heritage; it is rather an active principle, a principle we apply to solve particular problems, and as the problems change from age to age, so must the solutions." True; but what of the principle itself? There is a sleight-of-hand involved in an argument that can conclude (à propos surrealism) that modern art "only seems to be revolutionary because it insists on developing the central tradition of art." The point in question is begged: has not that centre and that principle somewhere been lost?

On many occasions, especially towards the end of his life, Herbert gave expression to something very like despair about the present situation: "It does not seem that the contradiction which exists between the aristocratic function of art and the democratic structure of modern society can ever be resolved. But both may wear the cloak of humanism, the one for shelter, the other for disguise. The sensitive artist knows that a bitter wind is blowing." "Reading, like walking, is one of the lost arts; one of the sacrifices we have made to speed, noise, and news." " . . . we may be leaving an epoch without taste to enter an epoch without art"; admissions, bitter enough, of the bankruptcy of the zeitgeist.

At the Eranos conference in 1958 Herbert Read gave a paper entitled *The Flower of Peace*; and in that late statement, made before a small group of Jungians, the reader feels that he was reverting to what he himself loved, to that "true voice of feeling" he had often been compelled to stifle under the sense of obligation to fight the battles of the Modern Movement. He had written, many years before, "I have a characteristic preference for the miniature, for the epitome, the episode, the epigram. Rhetoric, everything mouth-filling and pretentious, the imposing and the pompous, everything orotund and ornate, intimidates me, and what is intimidating cannot be lived with. Art must be intimate if it is to be a personal possession. It belongs to a private world." He disliked the Renaissance, Bernini and Michelangelo; loved the laconic *haiku*, the private voice of George Herbert, the "innocent eye" of Traherne. He quoted, in his Eranos paper, Henry Vaughan's "My Soul, there is a country, Far beyond the stars"; and George Herbert's "Sweet Peace, where dost thou dwell?" — and suddenly we know that he is no longer on the battlefield, but at home, speaking of what he himself loves.

In his Introduction to *The Tenth Muse* he beautifully states his own faith: " . . . my general outlook—of an attitude I would never venture to call a philosophy. . . . Never yield to habit, especially to habits of thought which polish away the rough edges of truth; remain open, innocent, original. Put away childish things, but retain, all the same, a core of childhood, a slender vein of vital sap, which the rings of growth may hide, but never destroy. Keep a reserve of simplicity, even of primitiveness, so that you do not meet elementary situations with sophistication. Your aim should be, not simply to be, but rather to be ever capable of becoming — not at rest, but moving with the moving world — always in touch with what is changing, changing one's self, open, like a child, to the whole world without, but with an inward reserve which the child does not possess, where one gathers a little strength, a certain order."

157

DONALD DAVIE

Emigrant, To the Receding Shore

for the shade of Herbert Read

The weather of living in an island
That is not an island in the ocean
Crackles in the hallway.   What is salt
And ancient in us dries
To an inland heat.   The Atlantic
Is a pond sunk in a garden,
A concrete mole has sealed the Aleutian vents
Browned already; only beside New Zealand
Sobs refresh a walled-up bind of waters.

Alfred in Athelney, Hereward in the Isle
Of Ely, learn to go mounted.

Tooling through second-growth Sherwood
In an Armstrong-Siddeley tourer,
Percheron of the twenties,
My grandfather unmeaning
Anything but well
Discharged his quiverful:
Aridity, and levels.

The anti-cyclone regions
Of population pressure,
Respondent to the pulse of
Asia, Arabia, Kansas,
Send out their motorized
Hordes, the freely breeding.

And the Age of Chivalry prinks
Pygmy-size to my daughter's
Gymkhana, though the Godolphin
Arabian has invaded
The forested, painfully cleared
Lands of the Clydesdale, the Suffolk
And the Shire horse, the old black English.

The great trees sail the oceans,
Spill acorns on Pitcairn Island.
And all of this is over.

ANTHONY KERRIGAN

The Green Child

A green child greenly stayed:
on a Cuban balcony, green:
beside a County Wicklow Georgian manor, green:
across a Yorkshire moor, green:
in a Venice full of performance, another shade
                of green: but green.

Fought battles always green
with the gentle give of a tree turned
and turned round and twisted and turned again.

Unless it be the "infinite brown" of Rembrandt
or the black background of the *Christ* of Velázquez
or the blue of certain Cézanne watercolour geometries,
accomplished silence is always green.

"Green silence" is the most yielding background,
as moist and deep as English grass remembered;
in the biggest bole of a Constable still a sapling,
a passage of counter-composition to a *nature morte*.

Robin Skelton

THE POETRY OF HERBERT READ

ERBERT READ's writings about poetry have overshadowed his actual compositions. The authority with which he wrote about the poetry of others and about the creative process makes it difficult for us to approach his poems with an open mind. We expect the poems to support the critical theories, and to evince the same wayward brilliance as the essays. We search for examples of Imagism, of Vers Libre, and Organic Form. We suppose that the philosophical and radical temper of the essays will appear with even more intensity in the poetry, and we are frequently disappointed.

It would be a sad disservice to the memory of so great a man to adopt a merely pietistic attitude to his work, and to praise that which deserves to be put aside. Herbert Read himself, though the kindliest of critics, was not the least rigorous, and in writing of his poetry I feel compelled to attempt standards of honesty which he himself set, and obliged to look at the poems themselves without attempting to justify their failures or magnify their achievements by relating them to their author's critical theories. What matters is the quality of the poetry as poetry, and not its relationship to other writings.

Reading and re-reading the canon of Herbert Read's poetry as he defined it himself in the two books, *Collected Poems* (1952) and *Moon's Farm* (1955), I find myself disturbed by the conviction that the poet has been ill served by the philosopher. The success of the poems is usually in inverse proportion to their length and to their degree of explicit intellectualism. Thus the section of "Longer

Poems" in the *Collected Poems* is the least satisfactory part of the book. Many times the struggle towards the intellectual formulation of a problem results in the disorganization of the imagery and the straining of language. "John Donne Declines a Benefice" opens with the lines:

> Shut out the sound. — These June birds shrill
> Their easy ecstacies too well
> To make a music for the thoughts
> That deep within discordantly delve
> This fallow mind....

The shift from images of music's ecstasy to images of delving the land is not sufficiently controlled by the creation of a credible persona for me to be able to accept it. The passionate voice of Donne, its rhythmic vigour and its humour, presented a fictive speaker whose mind could range easily and swiftly from abstract to concrete and mix metaphors and allusions with such speed and apparent spontaneity that our acceptance of oddity is at one with our admiration and understanding of his passionate intelligence. Read's speaker may imitate the Donnian mode in his brusque transitions, but does not share Donne's all-embracing gusto and zest for the grotesquerie of human energies. Moreover, the ringing originality of Donne's sudden violent perceptions is missing. Thus, later in the poem we find a concatenation of imagery whose violence cannot justify its absurdity, however much we tell ourselves that we are exploring a Jacobean intelligence. The trouble lies in the use of abstraction. An abstraction, such as "faithless lechery" unless given a novel conceptual twist by some device of wit, suggests the presence of a moral or philosophical assurance that is in direct opposition to any attempt to question the stability of the spiritual universe.

> Once I was Jack Donne, burned by the vast
> Energies of an eager lust,
> And leapt with zeal
> Into the mirage of a limpid pool
> Which my impinging body crackt
> Into a crater, a sulphurous hole
> Of faithless lechery.
> I reattained the fresh atmospheres
> By the perfection of a fair fantasy,
> This heart's concern, a sun to shine
> In the night of lust.

The final cliché emphasizes the essentially fustian quality of the lines. Read cannot make us believe in his Donne, but only in a man wishing to emulate Donne.

This is a harsh judgment, perhaps, but it appears to be almost equally true of the other dramatic monologues. It is as if the speaker of them were attempting to remind himself of the philosophical significance of his own existence by interpreting and qualifying each phenomenon with the aid of cleverly chosen but poetically debilitating abstract epithets. Thus, in the first section of "The End of A War" what might well have been a chilling presentation of the silence surrounding the dying German officer becomes a presentation of a jargon-ridden intelligence weakly attempting profundity.

> ... Now the silence
> is unholy.   Death has no deeper horror
> than diminishing sound — ears that strain
> for the melody of action, hear
> only the empty silence of retreating life.

If we cut out the words and syllables "for the melody of action" and "-ing life," we find ourselves approaching the sensation more nearly without in any way reducing the metaphysical implications.

The hunger after acceptable intellectual formulae mars many of these poems. In "The Analysis of Love" the sixth section opens with the lines:

> There are moments when I see your mind
>   Laps'd in your sex;
> When one particular deployment
>   Is the reflex of incomplete attainment.

This is, one may admit, clever stuff. It is also a useful component of the poem's total argument. It is also, however, versified talk of a peculiarly polysyllabic and dispassionate kind. The opening lines of the seventh section of the poem make the point:

> Since you are finite you will never find
>   The hidden source of the heart's emotion;
> It is a pool, secret in dusk and dawn,
>   Deep in the chartless forest life has grown.

Here we are told that there can be no intellectual formula for the numinous. The abstract language of philosophy cannot place us in communication with the sensation of living, only with the sensation of thinking — to make a useful but false distinction. Nevertheless, the human creature must somehow attempt that "intolerable wrestle with words and meaning." In "Beata L'Alma" we find the lines:

> . . . words lie. The structure of events alone is
>
> comprehensible and to single
>   perceptions communic-
> ation is not essential.
>   Art ends;
> the individual world alone is valid
>
> and that gives ease.   The water is still,
>   the rocks are hard and vein'd
> metalliferous, yielding
>   an ore
> of high worth.   In the sky the unsullied sun lake.

It is in the presentation of "the structure of events" that Read the poet excels, and not in the communication of opinions about them. Nevertheless, it seems there must be some justification for refusing to comment upon the significance of events. In "Mutations of the Phoenix" the question is asked.

> Why should I dwell in individual ecstasy?
> It is a hollow quarry of the mind
> rill'd with rock drippings, smooth'd with silt;
> and only the whorlminded Hamlet walks there
> musing in the gutters.

The answer given suggests that man is obliged, by his very nature, to attempt to bring unconscious perceptions and impulses into conscious awareness, for man's consciousness is his supreme and unique attribute.

> Mind wins deciduously,
> hibernating through many years.
> Impulse alone is immutable sap
> and flowing continuance
> extending life to leafy men.
> Effort of consciousness
>   carries from origin
>   the metamorphic clue.
> The cap is here

> in conscience humanly unique;
> and conscience is control, ordaining the strain
> to some perfection
>   not briefly known.

Unfortunately, however important the notion, it is here destructive of poetry. It is, indeed, only when the poem accepts the "phoenix" and accepts the warning that "you can't escape" that the poem, as poetry, surges forward into intensity of vision. This "vision is fire"; the phoenix "burns spiritually" in a world which is "finite" and in which "the eye is all" for time itself is "vision." One should involve oneself in the dionysiac energies of the impulse towards vision, not the Appolonian search after categories and order. This is certainly the theme of "The Lament of Saint Denis" who, rapt by his vision, called himself "master of all nature and knowledge," and who, containing in himself "the storm you met on the way," announces that at last he shall stand "in ordain'd radiance" and his eyes shall become "the light of reason."

The visionary element in some of these long poems thus contrives to overcome the intellectualization, but does not, still, provide the authority of most of the shorter poems in which the battle of Apollo and Dionysus is not joined. It is in these poems that the clarity and elegance of Read's sensibility is most effectively displayed. It is in these poems too that he balances his language so that the silences are ineluctably part of the poem's structure and meaning. Consider "April":

> To the fresh wet fields
> and the white
> froth of flowers
>
> Came the wild errant
> swallows with a scream.

We do not need to be told that this is more than a leaf from a poet's sketchbook. It is a classical feeling we have here; the flowers of April, in their innocence and fertility are inevitably to be visited by those swallows which, in myth, were born of predatory sexuality. The myth of Itylus is not mentioned. It does not need to be. It is all in that "scream" and that "errant." Again, in "Movement of Troops," a similarly glyptic poem describing a scene of the first world war the imagery calls up the living experience of myth.

165

> We entrain in open trucks
> And soon glide away
> > from the plains of Artois.
>
> With a wake of white smoke
> We plunge
> down dark avenues of silent trees.
>
> A watcher sees
> Our red light gleam
> Occasionally.

The accuracy of the picture, as a record of a scene, is breathtaking, but what is even more astonishing is the shift in viewpoint from that of the speaker to that of a watcher observing what is surely a descent into the inferno. The word "occasionally" is filled with poignancy. The watcher cannot see all the agony. He can only glimpse it from time to time. The soldiers can only from time to time hope that their pain may be observable and be recorded. Herbert Read's translations of contemporary scenes into living myth are among his finest achievements. That they occur most frequently in short poems should not blind us to the magnitude of his success.

Not surprisingly, it is in his War Poems that Read discovers mythic universality most frequently, and again, these are most impressive when least explanatory. "My Company," for example, hits home when we read:

> My men go wearily
> with their monstrous burdens.
>
> They bear wooden planks
> And iron sheeting
> Through the area of death.
>
> When a flare curves through the sky
> They rest immobile.
>
> Then on again,
> Sweating and blaspheming —
> "Oh, bloody Christ!"

But this image of suffering humanity which, by means of the imprecation, is compared to the suffering of Christ on his way to Calvary is then marred by an explicit piece of sermonizing, for this second section of the poem ends:

My men, my modern Christs,
Your bloody agony confronts the world.

The clean narrative development of "The Execution of Cornelius
Vane" does not permit of intrusive explanations and is, as a consequence a moving record of human confusion. "The End of a War,"
however, with its adoption of essentially Metaphysical methods suf-
fers from elaboration and even the "Ode Written During the Battle
of Dunkirk" and "A World Within a War" are marred by senten-
tiousness.

When we turn to the shorter poems, however, we discover that
the imagery carries the viewpoint and the mythic awareness beautifully. "Bombing Casualties in Spain" concludes with an image filled
with implications. We find ourselves wrily registering allusions to
frivolous folly, to childhood, and to the irrationality of collective
human passion.

> They are laid out in ranks
> like paper lanterns that have fallen
> after a night of riot
> extinct in the dry morning air.

In "The Heart Conscripted" the viewpoint is expressed succinctly
and in concrete imagery.

> I hear only the sobbing fall
> of various water-clocks
> and the swift inveterate wail
> of the destructive axe.

It is therefore in the short, passionate poems, in which the image is
presented, in Pound's words, as "an intellectual and emotional complex" that Read's power emerges most effectively. He can present
the nuances of a scene or personality as deftly as Pound in the best
of *Lustra*. "Penumbra" ends with an image quite as astonishingly
effective as that of the woman "like a skein of loose silk blown
against a wall" in Pound's "The Garden."

> She is gone
> a vestal her robes fluttering
> like a printed sheet
> in the gusty Tube

The more the poems depend upon the image and the symbol the
more disturbing they become. Consider the echoing of the images in
"Aubade":

Early light
beats down

my body is a beaten
silver leaf

If I rise
it will wrinkle
a tinsel pod

a wither'd caul
from the womb of night.

Images of the autumn, of birth, of death, and of male sexuality are here fused into a simple classically economic whole.

The word "classical" has often been applied to Read's poetry, and if we allow the word to refer to that extraordinary capacity for evocative particularity possessed by many of the authors of the Greek Anthology, as by Sappho, and, at a later date and in a different tongue, Virgil in his Georgics, the term is valid. The poems are uncluttered with epithets and tense with the dynamics of movement. Thus in "The White Isle of Leuce"

The oars beat off; Achilles cannot see
the prows that dip against the dim shore's line.
But the rowers as they rest on the lifting wave
hear the revelry of Helen and a voice singing
of battle and love.

Here all is active, nothing is passive. The poem is presenting a movement, and not a state, of perception. Again, in the first stanza of "The Ivy and the Ash," a scene which might well have been fixed into immobility by the recording eye is vital with movement.

The ivy and the ash
cast a dark arm
across the beck.
In this rocky ghyll
I sit and watch
the eye-iris water move
like muscles over stones
smooth'd by this ageless action.

The rigour which in the lengthier poems leads to a conscientious struggle towards intellectual formulae, here leads to a disciplined economy, a balance, and a tension which are totally convincing.

Moreover, Read can sum up in a phrase a whole world of implications, without losing touch with physical immediacy. "Song" opens

> So long my heart,
> This little polish'd ball of blood. . . .

He can combine precision of description with richness of allusion as when in "Death of a Greek Mercenary" he tells us how

> The startled goats left footprints
> pointed like the olive leaves

Here, even the speed of the scurrying goats is indicated by the shape of their spoor, and the locale is itself reimpressed upon us by the simile. Read has a penetrating eye for detail. In "The Death of Kropotkin" he shows us how he can make the vaguest and most abstract reference vividly particular and actual. The second stanza is, indeed, almost a critique upon Read's own method of translating the numen into the nomen.

> She said he had died in peace
> and the eternal intelligence on his brow
> had seemed like a light
> in the dark unlit hut.
> I imagined
> his steel-rimmed glasses on the side-table
> and a book abandoned.

This has the poignant detail of the passage in "The Mayor of Casterbridge" where the death of Mrs. Henchard is reflected upon. Hardy and Read were both keenly aware of the pressure of the natural world upon the sensibility of the human creature. Moreover both were fascinated and disturbed by stories of return. The man, after his long life, returns to the village of his youth, and the village reflects for him a vision of his own place in time and space that he would otherwise never have discovered. In one "Sonnet," Read tells his reader, or himself,

> One day you will intuitively come
> Home again driving westward. . . .

On that journey memory will be

> a dusty screen that blinds the vision

The waiting world will be full of remembrance and agony and

> It will be still and you will descend
> Into an arena of yellow corn
> That not a breath of wind stirs
>
> And a rock if it should swerve in the sky
> Will move the whole world momentously.

This is at once the "individual vision" and the universal moment of understanding. It is a poem in which the environment becomes totally meaningful, and almost heroic. In another "Sonnet" Read tells us how the landscape is in turmoil, in continual epic war-array

> Berries in hedges are splashes spilt
> In this massed conflict. Along the roads
> Beech-boles evade the shuffling mists
> Bearing into vision like furled masts.

The landscape of Read's poems is one of vitality and struggle, and though the poems may be about Greece or France or Italy they always remind one of the strong landscape of West Yorkshire, the moors, the stone walls, the dales, or of the Lake District. For Herbert Read

> The waters of the well of life
> Lie deep on a rock bed

The protagonists of the majority of the lyrics are acquainted more with the rough mountain track than with the city street. In "Inscription (for a book of memories)" the reader is directed to

> Think kindly of a man not able
> To face the fiery light
>
> He had wandered over mountains
> And bruised his feet on stones
> Had dreamt of wine-fed fountains
> That dulled the ache of bones.

Read's dreams of Classical Greece and of myth appear to be the result of an attempt to find a symbolism which will relate the struggle of man upon and against the resistant earth with the spiritual unity of the cosmos. Thus "Kalamis and Sosandra" ends with the ringing statement:

> A warm breeze blows across the lake
> It is the season of the grape

> The god the lion and the man
> They have a single shape

This search for a name for that life-force which "runs through all things" leads finally however past Heraclitus, past the Dionysiac energies of Ancient Greece, to Yorkshire and to the long "Dialogue for Three Voices," *Moon's Farm*. On a corrected proof in the University of Victoria Library Read labels the three as "Place", "Self" and "Time".

Moon's Farm was written for radio and, as a consequence, it is more leisurely in progress than many poems and, of course, more discursive. It is perhaps a little marred by passages in which the protagonist returning to Moon's Farm, the scene of his youth, attempts to puzzle out his own relationship to the idea of God, but even here while the poetic tension slackens the intellectual argument produces equivalent tensions of its own, and, moreover, relates directly to the more mysterious and visionary passages. Moreover two forces, those of Dionysus and of Apollo, of poetry and abstraction are here clearly identified, for the second voice, the Self, tells us:

> Yes: we have two voices
>> the instinctive voice that flows like water from a spring
>> or blood from a wound
> and the intellectual voice that blares like a fanfare
>> from some centre of the brain.

The third voice, Time, replies:

> I have only one voice
>> but it is new every day.

Moon's Farm is obviously a record of its author's own spiritual pilgrimage. Its directness and honesty are deeply moving. It records without pretention the struggle towards self-discovery and the final sense of inadequacy. As the Third Voice says: "There is not unity in human character." And yet *Moon's Farm* does end with an expression of unity for it is at Moon's Farm, the place of beginnings, the place of intuition, the place of simplicity where "men hold on to tangible things" and "live with the sun by day and the stars by night," that unity becomes almost possible. It is to Moon's Farm that we must return for assurance and for refreshment.

Read's poetry is at its greatest when it returns to those qualities of intuitive simplicity and direct experience which he finds at Moon's

Farm. It is this which can make dying bearable. The protagonist tells us that:

> I might die in pain
> > in weariness
> > > or in despair.
> But if at the last moment
> I could see some perfect form
> > it might be this fern at my feet
> > or a sparrow flickering past my window
> > or a painting on the wall
> > or some poet's vision of eternity
> > > *like a great Ring of pure and endless Light*
> > > *all calm as it was bright . . .*
> Granted that I could at the last moment
> see some bright image
> > I should die without fear and trembling.
> It is when we look into the abyss of nothingness
> > infinite nothingness
> that we lose courage
> > and die swearing
> > > or die praying.

Read's poems at their best provide that "perfect form" spoken of here, and also that directness of vision which relates man to his environment with the unanswerable logics of myth. There is in Read's poetry a fusion of the poet and the peasant. As the Self, the second voice of *Moon's Farm* tells us:

> I did not discover that I was a peasant
> > until I became a poet

One might also reverse the statement, for it is when the poetry takes on the mythic directness of the peasant, whose world is one of symbols and of omens as well as of the realities of sweat and labour, that Read's vision achieves dignity and power. It is at such moments that we can be told, as we are told by the first voice:

> Man is more than his fate.
> Man is moulded in a womb
> > and dissolved in earth
> His foundations are two tombs
> He is like earth uprisen.

Finally the intellect must give way to a more comprehensive method of understanding, a method that may be alien to the philosophers or even to our type of civilization, but which can be discovered in the poetry of Wordsworth and Traherne, in the mythology of the Greek peasant, and in childhood. In "Emblem" we read:

> Beauty has no other reason
>> than the eye can indicate
> Only the miraculous conception
>> is immaculate

The battle of the two voices which marred some of the longer and earlier poems of Herbert Read ends with this appeal to the profound human understanding that is inevitably present in perfect artistic form. Our recognition of artistic perfection is also our recognition of a type of understanding which transcends both intellectual formulae and the raw directness of intuition. In the poetry of Herbert Read this understanding is most intense when most lyrical and when the form of the lyric and its content are fused together in a gesture appropriate to both poet and peasant. It is this song which is for Herbert Read as a poet the ultimate expression of living man. Thus in "The Heart Conscripted" he celebrates the death of Lorca, a poet whose work was of the people,

> Lorca was killed singing,
> and Fox who was my friend.
> The rhythm returns: the song
> which has no end.

And thus what is perhaps the most crystalline and the most direct of all his songs is that made for the Anarchists in Spain. Freedom here is seen here not only in political terms, in terms of the ideal community of man with man, but also in terms of the intimate connection of man with the earth to which he is born and of which he is made.

A SONG FOR THE SPANISH ANARCHISTS

> The golden lemon is not made
>> but grows on a green tree:
> A strong man and his crystal eyes
>> is a man born free.
>
> The oxen pass under the yoke
>> and the blind are led at will:
> But a man born free has a path of his own
>> and a house on the hill

And men are men who till the land
and women are women who weave:
Fifty men own the lemon grove
and no man is a slave.

The poetry of Herbert Read, as I said at the beginning of this essay has been overshadowed by the more immediately obvious importance of his other writings, and it is true that in the canon of his work there are many flawed poems and many poems divided against themselves. Nevertheless the successes are many and among those successes are some of the most formidably rigorous, sensitively organized, and subtly perceptive short poems of our century. Herbert Read may never be listed as one of the Great Poets of our history but his achievement demands that he be ranked high among the poets of major importance.

Comparisons of stature are however ultimately ridiculous. He lived, as the voices of *Moon's Farm* bade him, "in the moment of attention" and "in the presence of things," and his work commands our reverence and praise.

ROBIN SKELTON

Song of Honour

i

The inventor of
barbed wire was
thinking of cattle.

My brother lay there
tripes skeined out
like silk.

ii

A question of
weight of
manpower,
      cannon-fodder:

Falstaff and
Talleyrand
watch us
      filling the pit.

iii

Passionate fear of
pity is also
pity

eating away the
vitals like a
fox.

iv

We do not live.
We die aloud

to flags and oaths.
The centuries

steal our graves.

ROY FULLER

The Final War

'People have this thing about being burned to death.' U.S. airman in
Vietnam. The Times, December 11, 1967

Dreaming that the final war had started (as
It has) I saw again balloons grey-skinned
As breathed-on mercury, a colander
For sky upturned on the disordered city.
A nonentity, some minor office colleague,
Was there encountered, in whose pointless aim
Of catching a train at the scheduled time of leaving
I was involved . . . Sufficiently alarming,
Such feeble bodying out of present fear
With images anachronistic.

And so begins my tertiary period.
But where is the devoted daughter-figure
To care for my frailty; the honours, the homage?

Those nightmares guard my sleep from sounds of harmless
Aircraft, and getaways at traffic lights
Beyond the opposite Augustan houses;
And when I wake breaks in not only man-made
Disasters but also the major forms of nature —
All, all inimical to organic life.
How fragile that experiment conducted
Under the heat of stars, in seconds of
Virtual eternity, glued to the globe.

What of the minor poets of Sumer?
What indeed of the major?   Better to
Have been the author of *This stone was laid
By Edward Pygge Esquire on August 3rd.*

How easily metabolism turns
The era's very joys to morbid waste.
No one would guess of my cachinnations at noon;
Mockery of Juggins, affection for Ponsonby.

Mysterious all the more my pains to guard
Against, to conquer, natural ills
And reach the days of general extinction —
As though my affinity were not with that
Basel historian who was prepared
At every moment to exchange his life
For a never-having-been, but more with him
Who threw his arms around the ill-used nag
And collapsed into madness, with the signatures
'The Crucified' and 'Dionysus'.
                              To see
In 1300 through the Little Ice-Age
To the threshold of a rational century,
Writing one's panegyrics of the Spring
Overcoated!
                    Though I've always slept with it,
Never have I been reconciled to death.
And now to come so late in life to death
By fire, death of the world, death of one's art!
I sense the pain of everything assaulted,
Even boughs licked in rubbish heaps of Autumn:
Their boiling sap's my own. If what we feel
Were so — if from a dream we merely wake
Into another! Even heroic Nietzsche
Would have preferred to be a Swiss professor
Rather than God.
                        Who's going to usher me
Into my dreamless sleep?

BEAUTY - OR THE BEAST?

A Conversation in a Tavern

There's no such thing as that we beauty call,
It is meer Cozenage all.   JOHN DONNE

Beauty; "That assemblage of graces, or proportion
of parts, which pleases the eye." SAMUEL JOHNSON

BONAMY: Is there anything wrong with your mixed grill?

HERBERT: No; I was merely contemplating it: I thought it looked rather beautiful.

BONAMY: I don't approve of this "still-life" attitude towards grub; it's too detached, and therefore bad for the digestion, which implies the closest possible intimacy. Mustard please!

HERBERT: Beauty, mustard, intimacy, detachment — what a flux of ideas! Here, at any rate, is the mustard.

BONAMY: You're very severe with me; but I see you funk the point.

HERBERT: The point is in the mustard; most people take their art with a condiment.

BONAMY: I query "most." In art, as in other things, there are two races of men. Half the world wants mustard with its art, the thrill, that is, the something queer, like Bacon with his "strangeness in the proportion"; the other half simply wants the familiar, Pope's "What oft was thought . . . ," in fact tidiness as the great desideratum in art. Are you for Pope or Bacon?

HERBERT: For Pope. But do not let us lose sight of a valuable analogy: I mean that between the digestion of food and the appreciation of art.

BONAMY: Analogy? I oppose them. The appreciation of art is the most highly conscious thing we do; we have, alas! lost the pleasures of digestion.

HERBERT: "The appreciation of art" is an odd phrase. Personally, I "appreciate" this mixed grill, I leave art to my unconscious moments.

BONAMY: The theory of the unhappy sponge, "simply absorb!" I'm convinced there must be some collaboration between creator and observer: the latter has to wrest something out of the work.

HERBERT: The theory of the unhappy sponger!

BONAMY: No, because one cannot wrest without payment. Beauty is the lover's gift — not the bribe he is offered.

HERBERT: Oh, beauty! I thought we were talking about art.

BONAMY: I admit the distinction of course: I never supposed that when you gazed so raptly at your mixed grill you thought it was a work of art. Beauty can exist without art — but can art exist without beauty?

HERBERT: That is the question. I have no hesitation in saying that it can. My only doubt is whether it ever exists with beauty.

BONAMY: George! Another double-brown please.

HERBERT: Beauty, you see, is such a bastard concept. Beautiful women, beautiful wine, beautiful skies, beautiful food — it seems to me that anything can be beautiful so long as it ministers to our senses. Beauty passes, beauty fades ... what is the line? — anyway, you know the sense: it has been the parrot-cry of every lyrical poet since Alcman. Everywhere and at every time beauty ' as been recognized as a transient phenomenon; something to be crooned over rather sadly, sentimentally. But art — surely a different thing! A work of art (how our very clichés express the difference — a *work* of art, a *thing* of beauty!) a work of art is by its very nature definite and enduring: it may be cruel, it may be difficult, it may be far from pleasing to the senses — but it endures — endures because it is the adequate expression of an enduring truth. Art satisfies the intelligence of men; beauty their senses.

BONAMY: I dislike the word beauty as a public counter as much as you do, though what sort of emotion it conveys is always clear from the context. You know quite well that when I talk of a beautiful beef-steak, or a beautiful Picasso, or a beautiful woman, or a beautiful mind, the same word-sign stands for quite different emotions; and you know in each case what sort of emotion it stands for.

I object to the word simply because I don't know what sort of emotion it stands for in other people's mouths; or rather because I know that with most people it means merely a vaguely diffused feeling of comfort or desire, and it is often used as a cloak for the mushiest sentimentality. But here's my beer. Now I don't quite know what an enduring truth is — but accepting that there is such a thing, will you prove to me that its "adequate expression" can exist without that something you and I would agree to call beauty?

HERBERT: I shall try; but let us avoid abstractions. Let us talk, not of beauty, not of art, but of definite things, a picture, a poem, a particular cathedral. Come; you shall select three examples of beauty, and I three examples of art. Then your task will be to reduce all six examples to the same category, mine to maintain an irreconcilable difference.

BONAMY: I like that! You're simply forcing me to assume your premises. I could select three examples of beautiful things which were not intended to be works of art — certain factory chimneys, for instance (which, by the way, express "enduring truths" of mechanics, and very adequately indeed), or a Vauban fortress. But if you ask me to select a picture, a poem and a cathedral, that is, things which are supposed to be works of art, it seems to me rather to shift the onus of proving things on to you. You must now prove to me that Ingres' portrait of Madame Rivière, Marvell's *To His Coy Mistress*, and well, to go on selecting rather haphazard, Salisbury Cathedral, though admittedly beautiful, are not works of art.

HERBERT: I see you don't mean to fall into my trap. Your selection, indeed, however random, seems to indicate that you unconsciously recognize the difference I have in view. At least two of them, Ingres and Salisbury Cathedral, are — at first glance — examples in which we shall find the elements of art and beauty freely consorted; mixed but not mingled. For I am going to admit frankly that art and beauty can cohabit and cohere; but I am also going to maintain, in opposition to the view you have expressed, that when art and beauty do cohabit, it is a casual union, not blessed by church or state, or by that personal harmony which sometimes usurps an official sanction in human relationships. You seem to regard art as a graceless masculine creature — a regular old ogre, in fact — who must somehow or other make love to a pretty girl before the world will tolerate his presence.

BONAMY: I didn't know ogres grew more agreeable by devouring maidens; however, I resent your imputation that I regard art as a sort of Caliban who is only tolerable when clothed at the Lyric Theatre, Hammersmith. Anyway, if art is all skeleton and tendons, let me know him with the usual pleasant additions of flesh and skin.

But all this play of yours with analogies and so forth, is to try to make me admit something I don't want to admit: I don't think my view is at the opposite pole to yours, so I cannot flatly contradict. But why manoeuvre for position like this? Tell me your three works of art which are not beautiful, and let me tell you what I feel about them.

HERBERT: Art is not all skeleton and tendons, but it differs from beauty in that it has these bones and sinews to give it not only life, but movement, action, momentum. But I must comply with my own challenge, and give you works of art to convert to beauty. Let us take a Greek tragedy for one — say *Oedipus Rex*; and for another let us take Picasso's stage-settings for *Mercure*; as for the third, you have already selected it, Salisbury Cathedral.

BONAMY: Not beauty! "What *is* beauty? saith my sufferings then." But I see what you're after, at least I think I do: and as our difference is only a distinction, though I believe an important one, perhaps I had better try to state some formula or theory.

My first difficulty is that there are so many roads of approach: but at any rate I don't think the creation of beauty is the artist's end; I think it is an accidental quality, an emotion in the recipient, which, however, it is essential he should feel if he is to grasp what the artist is at. Thus all decoctions made to please the senses, are not art at all — though that is no reason why we should despise them.

Now in face of the works of art you mention, I do feel this emotion which I call thinking a thing beautiful. It is almost a guarantee of my understanding it: it is not an emotion to which I attach any importance in itself: it has, possibly, something to do with the senses, and the senses, as you have written somewhere, can never be satisfied.

There are, I think, two possibilities, and they need not be mutually exclusive: each may apply to a slightly different realm. The first is this: that beauty is, as it were, the solvent of art: it permits the spectator to grasp the meaning of the work of art. It is, perhaps, the familiar element which throws a bridge over the chasm separating us from the newness of the work. It is, I will go so far towards you as to say, the cliché: that is why the public only hails as "beautiful" or "artistic," something which it recognizes as having seen before. But this element is necessary. You remember, no doubt, that Rémy de Gourmont said that a page of writing without clichés would be incomprehensible. Naturally, in a person more accustomed to consider works of art, the sense of beauty will only be given by something a little more recondite than the common favourites; though the emotion of beauty is necessary to put him into that state of mind in which he can grasp the intuition, the new thing, or relation, expressed in the work of art.

It is possible also that the emotion of beauty is that which we get on apprehending a work: art, you say, appeals to the intellect; well, perhaps it is this element I am trying to define, this recognition of an enduring truth (recognition, somehow, seems to come in again), which makes us see beauty in a theorem of Euclid, or any generalization so expressed as to seduce us utterly or immediately. These are but vague gropings. Perhaps you will help me to disentangle, or to destroy them.

HERBERT: I think it will help us if we get the question into some sort of historical perspective. You have only to reflect a minute to realize that beauty is something purely relative. What is beautiful for one age is not beautiful for another. What one age ignores is taken up and exalted by its successor. And even in one age, beauty is conditioned by climate, religion, social status, culture and sensibility. All this, you will agree, is obvious enough. Now I don't want to ask you whether you are a nominalist or a realist, but I would like to know whether you consider this solvent, beauty, is at all times constant in its function. Beautiful things, you must admit, vary infinitely: there is nothing in common between a painting by Angelica Kaufmann and a Cambodian idol. But is the function of beauty in these examples one and the same?

BONAMY: Well, for the sake of your argument, I will admit that it is so. The clichés are different (I rather fancy that Angelica Kaufmann is all cliché), but they are clichés none the less.

HERBERT: I am inclined to agree. Beauty is nothing if it is not fashionable, something which Mr. Clive Bell must fetch from Paris twice a year, like the dressmaker his models. And please don't despise the dressmaker.

BONAMY: God forbid!

HERBERT: Then I don't see that logically you can stop anywhere between Poiret's latest creation and the portrait of Madame Rivière. Beauty is a question of degree, the degree of sensibility of the observer. For the "artist" it is the same thing essentially: it is an instinctive manipulation of material. The sculptor with his stone, the painter with his oils, the poet with his words, the potter with his clay — it is all a question of instinctive play, so far as beauty is concerned. But now and then the artist is conscious of more than his constructive instinct: he is conscious of his intelligence, and then, if he is clever enough ("great" enough, the world would say), he makes his instinct serve his intelligence, and a work of art becomes possible. That is not the whole of the process; there are still more qualifications to be made — but enough for the moment.

BONAMY: Certainly if you had not cried "enough," I should have had to do so: you have raised a dozen issues. But I see we are agreed on the main point, namely that beauty, the fashionable thing, is in reality the beast against which every artist must guard. If he pursues it, he is lost. Culture is the enemy against which every generation of artists has to fight. Nearly every advance in art is greeted as "ugly" by the public, for it is something unaccustomed, and art is nothing if it is not an exploration of life — or if that sounds too grandiloquent, of the artist's mind.

But to go back to what you said about beauty, how it changes, and by what it is conditioned; I suggest that your sentences will be equally just if you substitute the word art for beauty. Art certainly has some connection with truth, but truth changes. You, of course (I say "of course" when I mean I infer), are out for the adequate expression of a metaphysical truth. But you who know much more about such things than I do, will surely not maintain that metaphysical truth is constant? There is only one truth which seems to me to be unchanging (for all the other truths involve values, which are always being transvalued); and that is, that Solomon and Caesar and Shakespeare, and Mr. Jones next door, were once living and are now dead; that you and I are now living and will some time be dead. It seems to me that the only arts which constantly and thoroughly express this, are ancient Egyptian sculpture and Greek tragedy: all the rest, according to you, are elaborate frivolity. I submit that other artists have also expressed this truth — Shakespeare, El Greco perhaps: but is it for that that they are great artists?

HERBERT: If this pot had not been to my lips when you uttered that blasphemy: "truth changes," I would have groaned out loud. As it was, I merely choked. παντα ρει is not my motto. Truth, if there is such a thing, is immutable and eternal. Truth, as wise men have remarked, is a difficult thing to define. Above all, logical and physical truth is a poor, contingent affair. But what I will call qualitative truth — metaphysical truth, if you like — persists in spite of the logicians. It is superior to probability and the laws of nature. It can be deduced from one observation at one time and in the mind of one person, thus confounding the relativists. In fact, metaphysical truth is so relative as to be absolute. In a word, it is a revelation, and revelation is precisely what art, as distinct from beauty, does give us. Revelation, of course, is a theological term, and I use it in a theological sense. But that is only an indication of the nearness of art and religion.

BONAMY: I confess I become lost and embrangled, to use a philosopher's phrase, when you lead me into these cloudy speculative regions, where I do not feel at all at home. Yet I believe you have delivered yourself into my hands. If truth is an intensely personal, unique, and momentary revelation, how on earth can a work of art express this to anyone else without some medium, without some symbol? And this medium is beauty, which does appeal to the senses, physical, emotional and intellectual, which, presumably, we all more or less share. If it is not beauty which is the means of communication, this solvent, what in heaven's name is?

HERBERT: You still misconceive the nature of truth and revelation. *Truth* is not "intensely personal, unique and momentary"; these terms only relate to the perception of it, to revelation. In revelation we, who are temporal accidents, gain a glimpse of those things which are timeless and eternal, absolute and universal. When that beatific vision is given to man, and when man has sufficient grace to give expression to his vision, then the result is art. You seize on the process of expression, hoping that beauty may be identified with it. But I think your hope is vain. I used the word "vision," but in no vague, mystical sense. The vision of the artist is an intellectual vision, and the expression of this vision is an exact — and exacting — discipline. Art is a process of materialization, the translation of vision into actuality, of ideas into shapes, sounds, and signs. It is a practical activity, a making, a craft. Art, you see, actually *is* expression, and art ends with expression. Beauty may be involved, but always incidentally, *unnecessarily*, and as reaction, perception, absorption, physical passivity. Art works from the mind within to the thing without; beauty from the thing without to the mind within. But I don't therefore imply that these activities are reciprocal: It seems to me that the highest delights of art end with their creation; the rest is whoring.

184

BONAMY: Well; what objection is there to that? if I'm not to despise the dressmaker.

HERBERT: That is an argument *ad hominem*.

BONAMY: Surely you admit that everyone may enjoy without being false to truth, or whatever this revelation may be?

HERBERT: We only begin to perceive the truth when we have done with enjoyment.

BONAMY: There I am with you: the beauty fades and the art remains, but the beauty is nevertheless essential. Before digesting my food, I must enjoy it; at least I do. And perhaps without the pleasure I would cease to eat. Art, if you wish, like a pretty problem in the calculus, appeals to the intellect, and beauty, like beefsteak, the perfume of a rose, or the fine lines of a cathedral, to the senses. So be it: then let me have beauty with my art, as for pure art (since, according to you, the only works of art I can really delight in are my own — an arid prospect) I don't care a fig. You may sneer at me for wanting my condiment, for I am a creature of the senses: I have taste, and sight, and hearing, and the imagination to grasp a printed page, that I know: and whatever else I may have has only these to build with. And just as without the senses there can be no thought, so without beauty there can be no art: it is skeleton without flesh, love without desire, a Dead Sea fruit which lacks even the bitterness. The senses, you say, are never satisfied: tell me, is the mind?

But the virtue of art, it seems to me, lies especially in that it reaches the mind through the senses, even sometimes through sheer sensuality. It works, as you say, from without to within. It is the one thing which reconciles mind and body, for it despises neither. Art, to personify it for the moment, is like the soul of man: if it despises the flesh it is ruined, and a great prince in prison lies. One can, of course, wallow in beauty as one can in the sensual sty, and many accredited poets, painters and critics of today do so, to the applause of the multitude, and of sects that ought to know better. It is *that beauty* which I despise, or rather care nothing for, since it opens no windows for me, and gives me no new reality. A great and fresh work of art is nearly always, I think, unacceptable at first, at any rate to my lazy self, for it involves a readjustment: it is a volcanic thing which may blow one's attitudes sky-high. And that, of course, is the really valuable thing in it. But the beauty I ask for I would relinquish as soon as the taste in this excellent cheddar — Yes please, George, two ports — for without it, all art, which is, I repeat, an exploration of experience, would be dry, and tasteless, and chilly, a universe of which the suns are dead.

HERBERT: You are so eloquent — and before the port! — that I begin to suspect you must be right.

BONAMY: Here *is* the port, so there's no need to be malicious.

HERBERT: I only make this reservation: the art I have envisaged is not arid, not chilly, not necessarily without sensuous appeal. Why, think of the passionate fire of the *Divine Comedy*, and that is the very summit and supreme type of art! It comes to this: you are for human standards; and I think a word you like, and it well describes your standards, is *gustation* . . .

BONAMY: Even if I use it in the theological sense?

HERBERT: . . . while I want a word more remote from human appetite; and yet I want the enchantment, the delight, the radiance. Will *delectation* do? I think it will. It implies Eden before the Fall, just as *gustation* is heavy with the fruit of the Tree of Knowledge. If we must be human, you have the advantage, for your beauty, however, transient, is real. But I think I am a transcendentalist, and in that airier region. . . .

BONAMY: . . . we do not have to pay our bills as we do here (they're both the same, we'll settle as we go along). And while I wait for the change, let me try and remember that phrase of Plotinus about approaching work of art, a phrase in which we can exist together, and pursue beauty-mongers to the death —

HERBERT: I had almost forgotten them; yes, down with them!

BONAMY: Let me see — not solemnly, but with a happy reverence is the idea: here it is! "With wonderment and a delicious trouble, longing and love and an awe blended with delight," though seeing the havoc recent writers have made of love in this connection, I would like to leave that word out. But otherwise, does it please you?

HERBERT: Please is the word; it is pleasant. But let "love" be, for Plotinus also has a right to the theological sense. Then the phrase will cover all the dark points of our dispute, and lie like the sunlight on these hollow houses.

Roland Penrose

HERBERT READ

PERHAPS THE MOST DISTURBING and terrifying thing about a death is its stark and irreversible finality, and yet in writing about Herbert Read I find that he continues for me to be so alive and his presence so real that I feel urged to look for reasons for this persistence which breaks through the normal barriers between conscious life and the silent void of death. There are of course the memories of moments spent in Herbert's company which carry with them an intense sense of pleasure, such as the clear winter morning when he took me to see Rievaulx Abbey not far from his home in Yorkshire. The fact that he was my guide but said very little as we wandered round that magnificent Gothic ruin or walked on the thin crisp covering of snow among the trees and on the hill above, visiting the frivolous elegance of the eighteenth-century temples which ornament the natural beauty of the site — the fact that he seemed to transmit with no unnecessary explanation and without passing judgment the significance of this contrast between medieval faith and serenity and Georgian aristocratic caprice, gave me a sense of his ability to appreciate equally, sublime simplicity and grandiose extravagance. This understanding, this acceptance of opposites, made me wonder. I was never in doubt about Herbert's reverence for the great mysteries of life but his quiet laugh that assured me so often of his taste for the absurd, the trivial and the ridiculous as their inevitable counterpart came as a refreshing and endearing surprise.

Beyond the casual incidents that remain as a continual delight there is a more profound and durable quality which keeps Herbert continuously alive, and this I think depends essentially on his penetration, as a poet and a sage, to the roots of life. This was somehow linked closely to his love of nature and of his friends. We find it expressed most convincingly in that story of his early life told so candidly in *The Innocent Eye*. We realize that in spite of his brilliant intellect and the great attraction that learning had for him he was deeply, in fact primarily, attached to the soil — what is more, the soil of Yorkshire where he was born and lived an idyllic childhood. The intense joy of being absorbed into the traditions of the countryside, his attachment to every tree, stone and brook and his understanding of their timeless function, thrived in his imagination and expressed itself in his poems and in that very personal fantasy, *The Green Child*. It is there that we can study a significant solution offered by Herbert for that problem which confronts us all, the problem of enjoying life to its full in all its diverse channels in spite of its outrageous risks and deceptions and yet being prepared to relinquish our all-absorbing passions with understanding and serenity.

The reversal of the belief in the supremacy of the soul that he unfolds at the end of the book allows him to expand on his pleasure in the harmonies and timeless perfection of inanimate nature with which his dying hero becomes identified. This purified condition of the human body which he achieves can only take place when the body has become liberated from the lusts of the spirit and the insatiable desires of the soul. The allegory has its source quite obviously in a fact as simple and primitive as an intense love of the soil — a love which he shared with many English poets and which descended on him especially from Wordsworth.

Herbert's ability to accept the dramatic contradictions of life and use them for his spiritual growth was one of his greatest qualities. We think of him as the happy son of Yorkshire farmers, tranquil and robust, and then abruptly in sharp contrast as the officer who could lead his men with calm and heroism through the hellish madness of war in Flanders. He is also the child of an unspoilt countryside who became a scholar of great repute and travelled widely, acclaimed in many countries as a philosopher who could give new meaning and importance to the arts. His love of order and peaceful understanding between men was balanced by his conception of anarchy which would unite mankind and resolve the menace of violence without the compulsion of the law. A fantastic portrait bust of him made by Eileen Agar in 1937 was reproduced beside a photo of Herbert in *The London Bulletin* and given the title "The Angel of Anarchy."

Herbert in his thought as well as his behaviour was marvellously fearless. I remember the authority with which he talked to us about fear in those days when war was again inevitably becoming a pre-occupation, how he told us that he had learnt in Flanders to detect in others the difference between fear and cowardice. His own capacity for detached concentration not only gave him great physical courage but allowed him also to have the courage to doubt even himself. This quality, due largely to his humility often made it difficult for him to make a final decision. At times when we worked together and it was necessary to make up our minds on some point I felt I became a crude insensitive opportunist when finally I insisted on a decision. Yet once a reasonably correct solution was made he seemed relieved and was always loyal and full of encouragement for the line chosen.

And here I should also mention Herbert's patience. His motives may have been various for doing so but it was extremely rare that he refused to see a poet or a painter who was asking for advice, and he was always eager to find some virtue in the work, however dim. This led often to hours of boredom but also to those many discoveries of talent due to Herbert's unending sense of inquiry.

I do not mean to imply by what I have said that Herbert lacked convictions. On the contrary, like many others, I have always thought of him as a leader who inspired us by the clarity of his thought and his unshaken faith in humanity. It was this that made him in the thirties such a close ally of the surrealists, both poets such as Paul Eluard, and among painters, Miro. Among other things their insistence on the integrity of the artist and of his social responsibility appealed greatly to Herbert in those days before the war when the world seemed inevitably divided into two camps — democracy and fascism.

I remember how closely he was involved, how he showed me one day a letter he had just received from George Orwell who was then fighting with the International Brigade in Spain, saying that we must prepare for a state of siege in which freedom of expression would be the most essential thing to defend and asking Herbert to examine the means of setting up a clandestine printing press in London. Among Herbert's friends were experienced and very sincere anarchists who included among them the indefatigable Emma Goldman. They could have provided the resourceful determination needed for the operation. But Herbert worked with great energy for a number of anti-fascist organizations and spoke with eloquence in public meetings, just as years later he was again among those who led nuclear disarmament demonstrations in Trafalgar Square. "We must fight these primary battles first," I remember him saying, "otherwise there will be nothing to fight for."

In spite of the time and energy that went into these things Herbert had an immense reserve that he dedicated to his poetry, his philosophy and that cause that he had deeply at heart, the understanding and the future of art. During his life he had witnessed the great revolution of the arts in this century and with the knowledge of an unbiased art historian he became, during the thirties, both the herald of abstract art and the champion of surrealism. He hailed with enthusiasm the freedoms won in earnest for the arts but he was not blind to the perils that now lie ahead. His last speech made in Cuba last January criticizing the fragmentation and frustration of the present "international" style shows this very clearly.

My first intimacy with Herbert grew from a combined effort to introduce surrealism to London in 1936 — a task in which we were joined enthusiastically by Henry Moore, Paul Nash, Humphrey Jennings, David Gascoyne, Peter Watson, E. L. T. Mesens and many other poets and painters. The great exhibition which took place in the New Burlington Galleries was supported by André Breton, Paul Eluard, Max Ernst, Miró, Dali and others from abroad, but it was the presence of Herbert Read and his opening speech that made this, for London, an event of great importance.

Using his gift for clarifying the confusion that can arise between groups that do not always agree but which have at heart the necessity for a revolution in the arts and in life, Herbert again took the leadership after the war of a cause which promised the fulfilment of his wish to encourage progressive experiment in the arts. He became a founder and the first president of the Institute of Contemporary Arts, an organization which he guided towards its present status as a centre for the growth and appreciation of the arts. In the late spring of 1968 he wrote to John Bodley after his first visit to the new premises the I.C.A. had just opened: "Wonderful — the fulfilment of a dream that has taken thirty years to realize." It was shortly after this visit that the cruel ravages of his illness caused his final return to the home he loved in Yorkshire and his end came as an inevitable and appropriate fulfilment of his life, a life dominated by the clarity of his intelligence, by the richness of his imagination, by his devotion to his friends and the ideals he shared with them. But perhaps above all this sense of fulfilment was due to his understanding of the eternal game of life and death. His death was beautiful in that it was the greatest accomplishment of life — a harmony such as he speaks of in *The Green Child* "that exists before life and after life: in worlds that are not yet formed and in worlds that are defunct" — a death which is a continuation of life and which engenders the eternal marriage of life and death — of heaven and hell.

Howard Gerwing,
with the assistance of Michael W. Pidgeon

A CHECKLIST OF THE HERBERT READ ARCHIVE IN THE McPHERSON LIBRARY OF THE UNIVERSITY OF VICTORIA

THE SIR HERBERT READ archive collection at the University of Victoria began in 1966 with the arrival at the Library of three trunks of typescripts, proofs, notebooks and letters. This stroke of good fortune was immediately followed up by the preparation of a desiderata list from the Library of Congress Catalogue, the National Union Catalogue, the British Museum Catalogue, and several other published checklists. The works on this list are now on order or are included in the non-circulating collection housed in Special Collections. It was decided to print this list along with the checklist of the unique materials, in order to give a full picture of the Sir Herbert Read archive at the University of Victoria, and a reasonably complete account of his publications.

Two of the trunks contained 47 bundles of papers, typescripts, notebooks and proofs. Since these bundles were put together either by Sir Herbert or his son Benedict it was decided to use these bundles as the basic units of the checklist. Though many of these bundles contained a variety of items such as letters, photographs, drawings, clippings and other printed materials, they were together because they had obvious connections with each other.

The third trunk contained correspondence filed in labelled folders. This material was listed as "letters to" Sir Herbert and "letters from" Sir Herbert, the latter being almost completely unsigned carbons. It is hoped that eventually many of the originals of the "letters from" will find their way into the archive. Each section of the correspondence list ends with an item labelled "miscellaneous letters." These letters are from correspondents still to be identified. The folders titled "Freedom Press" and "Freedom Defence Committee" were listed separately because they seemed to warrant such treatment. H.G.

192

SECTION ONE
Books by Sir Herbert Read

Ambush. London, Faber & Faber, 1930. 43 p.
(Criterion miscellany, no. 16) Contents: First blood; Man, melodion, snowflakes; Killed in action; Cloud-form; The raid; Cupid's everlasting honeymoon.

Anarchy and order; essays in politics. London, Faber & Faber, 1945. 235 p.

The anatomy of art; an introduction to the problems of art and aesthetics. New York, Dodd, Mead, 1932. 224 p.
London edition (Faber & Faber Limited) has title: The meaning of art.

Annals of innocence and experience. London, Faber & Faber, 1940. 211 p.
Includes the *Innocent eye,* and continues his reminiscences. "First published in November Mcmxl."

—. London, Faber & Faber, 1946. 236 p.
First published in November Mcmxl ... New revised and enlarged edition. Includes the author's *The innocent eye,* and his *In retreat;* both works also published separately. American edition (New York, H. Holt and company) has title: *The innocent eye.*

Aristotle's mother; an imaginary conversation. North Harrow, Middlesex, P. Ward, 1961. 14 p.
(Herbert Read reprints, no. 1)

Art and alienation: the role of the artist in society. London, Thames & Hudson, 1967. 176 p.
Bibliography: p. [166] - 169.

—. [1st American ed.], New York, Horizon Press, 1967. 176 p.
"Text references": - [166] - 169.

Art and education. Auckland, Paul's Book Arcade, 1964. 74 p.

—. Melbourne, F. W. Cheshire, 1964. 74 p.
Essays. Bibliographical footnotes.

Art and industry, the principles of industrial design. London, Faber & Faber, 1934. 143 p.
Title on 2 leaves.

—. London, Faber & Faber, 1944. 188 p.
"First published in October Mcmxxiv ... Second edition Mcmxliv."

—. [3rd ed., rev.]. London, Faber & Faber, 1953. 204 p.

—. [1st American ed.]. New York, Horizon Press, 1954. 239 p.
Based on the 3rd (revised) English edition.

—. [4th ed., rev.]. London, Faber & Faber, 1956. 205 p.

—. Bloomington [Ind.] Indiana University Press, 1961. 239 p.
(Midland Books, MB, 32)

—. [5th ed.]. London, Faber, 1966. 212 p.
Art and society. London, Heinemann, 1937. 282 p.

—. New York, Macmillan, 1937. 282 p.
"Printed in Great Britain."

—. London, Faber & Faber, 1945. 152 p.
"The substance of the book was originally delivered as lectures . . .
at the University of Liverpool, 1935-6." Pref. to the 2d ed.
"First published in Mcmxxxvi . . . New and revised edition published
in Mcmxlv."

—. [2nd ed.]. New York, Pantheon Books, 1950. 152 p.
Biographical footnotes.

—. [3rd ed.]. London, Faber & Faber, 1956. 152 p.

—. New York, Schocken Books, 1966. 152 p.
Bibliographical footnotes.

—. [4th ed.]. London, Faber, 1967. 152 p.
Bibliographical footnotes.

Art and the evolution of man; lecture delivered at Conway Hall, London, on April 10th, 1951. London, Freedom Press, 1951. 51 p.

Art now; an introduction to the theory of modern painting and sculpture. London, Faber & Faber, 1933. 144 p.

—. [new and rev. ed.]. London, Faber & Faber, 1936. 160 p.

—. New York, Harcourt, Brace, 1937. 160 p.
"Printed in Great Britain."

—. [rev. and enl. ed.]. London, Faber & Faber, 1948. 144 p.

—. [new and enlarged edition]. New York, Pitman, 1948. 144 p.

—. [rev. ed.]. London, Faber, 1960. 120 p.
Bibliographical footnotes.

—. [rev. and enl. ed.]. London, Faber & Faber, 1960. 131 p.
Bibliographical footnotes.

—. [rev. ed.]. New York, Pitman, 1960. 131 p.
Bibliographical footnotes.

The art of sculpture. London, Faber & Faber, 1956. 152 p.
(Bollingen series, 35. The A. W. Mellon lectures in the fine arts, 3)
Includes bibliographical references.

—. New York, Pantheon Books, 1956. 152 p.
(Bollingen series, 35. The A. W. Mellon Lectures in the fine arts, 3)
Includes bibliographical references.

—. [2nd ed.]. New York, Pantheon Books, 1961. 152 p. (Bollingen series, 35:3. The A. W. Mellon lectures in the fine arts, 3) Includes bibliography.

Arte y sociedad: Versión castellana de Agustín J. Alvarez; estudio preliminary de Alfredo E. Roland. Buenos Aires, G. Kraft, 1951. 307 p. (Biblioteca universal de sociologia, v. 2)

Arte, poesía, anarquismo. Buenos Aires, Editorial Reconstruir, 1955. 72 p. (Colección radar. Serie: Temas doctrinario de exposión y de critica, 8) Bibliographical sketch of author signed: C.D. Translation of *Poetry and anarchism.*

Byron. London, New York, published for the British Council by Longmans, Green, 1951. 43 p.

(Bibliographical series of supplements of *British book news*)
"Byron, a select bibliography": p. 35-43.

—. London, New York, published for the British Council by Longmans, Green, 1961. 43 p.

(Bibliographical series of supplements to *British book news on writers and their work*, no. 10)

—. London, published for the British Council and the National Book League by Longmans, Green, 1966. 43 p.

(Bibliographical series of supplements to *British book news*, no. 10) "Reprinted with additions to bibliography 1966". "Byron, a selected bibliography": p. 35-43.

A coat of many colours; occasional essays. London, G. Routledge, 1945. 352 p.

A coat of many colours; essays. [2nd ed., rev.]. London, Routledge & Paul, 1956. 352 p.

A coat of many colours. [1st American ed.]. New York, Horizon Press, 1956. 352 p.

Coleridge as critic. London, Faber & Faber, 1949. 40 p.

"Contribution to a Symposium on the Greater Critics, held at the Johns Hopkins University, Baltimore, but the text here printed is ... longer than the lecture actually delivered on April 14, 1948."

Collected essays in literary criticism. London, Faber & Faber, 1938. 366 p.
"First published in October Mcmxxxviii."

Includes essays first published in the author's *This sense of glory,* 1929, *Form in modern poetry,* 1932, and *In defense of Shelley.* The remainder of the essays are either from his *Reason and romanticism,* 1926, or have not hitherto appeared in book form. Contents: General theories: The nature of poetry; The nature of criticism. Particular studies: Froissart; Malory; Descartes; Swift; Vauvenargues; Tobias Smollett; Sterne; Hawthorne; Charlotte and Emily Brontë; Bagehot; Coventry Patmore; Gerard Manley Hopkins; Henry James.

—. [2nd ed.]. London, Faber & Faber, 1951. 381 p.
  Published in New York under title: *The nature of literature.*

—. [2nd ed.]. London, Faber & Faber, 1962. 381 p.

Collected Poems, 1913-25. London, Faber & Gwyer, 1926. 115 p.
  One of an edition of 56 copies. Signed by the author. 50 copies are
  for sale.

—. London, Faber & Gwyer, 1926. 115 p.

Collected poems. London, Faber & Faber, 1946. 201 p.
  First edition.

—. Norfolk, Conn., New Directions, 1951. 201 p.

—. [New ed.]. London, Faber & Faber, 1953. 203 p.

—. London, Faber, 1966. 286 p.

—. [1st American ed.]. New York, Horizon Press, 1966. 286 p.

A concise history of modern painting. London, Thames & Hudson,
  1959. 376 p.

—. New York, Praeger, 1959. 376 p.
  "Text references": p. 338-345. Bibliography: p. 346-348.

—. London, Thames & Hudson, 1961. 376 p.
  (The World of Art library) "Text references": p. 338-345. Bibliography: p. 346-348. First published 1959.

—. New York, Praeger, 1965. 378 p.
  (Praeger World of Art series) "Fourth printing 1965." "Text references": p. 339-346. Bibliography: p. 347-349.

A concise history of modern sculpture. London, Thames & Hudson,
  1964. 310 p.

—. New York, Praeger, 1964. 310 p.
  (Praeger World of Art series) "Text references": p. 279-282. Bibliography: p. 283-285.

—. New York, Praeger, 1965. 310 p.
  (Praeger World of Art series) Includes bibliographies.

Contemporary British art. Harmondsworth, Middlesex, Penguin Books,
  1951. 47 p.
  (Pelican Books, A 250) Bibliography: p. 47-48.

—. Harmondsworth, Middlesex, Penguin Books, 1954. 47 p.
  (Pelican books, A 250) Bibliography: p. 47-[48].

—. [rev. ed.]. Baltimore, Penguin Books, 1964. 61 p.
  (Pelican books, A 250) Bibliographical references included in footnotes.

The contrary experience; autobiographies. London, Faber & Faber,
  1963. 356 p.

Includes the author's *The innocent eye* and pt. 2 of his *Annals of innocence and experience*, with new and previously unpublished material. Bibliographical footnotes.

—. [1st American ed.]. New York, Horizon Press, 1963. 356 p.
Includes the author's *The innocent eye* and part 2 of his *Annals of innocence and experience*, with new and previously unpublished material.

Culture and education in world order. New York, published for the Committee on Art Education by the Museum of Modern Art, 1948. 14 p. Cover title. "Address . . . given for the Committee on Art Education at its Sixth Annual Conference, April 23-25, 1948."

Design and tradition. With a preface by F. H. K. Henrion. Hemingford Grey, Vine Press, 1962. 17 p.
(Society of Industrial Artists. Design oration, 1961)

Eclogues. A book of poems. London, C. W. Beaumont, 1919. 35 p.
Decorations designed by Ethelbert White. No. 23 of 30 copies printed on Japanese vellum.

Eclogues; a book of poems. Westminster, Beaumont Press, 1919. 35 p.
Cover and decorations designed by Ethelbert White. Limited to 200 copies. This is no. 123.

Education for peace. New York, C. Scribner's Sons, 1949. 166 p.
"Four . . . papers . . . originally delivered in 1947 or 1948 as lectures in various parts of the world . . . The final essay was originally published by the Freedom Press (London)." Bibliographical references included in "Notes" (p. 155-161). Contents: Education for peace; Education in things; Culture and education in a world order; The moral significance of aesthetic education; The education of free men.

—. London, Routledge & K. Paul, 1950. 131 p.
Bibliographical references included in "Notes" (p. 121-125)

The education of free men. London, Freedom Press, 1944. 32 p.
Inscribed by the author to T. S. Eliot. Annotated by Eliot. "This treatise is a shorter statement of the theory of education put forward by the author in Education through art, London, (Faber & Faber), 1943."

Education through art. London, Faber & Faber, 1943. 320 p.
"First published in Mcmxliii." Bibliography: p. 303-312.

—. [2nd ed.]. New York, Pantheon Books, 1945? 320 p.
Bibliography: p. 303-312.

—. [new rev. ed.]. London, Faber & Faber, 1958. 328 p.
Bibliography: p. 309-321.

—. London, Faber & Faber, 1961. 328 p.
(Faber paper covered editions)

The end of a war. London, Faber & Faber, 1933. 31 p.
A poem.

English prose style. London, G. Bell, 1928. 227 p.

—. New York, H. Holt, 1928. 229 p.

—. London, G. Bell, 1942. 227 p.
"First published May 1928 ... Cheaper edition 1931. Reprinted ... 1942." Minor revisions have been made in the various reprints of this book.

—. [New (rev.) ed.]. London, Bell, 1952. 216 p.

—. [New ed.]. New York, Pantheon Books, 1952. 216 p.

—. [New ed.]. Boston, Beacon Press, 1955. 216 p.
On cover: BPIO.

English stained glass. London & New York, G. P. Putnam's Sons, 1926. 259 p.
Frontispiece accompanied by guard sheet with descriptive letterpress. "Selected bibliography": p. 250-253.

Essential communism. London, S. Nott, 1935. 32 p.
(Half-title: Pamphlets on the new economics, no. 12) Discusses from the point of view of an artist, the trend toward collectivism; concludes by advocating social credit as "a mode for attaining essential communism."

Existentialism, marxism, and anarchism; chains of freedom. London, Freedom Press, 1949. 56 p.

Form in modern poetry. London, Sheed & Ward, 1932. 81 p.
(Essays in order, no. 11)

—. London, Vision, 1948. 85 p.

—. London, Vision, 1957. 85 p.

The forms of things unknown; essays towards an aesthetic philosophy. London, Faber & Faber, 1960. 248 p.
Includes bibliography.

—. New York, Horizon Press, 1960. 248 p.

—. Cleveland, World Pub. Co., 1963. 248 p.
(Meridian books, M168)

The future of industrial design. London, 1946. 8 p.
(Design and Industries Association. Booklet no. 1)

Geschichte der modernen Malerei. [Aus dem Englischen übertragen von Alfred P. Zeller]. München, Knaur, 1959. 368 p.
Includes bibliography.

The grass roots of art; four lectures on social aspects of art in an industrial age. New York, Wittenborn, 1947. 92 p.
(Problems of contemporary art, no. 2) "Delivered as the Woodward

and Trowbridge memorial lectures at Yale University during the spring of 1946" — Pref. Bibliographical footnotes. Contents: Society and culture; The social basis of great architecture; The aesthetic method of education; Towards a duplex civilization.

The grass roots of art. London, L. Drummond, 1947. 117 p.
(Transformation library, 1)

The grass roots of art; lectures on the social aspects of art in an industrial age. [Rev. and expanded]. London, Faber & Faber, 1955. 160 p.
Bibliographical footnotes.

—. [Rev. and expanded]. New York, G. Wittenborn, 1955. 160 p.
(Problems of contemporary art, no. 2) Bibliographical footnotes.

—. Cleveland, World Pub. Co., 1961. 160 p.
(Meridian books)

The green child; a romance. London, Toronto, Heinemann, 1935. 256 p.

—. [New ed.]. With illus. by Felix Kelly. London, Grey Walls Press, 1945. 137 p.

—. [Introd. Graham Greene] London, Eyre & Spottiswoode, 1947. 194 p.

—. With an introd. by Kenneth Rexroth. New York, New Directions, 1948. 194 p.

Henry Moore, sculptor, an appreciation. London, A. Zwemmer, 1934. 15 p.

Henry Moore; a study of his life and work. London, Thames & Hudson, 1965. 284 p.
(World of art library)

—. New York, Praeger, 1966. 284 p.
(A Praeger world of art profile) Bibliography 265-266.

High noon and darkest night. Middletown, Conn., Center for Advanced Studies, Wesleyan Univ., 1964. 18 p.
(Monday evening papers, 3)

Icon and idea; the function of art in the development of human consciousness. London, Faber & Faber, 1955. 161 p.
(Charles Eliot Norton lectures 1953-1954) Bibliography: p. 141-152.

—. Cambridge, Harvard University Press, 1955. 161 p.
(The Charles Eliot Norton lectures, 1953-1954) Bibliography: p. 141-152.

Imagen e idea; la función del arte en el desarrollo de la conciencia humana. Traducción de H. Flores Sánchez, México, 1957. 245 p.
(Breviarios del Fondo de Cultura Económica, 127)

199

In defence of Shelley & others essays. London, Heinemann, 1936. 282 p.
Contents: In defence of Shelley; Coventry Patmore; Gerard Manley Hopkins; Obscurity in poetry; Two notes on Swift; Diderot's love letters; Pablo Picasso; Parallels in English painting and poetry; English art.

In retreat. London, L. & Virginia Woolf, 1925. 42 p.
(The Hogarth essays, no. 6) Caption title: In retreat; a journal of the retreat of the Fifth army from St. Quentin, March 1918.

—. London, Faber & Faber, 1930. 46 p.
(Half-title: Criterion miscellany, no. 8)
Caption title: In retreat: a journal of the retreat of the Fifth army from St. Quentin, March, 1918. Published in 1925 as the Hogarth essays, VI. Reprinted in 1930 by Faber & Faber Limited: second impression September, 1930.

The innocent eye. London, Faber & Faber, 1933. 81 p.

—. New York, Holt, 1947. 268 p.
Includes the author's *The innocent eye*, and his *In retreat*; both works also published separately. British edition (London, Faber & Faber) has title: Annals of innocence and experience.

Julien Benda and the new humanism. Seattle, University of Washington book store, 1930. 33 p.
(Half-title: University of Washington chapbooks, ed. by G. Hughes, no. 37)

A letter to a young painter [and essays]. London, Thames and Hudson, 1962. 277 p.

—. [1st American ed.]. New York, Horizon Press, 1962. 277 p.
Essays.

Lord Byron at the opera; a play for broadcasting. Middlesex, Eng., Ward, 1963. 20 p.

Lynn Chadwick. Amriswill, Bodensee-Verlag, 1958. 23 p.
(Artists of our time, 4)
English and German.

The meaning of art. London, Faber & Faber, 1931. 150 p.
American edition (New York, Dodd, Mead & Co.) has title: *The anatomy of art*.

—. [2nd ed.]. London, Faber & Faber, 1936. 224 p.
American edition has title: *The anatomy of art*.

—. Harmondsworth, Middlesex, Eng., Penguin Books, 1947. 191 p.
American edition (New York, Dodd, Mead & Co.) has title: *The anatomy of art*. "First published 1931."

—. Harmondsworth, Penguin Books in association with Faber & Faber, 1949. 191 p.
(Pelican Books, no. 213)

200

—. [3rd ed., rev. and enl.]. London, Faber & Faber, 1951. 262 p.

—. New York, Pitman, 1951. 262 p.

—. Harmondsworth, Middlesex, Penguin Books, 1959. 196 p.
(A Pelican books, A213) Fifth reprint.

—. Baltimore, Penguin Books, 1959. 196 p.
(Pelican books, A213)

The modern art book. [n.p., 1966?]. 14 p.
(Columbiad Club. Keepsake, no. 78)
A lecture before the Columbiad Club, May 11, 1965. 50 copies.

Moon's Farm, and poems mostly elegiac. London, Faber & Faber, 1955.
77 p.

—. [1st American ed.]. New York, Horizon Press, 1956. 77 p.

Mutations of the Phoenix. [Poems]. Richmond, L. & V. Woolf, 1923.
51 p.

Naked warriors. [Poems]. London, Art & Letters, 1919. 59 p.

The nature of literature. [1st American ed.]. New York, Horizon Press,
1956. 381 p.
First published in London in 1938 under title: *Collected essays in
literary criticism.*

—. New York, Grove Press, 1958. 381 p.
(Evergreen books, E-92)
First published in London in 1938 under title: *Collected essays in
literary criticism.*

The origins of form in art. London, Thames and Hudson, 1965. 207-.
Bibliography: p. 189-197.

The parliament of women; a drama in three acts. Text by Herbert
Read; designed by Reg Boulton. Huntingdon, Eng., 1960. 113 p.
"One hundred copies printed and published in Great Britain by
Peter Foster and John Peters at the Vine Press . . . Number 34."

Paul Nash. Harmondsworth, Middlesex, Eng., Penguin Books, 1944.
16 p.
(On cover: The Penguin modern painters) At head of title: Herbert Read.

Phases of English poetry. London, L. & V. Woolf, 1928. 158 p.
(Half-title: Hogarth lectures on literature. (no. 7).

—. New York, Harcourt, Brace, [c. 1929]. 158 p.
(Hogarth lectures on literature, 7)

—. [Rev. ed.]. London, Faber & Faber, 1950. 148 p.

—. [Rev. ed.]. Norfolk, Conn., c. 1951. 192 p.
(Direction, 19)

The philosophy of anarchism. London, Freedom press distributors, 1940. 35 p.
"Special edition limited to 500 copies." Bibliographical footnotes.

—. London, Freedom Press, 1941. 35 p.
"First published September, 1940 . . . Second impression June 1941."

—. London, Freedom Press, 1947. 32 p.

The philosophy of modern art; collected essays. London, Faber & Faber, 1952. 278 p.

—. [Essays. 1st American ed.]. New York, Horizon Press, 1953. 278 p.

—. New York, Meridian Books, 1955. 309 p.
(Meridian books, M7)

—. London, Faber & Faber, 1964. 278 p.
(Faber paper covered editions)

The place of art in a University. An Inaugural Lecture given at the University of Edinburgh. Edinburgh, London, Oliver & Boyd, 1931. 28 p.

Poems, 1914-1934. London, Faber & Faber, 1935. 168 p.
First edition. Contents: Eclogues (1914-1918); War poems (1916-1932); Satirical verses (1919-1934); Lyrical poems (1919-1934); Longer poems (1920-1934).

Poems, 1914-1934. New York, Harcourt, Brace & Co., 1935. 168 p.
At the head of title: Herbert Read. Printed in Great Britain.
Contents: Eclogues (1914-1918); War poems (1916-1932); Satirical verses (1919-1934); Lyrical poems (1919-1934); Longer poems (1920-1934).

Poetry and anarchism. London, Faber & Faber, 1938. 126 p.
First published in June Mcmxxxviii.

—. [2nd ed.]. London, Freedom Press, 1947. 79 p.

Poetry and experience. London, Vision P., 1967. 160 p.
Bibliographical footnotes.

—. [1st American ed.]. New York, Horizon Press, 1967. 160 p.
Bibliographical footnotes. Contents: The faith of a critic; The attributes of criticism; The style of criticism; The definition of comedy; The disciples of Diderot; The dialogue; Poetry and experience; The resurrection of the word; American bards and British reviewers.

The politics of the unpolitical. London, Routledge, 1943. 160 p.
Contents: The politics of the unpolitical; The cult of leadership; Culture and liberty; To hell with culture; Art in an electric atmosphere; The vulgarity and impotence of contemporary art; Modern art and French decadence; a question of life or death; The collective patron; The freedom of the artist; The nature of revolutionary art; A civilization from under; Civilization and the sense of quality; A solemn conclusion.

202

Reason and romanticism. London, Faber & Gwyer, 1926. 229 p.
  Contents: The attributes of criticism; The nature of metaphysical
  poetry; Pure poetry; The future of poetry; Psycho-analysis and criticism; The disciples of Diderot; The definition of comedy; The dialogue; Charlotte and Emily Brontë; Tobias Smollett; The modern
  novel (cursory notes).

Reason and romanticism, essays in literary criticism. New York, Russell
  & Russell, 1963. 229 p.

*The redemption of the robot; my encounter with education through
  art.* New York, Trident Press, 1966. 254 p.
  (Credo series)
  Bibliographical footnotes.

Selected writings; poetry and criticism. With a foreword by Allen Tate.
  London, Faber & Faber, 1963. 406 p.
  "Select bibliography of the author's works compiled with the assis-
  tance of Philip Ward and Salma M. Ghanem: p. 402-406."

The sense of glory; essays in criticism. Cambridge, University Press,
  1929. 227 p.
  Contents: Froissart; Malory; Descartes; Swift; Vauvenargues; Sterne;
  Hawthorne; Bagehot; Henry James. Bibliographical footnotes.

—. Freeport, N.Y., Books for Libraries Press, 1967. 227 p.
  (Essay index reprint series)
  Bibliographical footnotes. Contents: Froissart; Malory; Descartes;
  Swift; Vauvenargues; Sterne; Hawthorne; Bagehot; Henry James.

The significance of children's art. Art as symbolic language. [1st ed.].
  Vancouver, University of British Columbia, 1957. 53 p.
  Includes bibliography.

Songs of Chaos. London, Elkin Mathews, 1915. 37 p.

Staffordshire pottery figures. London, Duckworth, 1929. 24 p.
  "Books": p. 24.

T.S.E., a memoir. Middletown, Conn., Center for Advanced Studies,
  Wesleyan University, 1966. 31 p.
  (Monday evening papers, no. 5)
  Cover title. "Reprinted from T. S. Eliot (1888-1965) edited by Alan
  Tate."

The tenth muse; essays in criticism. London, Routledge & K. Paul,
  1957. 330 p.

—. [1st American ed.]. New York, Horizon Press, 1958. 330 p.

Thirty-five poems. London, Faber & Faber, 1940. 80 p.
  Second impression 1941.
  Most of the poems were included in his *Poems, 1914-1934.* Includes
  bibliography.

To hell with culture; democratic values are new values. London, K. Paul, Trench, Trubner, 1941. 63 p.
(The democratic order, no. 4)

To hell with culture, and other essays on art and society. London, Routledge & K. Paul, 1963. 193 p.

—. New York, Schocken Books, 1963. 193 p.

The true voice of feeling; studies in English romantic poetry. London, Faber & Faber, 1953. 382 p.

—. New York, Pantheon Books, 1953. 382 p.
Appendix (p. 321-364): Concerning the relation of the plastic arts to nature, 1807 by Friedrich Wilhelm Joseph von Schelling; trans. by Michael Bullock, Bibliography: p. 365-366.

Vocal avowals. Worte sagen aus. St. Gallen, Tschudy-Verlag, 1962. unpaged.
Poems. German and English facing pages. Translated by Eva Van Hoboken.

Wordsworth. London, J. Cape, 1930. 271 p.
(The Clark lectures, 1929-1930)
Signed by the author.

—. New York, J. Cape and H. Smith, 1931. 271 p.
(The Clark lectures, 1929-30)

—. [New ed.]. London, Faber & Faber, 1949. 194 p.
Bibliography: p. 189-190.

—. [New ed.]. London, Faber & Faber, 1958. 194 p.
Includes bibliography. "New ed. . . . 149; reprinted."

A world within a war, poems. London, Faber & Faber, 1944. 50 p.
Signed by the author.

—. New York, Harcourt, Brace, 1945. 44 p.
"First American edition."

Zum 85. Geburtstag von Professor Dr. Carl Gustav Jung, 26. Juli 1960. Zürich, Rascher, 1960. 29 p.

SECTION TWO

Books edited by Sir Herbert Read

The anthology of English prose, selected and ordered by Herbert Read and Bonamy Dobrée. New York, Viking, 1931. 665 p.
Printed in Great Britain.

The collected works of C. G. Jung. Editors: H. Read, M. Fordham, Gerhard Adler. London, Routledge and Kegan Paul, 1953-.

SIR HERBERT READ AT STONEGRAVE, JULY 1966
Photo: Felicitas Vogler

" all that was left of them " -
Second Battle of the Somme - March 21-28 : 1918.

Back Row: Simpson - Stockell - The Padre - Davison -
Howard - Bingham - Hall.

Middle Row: Pickard (Q.M.) - Lunt (C.O.) - Read (Adjt) - White (M.O.)

Bottom Row: Roxby - "Nannie" - Hibbert.

April 1 - 1918.

SEE LOT 16

JACOB KRAMER

I hope you will forgive me if I make this an occasion
for some reminiscences, and for a personal tribute to our guest
of honour. Jacob Kramer occupies a very special place in my
life. He was the first artist I ever knew, and I have no doubt
that my conception of what an artist is and should be was
influenced by my early acquaintance with Jacob. We must
have first met in the year 1912, perhaps 1913, when I was a
student at the University here. Sir Michael Sadler, one of Jacob's
first patrons, was Vice-Chancellor, but I think the occasion of our
meeting must have been some event at the Arts Club, that lively
institution in Woodhouse Lane founded by A. R. Orage & Holbrook Jackson.
Or it may be that Frank Rutter, the director of the Art Gallery at that
time, brought us together. In any case, we soon became intimate friends,
and it must have been at this period that Jacob drew the portrait
of me which is included in the Exhibition. But we were soon to
be parted by the war, but to that circumstance I owe some
letters that Jacob wrote to me, ~~letters which I have always preserved~~
~~because~~ some of which ~~have survived~~. I have kept all
these years, for they ~~then, and still do~~ express, with great feeling & eloquence, the ideals
of a young artist at the outset of his career.

You must try to recover the creative enthusiasm of those
years immediately preceding the First World War. Cubism had
just effected a complete break with the artistic traditions of
the past. In Paris & in Munich great artists — Picasso,
Braque, Leger, Kandinsky — were arousing our enthusiasm

SEE LOT 47

I

Whether by contrast with the following tumult, or from some
quality quite their own, the days of the first three
weeks of March 1918 have left with me a sense
of wonderful peace and of the freshness of earth
hard to match in a ~~short~~ young life. They were days
of bright ~~sunshine~~ light, of sunlight unfettered even
by phage; and the ~~ruined~~ razed villages we mostly lived in
were shadowless. It was a wonder to us that the
month should be so warm & we began to despise
the dreary bleakness that ~~we could not help but~~ inevitably we associated with
~~associating called to mind when our thoughts were
of~~ our own land. At ETREILLERS, where we must
have been in reserve about the second week of the month,
the French who had recently occupied the sector,
had constructed from the wreckage a ~~jolly~~ comfortable mess, in
appearance like a Swiss cottage. ~~Outside was
an ingenious well~~, worked with an elevated tank. Every day it was
glorious enough to sit outside, a book on one's
lap, ~~hard to concentrate~~ open but ~~later~~ neglected; for how
~~could them~~ could not a lazy man help following the
~~revolution apparitions~~ of an old draught horse, ~~pulling round~~
the as, belaboured by a red-faced ~~suburban~~ groom, it
tugged round the ~~beam~~ shaft that worked the ~~ingenious
strange mechanism~~ of the village well? ~~And how could
we loose to help playing~~ with Nancy the derelict goat, ~~se~~
~~if energy must be expended, the joy of leisure~~
~~responsive to my hands from~~ which roped about the yard.
~~And~~ The line itself ~~when we were in it~~ was
almost as idyllic. We were doing then, I think,
eight-day tours, and the last time we were in

—. —. [2nd ed.]. New York, Pantheon Books, 1966.
(Bollingen series, 20)

Encyclopaedia of the arts. Consulting editor: Herbert Read. New
York, Meredith, 1966. 966 p.
London edition has title: *The Thames and Hudson encyclopaedia
of the arts.*

English master painters. Edited by Herbert Read. London, Kegan
Paul, 1940.

The English vision; an anthology. Edited by Herbert Read. London,
Eyre and Spottiswoode, 1933. 364 p.
"My aim has been to present the English ideal in its various aspects
as expressed by representative Englishmen ... I have chosen little
poetry."

—. London, G. Routledge, 1939. 364 p.
First published in 1933.

Form in Gothic. Authorized translation by Bernard Rackham of
"Formprobleme der Gotik" by Wilhelm Worringer. Edited with an
introduction by Herbert Read. London, G. P. Putnam's, 1927. 181 p.

—. —. —. London, A. Tiranti, 1957. 181 p.

—. Authorized translation edited with an introduction by Sir Herbert
Read. Containing the original illustrations. New York, Schocken,
1964. 181 p.

—. —. —. [Rev. ed.]. New York, Schocken, 1964. 180 p.

Gaugin (1848-1903). With an introduction and notes by Herbert
Read. London, Faber & Faber, 1949. 24 p.

—. —. New York, Pitman, 1951. 24 p.

—. —. London, Faber & Faber, 1949-58. 2 vols.
Vol. 2: Introduction and notes by Pierre Courthion.

Klee (1879-1940). With an introduction and notes by Herbert Read.
London, Faber & Faber, 1948. 2 vols.
Vol. 2 — Introduction and notes by Andrew Forge.

—. —. New York, Pitman, 1949. 24 p.
The Pitman gallery.

The knapsack; a pocket-book of prose and verse. Selected by Herbert
Read. London, G. Routledge, 1939. 622 p.

*The London book of English prose, selected and ordered by Herbert
Read and Bonamy Dobrée.* London, Eyre and Spottiswoode, 1931.
665 p.

—. [2nd ed.]. London, Eyre and Spottiswoode, 1949. 572 p.

—. —. New York, Macmillan, 1949. 572 p.

—. —. London, Eyre and Spottiswoode, 1951. 572 p.

209

—. London, Eyre and Spottiswoode, 1963. 522 p.

The London book of English verse, selected by Herbert Read and Bonamy Dobrée. London, Eyre & Spottiswoode, 1949. 874 p.
"Notes" (bibliographical) : p. 838-855.

—. [2nd rev. ed.]. New York, Macmillan, 1952. 891 p.

—. —. London, Eyre & Spottiswoode, 1956. 874 p.

—. —. London, Eyre & Spottiswoode, 1965. 874 p.
Bibliographical references included in "Notes" p. 840-857.

Orage, Alfred Richard. Selected essays and critical writings. Edited by Herbert Read & Denis Saurat. London, Stanley Nott, 1935. 216 p.

The practice of design, by Alastair Morton and others. With an introduction and edited by Herbert Read. London, L. Humphries, 1946. 227 p.

A sentimental journey by Laurence Sterne. Edited, with an introduction by H. Read. London, Scholartiss Press, 1929. 230 p.

Speculations. Essays on humanism and the philosophy of art by T. E. Hulme. Edited by Herbert Read. London, International Library of psychology, philosophy, and scientific method, 1924 [1923]. 271 p.

—. —. —. [2nd ed.]. London, Kegan Paul, 1936. 271 p.

—. —. Edited by Herbert Read, with a frontispiece and foreword by Jacob Epstein. London, Routledge and Paul; New York, Humanities Press, 1965. 271 p.

The styles of European art, introduced and edited by Herbert Read. London, Thames and Hudson, 1965. 468 p.

Surrealism; edited with an introduction by Herbert Read; contributions by André Breton, Hugh Sykes Davies, Paul Eluard, Georges Hugnet. London, Faber & Faber, 1936. 251 p.

The Thames and Hudson encyclopaedia of the arts, consulting editor Herbert Read. London, Thames and Hudson, 1966. 976 p.
American ed. (New York, Meredith) has title: *Encyclopaedia of the arts*.

This way, delight; a book of poetry for the young. Selected by Herbert Read. Illustrated by Juliet Kepes. New York, Pantheon, 1956. 155 p.

—. —. Illustrated by C. Stewart. London, Faber, 1957. 192 p.

—. —. Illustrated by Juliet Kepes. New York, Pantheon, 1961. 155 p.

Unit 1, the modern movement in English architecture, painting, and sculpture, edited by Herbert Read. London, Toronto, etc., Cassell, 1934. 124 p.

SECTION THREE

Books contributed to by Sir Herbert Read

Art in Britain, 1930-40, centered around Axis, Circle and Unit One. London, New York, Marlborough Fine Art, Ltd., 1965. 92 p.
"Catalogue of an exhibition, March-April 1965, dedicated to Herbert Read as a belated tribute to his 70th birthday."

Atelier 17. Contributions by Herbert Read [and others]. New York, Wittenborn, Schultz, 1949. 31 p.
Fourteenth exhibition of prints by members of the Atelier 17 group, March 14 to April 1, 1949, Laurel Gallery, New York.

Australia: aboriginal paintings, Arnhem Land. Introduction by Sir Herbert Read. Greenwich, Conn., New York Graphic Society, 1954. 14 p.
(UNESCO world art series, 3)

Ben Nicholson — Paintings, reliefs, drawings. With an introduction by Herbert Read. London, Lund, Humphries, 1948. 32 p.

Ben Nicholson. With an introduction by Herbert Read. London, Lund, Humphries, 1955. 2 vols.
Vol. 1, 2nd ed.; vol. 2, 1st ed.
Includes bibliographies.
Contents: vol. 1. Paintings, reliefs, drawings. vol. 2. Work since 1947. 1947.

Child art; the beginnings of self-affirmation by Sir Herbert Read [and others]. Edited by Hilda Present Lewis. Berkeley, California, Diablo Press, 1966. 127 p.
"Grew out of a conference held on the Berkeley campus of the University of California on May 7, 8, 9, 1965." Includes bibliographical references.

The creative arts in American education: the interrelation of the arts in secondary education by Thomas Munro; the third realm of education by Herbert Read. Cambridge, Harvard University Press, 1960. 65 p.
The Inglis lecture and the Burton lecture, 1960.

Dutch tiles. The Van den Bergh gift. A guide by B. Rackham with the help of Mr. Herbert Read. London, South Kensington Museum, 1923. 32 p.

English pottery: its development from early times to the end of the eighteenth century by Bernard Rackham and Herbert Edward Read. With an appendix on the Wrotham potters by Dr. J. W. L. Glaisher. London, Ernest Benn, 1924. 142 p.
One of an edition of 75 copies.

Essays and studies by members of the English Association. Vol. 21. Collected by Herbert Read. Oxford, Clarendon Press, 1936. 168 p.

5 *on revolutionary art.* Essays by Herbert Read, F. D. Klingender, Eric Gill, A. L. Loyd, Alick West. Edited by Betty Rea. London, Wishart, 1935. 87 p.

Flicker. Three essays on the cinema by Herbert Read, Toni del Renzio and R. S. O. Poole. Croydon, Eng., R. S. O. Poole, 1944.

Four lectures on design. The future of industrial design. London, Hutchinson, 1943. 32 p.
(Design and Industries Association)

History of modern painting . . . text by Maurice Raynal [and others]. Translated by Stuart Gilbert (Douglas Cooper). 2nd ed. With an introduction by Herbert Read. Geneva, Albert Skira, 1949. 3 vols.

Hepworth. Exhibition, October-November 1959. Introduction by Sir Herbert Read. New York, Galerie Chalette, 1959. 24 p.

Henri Matisse. Texts by Jean Leymarie, Herbert Read, William S. Liebermann. Berkeley, University of California Press, 1966. 207 p.

Henry Moore. With an introduction by Herbert Read. London, P. Lund, Humphries, 1957. 2 vols.

—. —. [2nd ed. rev.]. London, P. Lund, Humphries, 19—.
Contents: v. 2. Sculpture and drawings 1949-1954.

Henry Moore: Mother and child. Introduction by Herbert Read. New York, New American Library, by arrangement with UNESCO, 1966. 24 p.

—. —. London, Collins in association with UNESCO, 1967. 30 p.

Henry Moore: Sculpture and drawings. With an introduction by Herbert Read. London, Lund, Humphries, Zwemmer, 1944.

—. —. [3rd rev. and much enl. ed.]. London, Lund, Humphries, 1949. 44 p.

—. Edited by Alan Bowness. With an introduction by Herbert Read. [1st ed.]. New York, G. Wittenborn, 1965-.
Contents: v. 3′ Sculpture, 1955-64, edited by Alan Bowness.

Kandinsky (1866-1944). With an introduction and notes by Herbert Read. London, Faber & Faber, 1959. 24 p.

—. —. New York, G. Wittenborn, 1959. 24 p.

Moments of vision, a cura di Herbert Read, luglio-novembre, 1959. Roma, Rome-New York Art Foundation, 1959. Unpaged.
English, Italian, or French.

New trends in British art; Nuove tendenze dell'arte inglese. Presentate do Sir Herbert Read e Lawrence Alloway. Roma, Rome-New York Art Foundation, 1958? Unpaged.
English and Italian.

Outline, an autobiography, and other writings by Paul Nash. With a preface by Herbert Read. London, Faber & Faber, 1949. 271 p.

Paintings by Felix Kelly. Introduction by Herbert Read. London, Falcon Press, 1946. 10 p.

Paul Nash. Ten coloured plates and a critical appreciation by Herbert Read. London, Soho Gallery, 1937.
(Contemporary British painters, no. 1)

Paul Nash. With an introduction by H. E. Read. Harmondsworth, Penguin, 1944. 16 p.
(Penguin modern painters)

Paul Nash. Paintings, drawings and illustrations. Edited by Margot Eates. With essays by Herbert Read [and others]. London, Lund, Humphries, 1948.

The Peggy Guggenheim collection at the Tate Gallery 31 December 1964 to 7 March 1965. [2nd ed.]. Preface by Herbert Read. London, Arts Council of Great Britain, 1965. 99 p.

Pioneering in art collecting. By Sir Herbert Read, James Johnson Sweeney [and others]. Edited by David Darryl Galloway. Buffalo, New York, Albright-Knox Art Gallery, 1962. 34 p.
Five lectures delivered at a symposium in art collecting convened by the Albright-Knox Art Gallery in January 1962, under the auspices of the Buffalo-Fine Arts Academy.

The quest and the quarry, a cura di Herbert Read. Exhibition magg. - sett., 1961. Roma, Rome-New York Art Foundation, 1961. unpaged. English, Italian or French.

Radio. By Rudolf Arnheim. Translated by Margaret Ludwig and Herbert Read. London, Faber & Faber, 1936. 296 p.

Recent paintings by Reybeyrolle. Introduction by Herbert Read. London, Marlborough Fine Art Ltd., 1961. 16 p.

Truth is more sacred; a critical exchange on modern literature: James Joyce, D. H. Lawrence, Henry James, Robert Graves, T. S. Eliot and Ezra Pound. By Edward Dahlberg and Herbert Read. New York, Horizon Press, 1961. 222 p.

—. —. London, Routledge and K. Paul, 1961. 222 p.

SECTION FOUR

Unique Materials in the Sir Herbert Read Collection in the McPherson Library of the University of Victoria

1 Nihilism and renewal in the art of our time. Eranos Lecture —
    August 1959.
    Holograph manuscript with corrections. Section I titled "The
        scream of Juno's Peacock"; Section II titled "The Principle
        of Speculative Volition". 51 l.
    Typescript with corrections. 34 l.

2 The third realm of education.
    Holograph manuscript with corrections. 39 l.
    Typescript copy, "uncorrected". 27 l.
    2nd typescript copy, "uncorrected". 27 l.
    Typescript with holograph correction. 32 l.

3 The origins of form in art. Eranos Lecture — August 1960.
    Holograph manuscript with corrections. 31 l.
    Typescript with corrections. 41 l.

4 British art since 1945.
    Holograph manuscript. 48 l.
    Typescript with corrections. 33 l.

5 The poet and his muse. Eranos Lecture — 1962.
    Holograph with corrections; looseleaf sheets in binder. 47 l.
    Typescript with corrections. 56 l.

6 Beauty and the beast. Eranos Lecture — August 1961.
    Holograph manuscript with corrections. 51 l.
    Two programmes of the Eranos conference, 1961, enclosing
        seven pages of holograph notes and six reprints of articles by
        various authors dealing with psycho-analysis.

7 Power politics and human values. ("A Conference at Jordans,
        May 20-21, 1944")
    Typescript with corrections. 25 l.
    Typescript copy with corrections. 24 l.
    Art and leisure.
    Typescript copy with corrections. 13 l.
    2nd typescript copy with corrections. 13 l.
    Existentialism, Marxism and anarchism.
    Typescript copy with corrections. 18 l.
    The ethics of power.
    Typescript with corrections. 9 l.
    Typescript copy with corrections. 13 l.
    Phases of English poetry.
    "Revised text for page 81". Typescript copy. 2 l.

Ode on melancholy by John Keats.
Typescript. 1 l.

Emblem by Frances Quarles.
Typescript. 2 l.

Song by Thomas Carew.
Typescript with holograph notes. 1 l.

Wordsworth's philosophy.
Typescript copy. 20 l.

Neither liberalism nor communism — a third way.
Typescript with corrections. 15 l.

Presuppositions.
Typescript copy. 1 l.

A one-man manifesto.
Typescript with corrections. 6 l.

A primer of dialectics.
Typescript copy. 6 l.

At the moment of writing.
Typescript copy. 6 l.

First aid for authors.
Typescript with corrections. 6 l.

Politics and the writer.
Typescript copy with corrections. 5 l.

The way of the world.
Typescript copy. 12 l.

Conversations in Germany.
Typescript copy. 10 l.

William Godwin.
Typescript copy. 5 l.

Education for peace.
Typescript copy with corrections. 15 l.

Kropotkin.
Typescript copy. 15 l.

To the Editor of the *New Statesman*.
"Before Dawn," dated 17.5.41. Typescript copy. 3 l.

Review of *The Peckham experiment: a study in the living structure of Society*, by Innes H. Pearse and Lucy H. Crocker.
Typescript copy with corrections. 4 l.

Freedom Press defence: speech for May 13, 1945.
Typescript copy with corrections. 7 l.

On justice.
Typescript copy. 7 l.
2nd typescript copy. 7 l.

Unto the new Caesar . . . a plea for a policy of meekness.
Typescript copy. 8 l.

215

Broadcast Review [of] *Science, Liberty and Peace* by Aldous Huxley and *War, Sadism and Pacifism* by Edward Glover.
Typescript copy. 8 l.

Anarchism.
Typescript copy. 4 l.

Ebeneezer Howard.
Typescript copy. 2 l.

The modern scene. On the threshhold of a new world. Renaissance or decadence.
Typescript copy. 10 l.

War and crisis.
Typescript copy. 7 l.

The method of revolution.
Typescript copy. 3 l.

Review of *The open fields* by C. S. & C. S. Orwin.
Typescript copy. 5 l.

8   Moon's farm and poems mostly elegiac.
Page proof with pencilled corrections. 40 l.

9   The true voice of feeling.
Typescript with corrections. 205 l.

Wordsworth's philosophical faith.
"Essay II" pencilled above title. Printed pages numbered 564 to 585 with holograph corrections. 12 l.

Five letters from Faber and Faber, publishers of *The true voice of feeling*.
September 8, 1952 - October 1, 1952.

10 Spiral Notebook 1. Holograph (46 l.) containing:
Rome-New York Art Foundation, 4 p.
Review of *Sources of Modern Art*. 6 p.
The secret of success in art. 24 p.
Does pornography matter. 35 p.
Review of *Paul Klee: the thinking eye*. 5 p.

Spiral Notebook 2. Holograph (39 l.) containing:
Vedova. 3 p.
The critic's dilemma. 4 p.
An appeal to fellow members of the Committee of 100. 7 p.
A note on policy submitted to the meeting of the Committee of 100 to be held on December 17, 1961. 5 p.
Review of *Nature of film*. 5 p.
Symposium on collecting. "Buffalo: January 20, 1962". 13 p.
Review of *The biology of art*. 6 p.
Review of *A sea ringed with visions*. 4 p.
Review of *Letters to T. E. Lawrence*. 4 p.
Review of *British art since 1900*. 8 p.
Review of *The ordeal of consciousness in Henry James*. 5 p.

216

Spiral Notebook 3. Holograph (49 l.) containing:
"President Kennedy, in his State of the Union address, uttered
 what was obviously a genuine note of alarm." 5 p.
John Hoskin. 3 p.
Review of *Essays and Introductions* by W. B. Yeats. 5 p.
Rebeyrolle. 4 p.
We believe. 1 p.
Cirlot. 3 p.
Review of *Three essays on the painting of our time* by Adrian
 Stokes. 4 p.
Review of *The poetry of Corbusier.* 4 p.
Review of *Muntu. An outline of neo-African culture.* 3 p.
Coleridge. 6 p.
Walter Daniel. Talking of books. 6 p.
Unbounded and immortal things. Talking of books. 6 p.
"Claude Fatherly, 'the Major who gave the "go ahead" to de-
 stroy Hiroshima' . . . " 2 p.
Review of *Benedetto Croce* by Gian N. G. Orsini. 5 p.
Henry Moore. Berlin — 1961. 10 p.
International Council of Societies of Industrial Designers.
 Venice: September 14, 1961. 16 p.
Spiral Notebook 4. Holograph (50 l.) containing:
Art in an Australian University. 11 p.
Review of *Henry James: Selected literary criticism,* edited by
 Morris Shapiro. 6 p.
Richard Aldington. 16 p.
From Futurism to Surrealism — Chap. IV of the *Concise His-
 tory of Modern Sculpture.* 29 p.
Spiral Notebook 5. Holograph (50 l.) containing:
Vincent Van Gogh. 23 p.
Lynn Chadwick — 1961. 7 p.
Spiral Notebook 6. Holograph (50 l.) containing:
Contemporary British art. 14 p.
A note on the plates. 2 p.
Edvard Munch. 14 p.
The Editors, *Encounter.* 4 p.
Foreword (Mrs. Ashton Warner). 5 p.
My first acquaintance with the philosophy of Bertrand Russell.
 13 p.
Review of *Of divers arts* by Naum Gabo. 5 p.
Two masters of modern art, a review of Georges Roualt by
 Pierre Courthion and Joan Miró by Jacques Dupin. 14 p.
Spiral Notebook 7. Holograph (51 l.) containing:
To quote or not to quote. 9 p.
Louis Le Brocquy. 5 p.
The voices of silence. 14 p.
Letter to Peace News. 3 p.

Ben Nicholson. 12 p.
(2nd) Review of *Of divers arts* by Naum Gabo. 4 p.
Review of *Born under Saturn* by Rudolf & Margot Wittkower.
   5 p.
Eileen Agar. 4 p.
Ars Una. 12 p.
Spiral Notebook 8. Holograph (50 l.) containing:
   Tolstoy's theory of art. 29 p.
   IV International Congress of Aesthetics. 12 p.
   Aldous Huxley. 8 p.
   To Huntington, Sage of the Potomac, Prosperity. 3 p.
   Civil disobedience. 4 p.
   A call to civil disobedience. 6 p.
   Books and the child. 9 p.
Spiral Notebook 9. Holograph (50 l. + 3 l. typescript) containing:
   Preface — The resurrection of the word. 21 p.
   Max Raphael. 19 p. + 4 p. corrected typescript.
   Michelangelo. 11 p.
   English poetry. 6 p.
Spiral Notebook 10. Holograph (50 l.) containing:
   The limits of painting. 52 p.
   A short note on *Zen*. 1 p.
   Clarification supplied. 3 p.
   Anarchism in the affluent society. 25 p.
Spiral Notebook 11. Holograph (97 l. + attachment) containing:
   A toy for God. 10 p.
   The moral significance of aesthetic education. 26 p.
   A broadcast review of *Science, Liberty and Peace* by Aldous
      Huxley and *War, Sadism and Pacifism* by Edward Glover.
      7 p.
   Wordsworth's philosophy. 15 p.
   Plato. 3 p.
   Coleridge. 59 p.
   Erni. 2 p.
   The crisis in bookcraft. 12 p.

11   Icon and Idea.
   Holograph. 7 l.
   Typescript with holograph corrections. 14 l.
   Holograph. 2 l.
   Typescript with holograph corrections. 3 l.
   Holograph. 35 l.
   Typescript. 2 l.
   Holograph. 32 l.
   Typescript with holograph corrections. 1 l.
   Holograph. 110 l.
   Typescript. 1 l.

12   The true voice of feeling.
     A cloth-bound notebook containing:
       The cult of sincerity. Studies in English romantic poetry.
         Holograph. 194 p.
       Inserted: Introduction. Typescript with holograph correction.
         3 l.
       Coleridge's dejection. Typescript copy with holograph correction. 5 l.
       "Blêw mímic hóotings to the sílent ówls, ... " Mimeograph. 2 l.
       " ... own time the best poetry, ... " Typescript copy with correction. 3 l.
       Dylan Thomas poem. Typescript. 2 l.
       Introductory remarks. Typescript. 2 l.
       Page from a book with coloured plates by Margaret Duncan and Richard Walker.

   Wordsworth.
     Dismantled copy with holograph corrections in green cloth case. 264 p. Jonathan Cape publisher's list. 47 p.
     Proof copy with holograph correction in dust wrapper illustrated with Wordsworth's death mask. Faber & Faber. 190 p. Index with corrected page numbers from dismantled copy. 5 p.
     Holograph letter from E. M. Hatt, proof reader for Faber & Faber. 1 l.
     Preface to a new edition. Typescript with corrections. 9 l.

13   Notebook 1 with black hard cover (217 l.) containing:
     The place of art in a university. An inaugural lecture given at the University of Edinburgh on October 15, 1931.
     Unbound printed pamphlet enclosed. 15 l.
     In pencil "Appendix D"
     The place of art in the educational system. In pencil: The Aesthetic principles of education and Education through art. Holograph. 341 p.
     Ebenezer Cooke. Holograph. 4 p.
     Enclosed a holograph letter (2 l.) from Gwendolyn M. Fry dated October 11, 1941, and three copies of a drawing showing a personality graph.

   Notebook 2 with blue hard cover (81 l.) containing:
     "Discipline (cont.)" (Education through art). Holograph 71 p.
     Sociology and Architecture. Holograph 24 p. with typed page pasted in titled "Hitler Speech, Nuremberg, 6 Sept. 38."
     Henry Moore. Holograph 14 p. Typed ½ p. Holograph. 1 p.
     Typed 5 p. Holograph 14 p. Enclosed sheet with some typing titled "Eden on Italy" and holograph notes of page references.

To the editor of the *Times*. Holograph. 2 p.

Dear Mr. Keyes. Holograph. 1 p.

Notebook 3 with red hard cover (80 l.) containing:

The problem of perception. Holograph. 120 p.

Enclosed a typescript (5 l.) titled "The perceptive problem in the aesthetic appreciation of single colours" by Edward Bullough.

Possible titles. Holograph. 3 p.

Preface. Holograph. 2 p.

N.E.W. Holograph. 3 p.

Reply to Canon Smyth's letter of September 19. Holograph. 2 p.

Shaw on the use of land. Holograph. 6 p.

Five newspaper clippings enclosed.

14 Education through art.

Proof copy with corrections. Unbound in multicoloured cloth case. 320 p.

82 letters concerned with *Education through art.*

15 Education through art.

Typescript with corrections. 484 l.

Galley proof page. List of plates. Contents.

16 In retreat.

Typescript with corrections. 50 l.

A journal of the retreat from St. Quentin to Amiens in March, 1918.

Holograph. 30 l. plus 9 'Messages and Signals' forms enclosed.

Army Book 136. 34 l.

Holograph. 12 p. plus group photograph enclosed.

Messages and Signals. 22 l.

Holograph.

Stanley Redoubt. Detail of Battalion defences. 1 l.

Holograph. 2 p.

Three War Office Maps.

17 A world within a war. 51 l. loose in black folder.

Typescript with corrections. 29 l.

Printed cut-outs pasted on notebook pages with corrections. 12 l.

18 Henry Moore. A study of his life and work.

Typescript with corrections. 120 l.

Two letters (April 5, 1965; May 21, 1965) signed "Pat" and eight photograph snaps of Henry Moore sculpture.

Holograph in black looseleaf notebook. 149 l. Enclosed a typed 'Preface' (2 l.), and a quote from Henry Moore, typed (1 l.).

19 Intimations of a new humanism. Eranos Lecture — August 1957.

Holograph. 68 l.

20   Adventures of the mind. Art and life.
       Holograph. 26 l.
       Typescript with corrections. 22 l.
       2nd typescript with corrections. 23 l.

21   Old lovers' ghosts. "Unfinished play".
       Holograph. 36 l.

22   The parliament of women. A drama in three acts.
       Holograph in brown notebook. 122 l. Includes pasted in design
         on front cover and five separate sheets of notes and *The death
         of Kropotkin*, holograph. 3 p.
     The parliament of women. A drama in four acts.
       Typescript with corrections in red binder. 86 l.
     The parliament of women. A drama in three acts.
       "first draft-revised". Typescript with corrections in orange bin-
         der. 110 l. Includes a G. Wilson Knight letter (2 l.); Knight's
         criticism of *The parliament of women* (4 l.); Read's reply
         (1 l.).
     The parliament of women. A drama in three acts.
       "final version". Typescript copy in blue folder. 86 l.
     The parliament of women.
       "Copy No. 4 + discarded scenes". Typescript copy. 17 Scenes.

23   The flower of peace.
       Typescript copy with corrections. 54 l.
     Beige clothbound notebook. Holograph (123 l.) containing:
       Penny wise and pound foolish. 33 p.
       Lord Byron at the opera. 37 p.
       The flower of peace II. 38 p.
       The flower of peace I. 24 p.
       Kandinsky. 28 p.
       The ambiguity of modern sculpture. 28 p.
       Notes. 2 p.

24   Spiral notebook 1. Holograph (49 l.) containing:
       American bards and British reviewers. 61 p.
       Kokoschka in London. 7 p.
       The war in the psyche. 13 p.
     Spiral notebook 2. Holograph (39 l.) containing:
       Art and communication. 53 p.
       Typescript copy with corrections enclosed. 19 l.
     Spiral notebook 3. Holograph (37 l.) containing:
       Gauguin. 15 p.
       Rysdale — Past and present. 13 p.
       Review of *The fire and the fountain* by John Press. 6 p.
       Bowra. 5 p.
     Spiral notebook 4. Holograph (50 l.) containing:
       Concise history of modern sculpture. 76 p.

Spiral notebook 5. Holograph (46 l.) containing:
  Modern sculpture illustrated. 69 p.

Spiral notebook 6. Holograph (51 l.) containing:
  Sc. V & VI. 72 p.

Spiral notebook 7. Holograph (52 l.) containing:
  Sculpture: an art transformed. 55 p.
  The paintings of Van Le Witt. 8 p.
  Review of *The beginnings of art* by S. Giedion. 8 p.

Notebook 8 with blue paper wrappers. Holograph (29 l.) containing:
  Gauguin. 2 p.
  Sotto voce: a plea for intimacy. 14 p.
  Wordsworth. 15 p.
  Byron. 4 p.

Notebook 9 with green cloth cover. Holograph (46 l.) containing:
  Introduction to Dahlberg. 12 p.
  Review of *The collected poems of Wilfred Owen.* 5 p.
  Introduction to the Czech/Jugoslavian edition. 12 p.
  Review of *The necessity of art: a Marxist approach* by Ernst Fisher. 16 p.
  Review of Australian aboriginal art edited by Ronald M. Berndt. 11 p.
  Preface Cash's Sterne. 6 p.

25 A history of modern painting.
    Holograph. 209 l.

    A concise history of modern painting.
    Typescript copy with correction. 259 l.
    Galley proof. 49 l.

26 The art of sculpture.
    Holograph. 110 l.
    Typescript with corrections. 207 l.
    Page proof. 131 l.

27 The sense of glory: essays in criticism.
    Page proof corrected and loose in purple cloth case. 134 l.

    Phases of English poetry.
    Hogarth lectures, No. 7. Page proof corrected and loose in orange cloth case. 76 l.
    Page proof (Faber & Faber) corrected. 111 l.

    Notebook 1. Holograph (32 l.) containing:
    Jung. 42 p.

    Notebook 2. Holograph (136 l. plus 1 l. typescript) containing:
    The constructive art of Naum Gabo and Antoine Pevsner. 22 p.
    Paul Nash. 18 p.
    Realism and abstraction in modern art. 33 p.

222

Psycho-analysis and the problem of aesthetic value. 32 p. + 1 p.
typescript.
Art and the evolution of man. 49 p.
Introduction: a defence of political idealism. 45 p.

28 The contrary experience.
A diary of the First World War.
Holograph. 20 l.
Autobiographies.
Typescript with corrections. 109 l.
Introduction.
Typescript with corrections. 8 l.

The innocent eye. Book Three. A dearth of wild flowers.
Holograph. 95 l.

The innocent eye. (pages 13-61 from *Annals of Innocence and
experience*)
Typescript with corrections. 144 l.

Riveaulx Abbey.
Two reproductions of the paintings of the Abbey by J. M. W.
Turner.
A letter to Sir Herbert Read dated January 27, 1961 from the
librarian and curator of the County Borough of Bury.
Typescript. 1 l.
A letter to P. M. R. Pouncey dated March 10, 1961 from Her-
bert Read.
Typescript copy. 1 l.

Annals of innocence and experience.
Dismantled copy (Faber & Faber, 1946) with corrections, 115 l.

29 The tenth muse: essays in criticism.
Typescript with corrections. 329 l.
(Includes typescript copy, pasted-in clippings, and printed
pages from other publications).
Page proof with corrections. 18 l.
Correspondence. 22 l.

Frank Lloyd Wright.
Typescript copy. 5 l.

Against the betrayal of architecture.
Review of *The future of architecture* by Frank Lloyd Wright.
Typescript copy. 6 l.
Two clippings from *New Republic*.

Review of *Notes toward the definition of culture* by T. S. Eliot.
European Service mimeograph. 4 l.

Review of *The letters of W. B. Yeats* edited by Allen Wade and
The identity of Yeats by Richard Ellmann.
Typescript copy. 3 l.

Graham Sutherland.
Typescript copy. 2 l.
Jung.
Typescript copy. 3 l.
An eightieth birthday.
Typescript copy. 4 l.
The art of art criticism.
Typescript copy. 11 l.
Tradition and revolt in modern English poetry.
Typescript copy. 42 l.
The cult of sincerity.
Typescript. 39 l.
Michelangelo and Bernini.
Typescript copy with corrections. 13 l.
The romantic revolution.
Typescript copy with corrections. 11 l.
Barbara Hepworth.
Typescript copy. 2 l.
Review of *The poetry of Ezra Pound* by Hugh Kenner.
Typescript copy with corrections. 4 l.
Ezra Pound as critic. A review of *Make it new* by Ezra Pound.
Typescript copy. 7 l.
Ezra Pound.
Typescript copy with corrections. 13 l.
Review of *Guide to Kulchur* by Ezra Pound.
Typescript copy. 3 l.
Reviews of *Seventy Cantos* by Ezra Pound.
Clippings. 4 l.
C. G. Jung.
Page proof from *Hudson Review*. 7 l.

30   Recent trends in English art.
Typescript with corrections. 37 l.

The present situation of art in Europe.
Typescript with corrections. 37 l.

Henry Moore and the renaissance of sculpture in England.
Typescript with corrections. 22 l.
Typescript with corrections. 14 l.

The limits of painting.
Typescript with corrections. Xerox copy. 31 l.

31   Poetry and philosophy — reading from Shelley.
Typescript copy with corrections. 4 l.

Poetry and philosophy: Shelley. BBC Third Programme Lecture.
Typescript with corrections. 9 l.

Talk for Canadian Broadcasting Corporation.
    Typescript copy with corrections. 9 l.
    Typescript copy with corrections. 5 l.

Lord Byron at the opera. BBC Third Programme: Imaginary
    Conversation series.
    Typescript copy with corrections. 29 l.

Aristotle's mother: an argument in Athens. BBC Third
    Programme: Imaginary Conversation series.
    Typescript copy. 16 l.

Personal anthology — chosen and introduced by Herbert Read.
    BBC Third Programme.
    Typescript copy. 20 l.

T. S. Eliot und die moderne Bewegung in der englischen Dich-
    tung.
    Typescript with corrections. 5 l.
    Typescript copy with corrections. 5 l.

Modern art and public taste. Speakers: Herbert Read, Eric New-
    ton. Chairman: Anne Symonds.
    Typescript copy with deletion. 8 l.

Changing conceptions of art. Music, poetry, and the visual arts of
    the 20th century, lecture No. 1.
    Typescript with corrections. 5 l.

It's good English. A lecture for weekly programme 'It's good
    English'.
    Typescript with corrections. 5 l.
    Typescript copy. 5 l.

Review of *Notes towards the definition of culture* by T. S. Eliot.
    Typescript copy with corrections. 7 l.

Writers in exile. A lecture for 'For your leisure'.
    Typescript copy. 3 l.

The ethics of power. A lecture for the BBC series 'Power — an
    aspect of social organisation'.
    Typescript copy with corrections. 10 l.

Book Talk: *Science, Liberty and Peace* by Aldous Huxley and
    War, Sadism and Pacifism by Edward Glover. For the BBC's
    series 'Book Talk'.
    Typescript copy with corrections. 7 l.

For the spirit. A discussion for the BBC series 'What is art for?'
    between Herbert Read and Eric Newton.
    Typescript with corrections. 7 l.

The dialogues of Plato. BBC Third Programme. The sixth of the
    series 'The dialogues of Plato'. Translated by A. E. Taylor.
    Arranged, with a prefatory note by Herbert Read.
    Typescript copy with corrections. 35 l.

New Judgment on Wordsworth. Telediphoned copy from BBC discussion between Herbert Read, Fuller and Bronowski.
Typescript copy with corrections. 15 l.

Poetry and philosophy — readings in Shelley. BBC Third Programme lecture. Chosen and introduced by Herbert Read.
Typescript copy with corrections. 14 l.

Moon's farm. BBC Third Programme, series 'The Inward Eye'.
Typescript copy. 26 l. with small printed review attached.

Wordsworth: an introductory talk.
Typescript copy with corrections. 14 l.

Wordsworth's philosophical faith. A lecture for 'The Wednesday Book Programme'.
Typescript copy with corrections. 19 l.

Wordsworth's philosophy.
Typescript copy with corrections. 12 l.

A new judgment of Wordsworth. A discussion between Read, Fuller and Bronowski. Transcribed from a telediphone recording.
Typescript copy with corrections. 17 l.

Longer poems. BBC Third Programme, 'Herbert Read Poetry Programme'.
Typescript copy with corrections. 32 l.
Typescript copy with deletion. 32 l.

32 The ambiguity of modern sculpture.
Typescript with corrections. 23 l.
Typescript with corrections and holograph. 22 l.
  (typescript with corrections 13 l., holograph 9 l.)
Typescript copy with corrections. 11 l.
Typescript copy with correction, typescript with corrections and holograph. 23 l. (typescript copy with corrections 20 l., typescript with corrections 1 l., holograph 2 l.)
Typescript copy 9 l. (2 copies).

Zur Theorie des Künstlerischen.
Typescript copy with corrections. 14 l.

Sculpture — an art transformed.
Typescript copy with corrections. 32 l.
List of slides to accompany above. Typescript. 1 l.

Die Plastik, eine Kunst in der Umwandlung. German translation of *Sculpture — an art transformed*.
Typescript copy. 20 l.

Lists of slides.
Typescript copy with corrections. 1 l.
Typescript. 1 l.
Holograph with corrections. 1 l.
Holograph. 1 l.

Sergel. From book *A survey of Swedish art.*
  Xerox copy of chapter five. Positive. 3 l.
  Xerox copy of chapter five. Negative. 3 l.

Johan Tobias Sergel. From a dictionary of Swedish artists, in French.
  Xerox copy of Sergel entry. Positive. 2 l.
  Xerox copy of Sergel entry. Negative. 2 l.

33 To hell with culture and other essays of art and society.
  As assembled for printing. Typescript with corrections, type-
    script copy with corrections, printed, from an earlier version,
    with corrections. 206 l.

34 A letter to a young artist.
  Typescript copy with corrections. 50 l.
  Typescript with corrections inter-paged with typescript copy.
    44 l. each. Also 4 l. holograph and a list of paintings, type-
    script copy. 2 l.

Existentialism, Marxism and anarchism.
  Typescript with corrections. 18 l.

Chains of freedom.
  Typescript with corrections, print with corrections, typescript
    copy with corrections. 45 l.

Poetry and love.
  Typescript with corrections. 23 l.

The inspired tinker. BBC Third Programme.
  Typescript copy with corrections. 8 l.

De Stijl.
  Typescript copy with corrections. 5 l.

Art and the evolution of man.
  Typescript copy with corrections. 38 l.

Review of *The problem of Knowledge* by A. J. Ayer.
  Typescript copy with corrections. 9 l.

Gauguin: the return to symbolism.
  Typescript copy with corrections. 1 l.
  Typescript with corrections. 9 l.

Shelley's philosophy.
  Typescript copy with corrections. 8 l.

Wordsworth's philosophy.
  Typescript copy with corrections. 19 l.

The fundamental conflict in contemporary art.
  Typescript copy with corrections. 22 l.

35 Reviews of *The life of John Middleton Murry* by F. A. Lea, *To
  keep faith* by Mary Middleton Murry and *Katherine Mansfield
  and other literary studies* by J. Middleton Murry, for *The London Magazine.*
  Proof sheets with corrections. 2 l.

227

Preface. (Karel Appel)
  Typescript copy with corrections. 3 l.
Karel Appel.
  Typescript copy. 2 l.
  2nd Typescript copy. 2 l.
The architect as universal man.
  Typescript copy with corrections. 13 l.
  2nd typescript copy with corrections. 13 l.
Review of *The poem itself* edited by Stanley Burnshaw.
  Typescript copy with corrections. 6 l.
British art since 1945.
  Typescript copy. 32 l.
A call to civil disobedience.
  Typescript copy with corrections. 3 l.
  2nd Typescript copy with corrections. 3 l.
The informal image in modern art. The IV International Congress of Aesthetics.
  Typescript with corrections. 11 l.
Review of *Yulengor: nomads of Arnhem land* by William S. Chaseling.
  Typescript copy with corrections. 3 l.
  2nd Typescript copy with corrections. 3 l.
Art and design. NUT conference. (notes)
  Typescript with corrections and one small paper clipping. 3 l.
Tourism unlimited.
  Typescript copy with corrections. 7 l.
Review of *Art* by Aldous Huxley.
  Typescript copy with corrections. 4 l.
Review of *Seeing and believing* by Frank Avray Wilson.
  Typescript copy. 1 l.
Middelheim. Speech to the people of Antwerp, 5th Biennial at Middelheim.
  Typescript copy with corrections. 6 l.
  Typescript copy with corrections, holograph. 6 l.
Introduction [to the work of John Warren Davis].
  Typescript copy with corrections. 2 l.
Review of *Safe conduct* by Boris Pasternak, translated by Alec Brown.
  Typescript copy with corrections. 3 l.
The future for poets.
  Typescript copy with corrections. 3 l.
Review of *The use of imagination: educational thought and the literary mind* by William Walsh.
  Typescript copy with corrections. 4 l.

228

Review of *Walter Bagehot* by Norman St. John-Stevas.
  Typescript copy with corrections. 4 l.

Review of *Havelock Ellis* by Arthur Calder-Marshall and *An
  artist on life: the life and work of Havelock Ellis* by John
  Stewart Collis.
  Typescript copy. 4 l.
  As printed in *The Listener*, January 29, 1959. 1 l.

Introduction [to Baker's *Stained Glass*]
  Typescript copy with corrections. 9 l.

Review of *Picasso: his life and work* by Roland Penrose.
  Typescript copy with corrections. 3 l.

[Untitled essay on INSEA]
  Typescript copy with corrections. 4 l.

Review of *The letters of John Keats*, edited by Hyder Edward
  Rollins.
  Typescript copy with corrections. 3 l.

Poet of felicity. Review of *Centuries, Poems and Thanksgiving* by
  Thomas Traherne, edited by H. M. Margoliouth.
  Typescript copy with corrections. 4 l.

Review of *The Court and the Castle* by Rebecca West.
  Typescript copy with corrections. 3 l.
  Holograph. 2 l.

Fautrier.
  Typescript copy with corrections. 3 l.

Review of *Art and reality* by Joyce Cary.
  Typescript copy with corrections. 3 l.

What's wrong with industrial design?
  Typescript copy with corrections. 9 l.

Reviews of *Children's art* by Miriam Lindstrom, *Art of the young
  child* by Jane Cooper Bland, *Creative and mental growth* by
  Viktor Lowenfeld and *Art and visual perception: a psychology
  of the creative eye* by Rudolf Arnheim.
  Typescript copy. 3 l.

Foreword [*To the Gothic Flame* by Dr. Varma]
  Typescript copy 2 l.

On breaking through.
  Typescript copy. 1 l.

Review of *A Henry Adams Reader* edited by Elizabeth Stevenson.
  Typescript copy with corrections. 3 l.

Review of *The works of Henry Vaughan* edited by L. C. Martin.
  Typescript copy with corrections. 4 l.

Review of *The diaries of John Ruskin*, Volume II, 1848-1873, selected and edited by Joan Evans and John Howard Whitehouse.
  Typescript copy with corrections. 3 l.

229

The British Pavilion, 1958.
Typescript copy with corrections. 7 l.

Review of *Politics and the poet* by F. M. Todd and *Wordsworth's Cambridge Education* by Ben Ross Schneider, Jr.
Typescript copy. 2 l.

My favourite picture.
Typescript copy. 2 l.

Review of *Art in crisis: the lost centre* by Hans Sedlmayr.
Typescript copy with corrections. 6 l.

Castello Sforzesco.
Typescript copy with corrections. 8 l.

Review of *Records of the American-Australian Scientific Expedition to Arnhem land: art, myth and symbolism* by Charles P. Mountford.
Typescript with corrections. 5 l.

Review of *The poetry of living Japan* by Takamichi Ninomiya and D. J. Enright.
Typescript copy with corrections. 2 l.

Vie quotidienne et valeur des Formes-Resumé.
Typescript copy. 3 l.

Anti-Malraux.
Typescript copy with corrections. 6 l.

Review of *A portrait of the artist as a martyr: letters of James Joyce,* edited by Stuart Gilbert.
Typescript copy with corrections. 5 l.

Lone Wolf.
Typescript copy with corrections. 3 l.

Art, industry and national decay.
Typescript copy with corrections. 9 l.
2nd Typescript copy with corrections. 10 l.

Walter de la Mare.
Proof copy. 1 l.
Typescript copy. 2 l.

Victor Pasmore Mural — Newcastle-upon-Tyne.
Typescript copy with corrections. 5 l.
Typescript with corrections. 5 l.

Review of *The author and the public: problems of communication.*
Report of Twenty-eight International P.E.N. Congress.
Typescript copy. 2 l.

Introduction, Sao Paolo 1957.
Typescript copy with corrections. 4 l.

Talk for BBC General Overseas Service.
Typescript with corrections. 3 l.

Review of *Towards science in aesthetics* and *Art Education: its*

230

philosophy and psychology, both by Thomas Munro.
Typescript copy. 1 l.

Review of *Love, freedom and society,* by J. Middleton Murry.
Typescript copy with corrections. 4 l.

Review of *William Wordsworth: the early years, 1770-1803* by Mary Moorman.
Typescript copy with corrections. 5 l.

Präraffaelitische Brüderschaft.
Typescript copy with corrections. 3 l.

Review of *Stained Glass* by E. Liddall Armitage.
Typescript copy. 1 l.

Review of *The diary of Benjamin Robert Haydon,* edited by Willard Bissell Pope.
Typescript copy with corrections. 4 l.

Art education. Review of *Art and the child* by Marion Richardson.
Holograph. 9 l.

Review of *Guy Burgess: a portrait with a background,* by Tom Driberg.
Typescript copy with corrections. 3 l.

Nature and art.
Typescript with corrections. 6 l.

Wilfred Rowland Childe.
Printed version. 2 l.

The mystery of landscape.
Typescript copy with corrections. 8 l.

Laing Art Gallery, Newcastle-upon-Tyne.
Typescript copy with corrections. 8 l.

King's College, Newcastle-upon-Tyne.
Address by Sir Herbert Read on the occasion of the viewing of Mr. Victor Pasmore's mural constructions in the Stephenson Building, April 3, 1957.
Typescript copy. 3 l. (6 copies)

Introduction. Rome-New York Art Foundation.
Typescript copy. 3 l.

Review of *Three essays on the painting of our time* by Adrian Stokes.
Typescript copy with corrections. 4 l.

Introduction. Cirlot.
Typescript copy. 2 l.

Review of *Essays and introductions* by W. B. Yeats.
Typescript copy with corrections. 4 l.

Review of *Neue Figurationen* by Hans Platschek.
Typescript copy, initialled. 1 l.

Cecil Stephenson.
Typescript copy with corrections. 2 l.

Preface (to *The teaching of mathematics* by Z. P. Dienes).
Typescript copy. 3 l.

Answers to "Volonta."
Typescript copy. 2 l.

Präraffaelitische Brüderschaft.
Typescript copy with corrections. 3 l.

Gregory Memorial Exhibition.
Typescript with corrections. 6 l.
Typescript copy with corrections. 6 l.

Review of *The banquet years* by Roger Shattuck.
Galley proof with corrections for *The London Magazine*. 2 l.
Typescript copy with corrections. 6 l.
Typescript with corrections. 6 l.

Preface (to catalogue of works by Henrion)
Typescript copy. 2 l.

Review of *Kunst und Konstruktion* by Herbert W. Franke.
Typescript copy. 3 l.

Review of *Der Raumsatz* by Wolfgang Th. Otto.
Typescript copy with corrections. 3 l.

Review of *Epoch and artist* by David Jones.
Typescript copy with corrections. 4 l.

Ruskin. Review of *The lamp of beauty, writings on art by John Ruskin*, selected and edited by Joan Evans.
Typescript copy with corrections. 4 l.

Foreword or Introduction (about St. Ives, Cornwall).
Typescript copy. 2 l.
Typescript copy with corrections. 3 l.
2nd Typescript copy with corrections. 3 l.

Review of *Indian Miniatures* by W. G. Archer.
Typescript copy with corrections. 3 l.

Reviews of *The life of John Middleton Murry* by F. A. Lea, *To keep faith* by Mary Middleton Murry and *Katherine Mansfield and other literary studies* by J. Middleton Murry.
Typescript copy with corrections. 8 l.
As printed. 3 l.

Introduction (for an exhibition for the Committee of Art of the Congress for the Liberty of Culture).
Typescript copy with corrections. 5 l.

Report. A review of *The life and opinions of Thomas Ernest Hulme* by A. R. Jones.
Typescript copy. 2 l.
Holograph. 3 l.

A letter to Sir Herbert Read dated July 13, 1959 from Victor
    Gollancz Ltd. Typescript, initialled. 1 l.
Ruth Francken.
    Typescript copy. 2 l.
Drian Gallery, Ruth Francken Exhibition. Preface.
    Typescript copy with corrections. 4 l.
Introduction (to the work of Jovan Obican).
    Typescript copy. 3 l.
    As printed. 2 l.
    Printed brochure of a ceramic sculpture exhibition by Jovan
        Obican, Venice, October 1-25, 1957. 1 l.
    Printed brochure of an exhibition of paintings and sculpture by
        Jovan Obican, Woodstock Gallery, London, June 1-13, 1959.
        1 l.
Isaac Rosenberg.
    Typescript copy with corrections. 4 l.
Review of *The business of criticism* by Helen Gardner. For *The
    Listener*, May 28, 1959.
    Proof copy with corrections. 1 l.
    As printed. 2 l.
Review of *The nature of experience* by Sir Russell Brain.
    Typescript with corrections. 4 l.
The Apollinaire of action painting. Review of *The tradition of the
    new*.
    Typescript copy with corrections. 5 l.
    As printed. 2 l.
Introduction (to *The Parliament of Women*).
    Typescript copy. 4 l.
Prints as a medium of cultural exchange.
    Typescript copy. 4 l.
Review of *Modulor 2: 1955* by Le Corbusier and *The work of
    G. Rietveld architect* by Theodore M. Brown.
    Typescript with corrections. 4 l.
Austin Cooper.
    Typescript copy with corrections. 3 l.
Harrogate.
    Typescript with corrections. 8 l.
    Typescript copy with corrections. 8 l.
James Lloyd.
    Typescript copy. 3 l.
Preface (about the Museum of Modern Art).
    Typescript copy with corrections. 3 l.
    2nd Typescript copy with corrections. 1 l.
    3rd Typescript copy with corrections. 16 l.
    4th Typescript copy with corrections. 5 l.

233

A letter to Mr. Drexler dated June 5, 1957. (Typescript copy unsigned. 1 l.)

Report on the translations of Paul Valery's poems made by Louise Bogan and May Sarton.
Typescript copy. 4 l.

Fifty years of British art, Olso and Copenhagen, 1956.
Typescript copy with corrections. 7 l.

The British Pavilion — XXVI Biennale, 1954.
Typescript copy with corrections. 5 l.

The English contribution to Twentieth Century art.
Typescript copy with corrections. 8 l.

The estate of man. Radio script.
Typescript copy with corrections. 11 l.

Coming to London, extracts from a diary.
Typescript with corrections. 9 l.

Council for the preservation of rural England, Ryedale Branch, Annual Report 1955-56 and Ryedale — Past and present by Sir Herbert Read.
Printed pamphlet.
Typescript with corrections. 8 l.
Typescript with corrections, holograph. 11 l.

Mr. Wyndham Lewis and the I.C.A.
Typescript copy with corrections and additions. 2 l.
Typescript with corrections. 5 l. (Title: A reply to Wyndham Lewis)
Typescript copy with corrections. 5 l. (Title: A reply to Wyndham Lewis)

(Untitled, about amateur and professional painting)
Typescript with corrections with small newspaper clipping attached. 4 l.

Gropius.
Typescript copy with corrections. 4 l.

Adolescent expression in art and craft. Society for education through art, Easter Conference, April 3-7, 1956.
Holograph. 2 l. In printed wrapper.

The unity of the arts.
Typescript with corrections. 4 l.

Life without a shoehorn.
Typescript copy with corrections. 6 l.

Review of *Busman's holiday* by Dorothy L. Sayers, *Hamlet, revenge!* by Michael Dunes, *The theft of the crown jewels* by Edgar Jepson and *Murder in hospital* by Josephine Bell.
Typescript copy. 4 l.

The informal image in art.
Unbound proof sheets with corrections. 3 l.

234

Review of *Muntu: an outline of neo-African culture* by Janheinz Jahn.
Typescript with corrections. 3 l.

Cecil Franklin: publisher of high standards. A letter to the editor, *The Times*, February 2 (?).
Newspaper clipping. 1 l.

A culture out of chaos. Review of *Aldous Huxley on art and artists*, edited and introduced by Morris Philipson.
As printed in *The Saturday Review*. 1 l.

Esthetics: an enemy of violence? In the series 'The creative arts and peace'.
As printed in *The Saturday Review*, December 24, 1960. 2 l.

Adult education and the arts. In *Scottish Adult Education*.
No. 18, December 1956.
Printed. 9 pp.

Archetypal images. Review of *Jackson Pollock* by Bryan Robertson.
Typescript copy with corrections. 3 l.

Preface (about artists of Ceylon).
Typescript copy. 3 l.

Letter to the editor about modern literary criticism.
As printed. 1 l.

The informal image in modern art. IV International Congress of Aesthetics communication.
Typescript copy with corrections. 11 l.

Rock paintings in South Africa. Review of *The Tsisah Ravine* by Abbé Henri Breuil.
As printed in *The Listener*, February 11, 1960. 1 l.

Art, industry, and national decay.
As printed in *The Listener*, January 31, 1957. 2 l.

What's wrong with industrial design.
Proof sheets with corrections. 2 l.

An art of internal necessity: recent trends in non-figurative painting.
Typescript. 22 l.

Review of *The Modern Dilemma* by Christopher Dawson.
As printed in *The Cambridge Review*, February 3, 1933. 2 l.
Letter to the editor of *The Cambridge Review*, February 17, 1933 from Christopher Dawson about Sir Herbert Read's review of his book *The Modern Dilemma*. As printed. 1 l.
Letter to the editor of *The Cambridge Review* about Christopher Dawson's reply to his review. Typescript copy initialled. 2 l.
As printed. 1 l.

Letter to the editor of *The Cambridge Review* from G. G. Coulton concerning Christopher Dawson's *The Modern Dilemma*. As printed. 1 l.

A rather beautiful animal. Review of *NRF — the most significant writings from the Nouvelle Revue Française, 1919-1940*, edited by Justin O'Brien.
As printed in the *New Statesman*, November 29, 1958. 1 l.
Proof sheets with corrections. 2 l.

Introduction (about stained glass).
Typescript with corrections. 9 l.

Henry Moore (an entry for an artists' dictionary in German).
Proof copy. 1 l.

The problem of aesthetic consciousness.
Proceedings of the Third International Congress of Aesthetics.
As printed. 4 pp.

An interview with Herbert Read by K. S. Toulson. *Writing Today*, No. 4, July 1958.
As printed. 1 l.

The prehistoric artist.
Unbound proof copy with corrections. 19 l.

British art since 1945.
Typescript with corrections. 43 l.
Unbound proof copy with corrections. 18 l.

Fables from Flanders.
Typescript with corrections. 7 l.

A painter known as Grünewald. Review of *Grünewald* by Nikolaus Pevsner and Michael Meier.
As printed in *The Listener*, July 17, 1958. 1 l.

Untitled notes about censorship.
Holograph. 5 l.

Review of *The problem of Knowledge* by A. J. Ayer.
Proof sheets with corrections. 2 l.

Préface à la section britannique/Preface to the British Section.
United Nations Educational, Scientific and Cultural Organization exhibition of contemporary painting, Paris 1946. In English and French, translated by Simone Boisecq.
Printed pamphlet. 13 pp.

The language of the eye.
Typescript copy. 4 l.
As printed in the pamphlet 'An exhibition of British painting since 1900, Bridgend, May 30 - June 22, 1940'. (Called 'Art for the people'.) 3 pp.

Fifty years of British art, Oslo and Copenhagen, 1956.
Typescript copy. 3 l.

Review of *Art in crisis: the lost centre* by Hans Sedlmayr.
As printed in the *New Statesman*. December, 14, 1957. 2 l.

Untitled piece about Sam Francis. Brochure for an exhibition of oil paintings and watercolours by Sam Francis, Gimpel Fils, May-June 1957.
As printed. 1 p. (2 copies)

Constantin Brancusi: 1876-1957.
As printed in *The Listener*, April 4, 1957. 1 l.

A portrait of the artist as a martyr. Review of *Letters of James Joyce*, edited by Stuart Gilbert.
As printed in *The New Statesman and Nation*, May 25, 1957. 2 l.

The Duveen era. Review of *Duveen* by S. N. Behrman.
As printed in *The Listener*, July 17, 1952. 1 l.

A cobalt bomb. Review of *The crowning privilege* by Robert Graves.
As printed in *The Listener*, October 6, 1955. 1 l.

Presentation of the Royal Gold Medal to Corbusier (Charles Edouard Jeanneret), R.I.B.A., March 31, 1953. (includes a tribute by Sir Herbert Read.)
As printed in the *R.I.B.A. Journal*, April 1953. 2 l.

A call to discipline. In the series 'Books and leisure'.
As printed in *Public Opinion*, March 16, 1951. 1 l.

The unity of the arts.
As printed in the *Penwith Society Broadsheet No. 4*. Summer, 1953. 1 p.

Art (article for an encyclopaedia).
Typescript copy with corrections. 8 l.

Art and healing.
Typescript copy with corrections. 4 l.

Painting (article for an encyclopaedia).
Typescript with corrections. 11 l.

Art education (article for an encyclopaedia).
Typescript with corrections. 9 l.

Education, theory of (from *Chamber's Encyclopaedia*).
Proof sheets with corrections. 2 l. (7 copies)
Letter to Sir Herbert Read from the assistant editor of *Chamber's Encyclopaedia*. Typescript. 1 l.

Aesthetics (article for *Chamber's Encyclopaedia*).
Proof sheets. 3 l.
2nd proof sheets glued into pages. 2 l.
Proof sheets with corrections. 3 l. (3 copies)
Proof sheets glued onto sheets with corrections. 3 l. (2 copies)
Other proof sheets glued onto sheets with corrections. 3 l.
Other proof sheets glued onto a sheet with corrections. 1 l.

Critic's choice 1955, selection by Eric Newton.
Pamphlet with notes.

36 Innocence and experience.
Typescript with corrections and ten leaves of printed text. 195 l.

37 Introduction (about Heinrich Wölfflin).
Typescript with corrections. 7 l.

Introduction to the Critic's Choice Exhibition.
Typescript copy with corrections. 6 l.

Fifty years of modern poetry.
Typescript copy with corrections. 6 l.

A call to discipline.
Typescript copy with corrections. 6 l.

The challenge of Boimondau.
Typescript copy (with one leaf of typescript) with corrections.
7 l.

The church and the world. A review of *Christ and culture* by
H. Richard Niebuhr.
Typescript copy with corrections. 4 l.

Wilfred Rowland Childe.
Typescript copy. 5 l.

Tombstones.
Typescript copy with corrections. 4 l.

Review of *Technics and civilization* by Lewis Mumford.
Typescript copy. 7 l.

Review of *D. H. Lawrence: selected literary criticism*, edited by
Anthony Beal.
Typescript copy with corrections. 3 l.

Review of *The life and work of D. H. Lawrence* by Harry T.
Moore.
Typescript copy with corrections. 4 l.

1900-1950: Poetry. European Service General News Talk.
Typescript copy with corrections. 5 l.

Sacred discontent. Review of *From the other shore* by Alexander
Herzen.
Typescript copy. 4 l.

Review of *The Englishness of English art* by Nikolaus Pevsner.
Typescript copy with corrections. 3 l.

Stained glass at Canterbury and Oxford. Review of *The ancient
glass of Canterbury Cathedral* by Bernard Rackham and *Medieval glass at All Souls College* by F. E. Hutchinson.
Typescript copy with corrections. 5 l.

Review of *The Lascaux cave paintings* by Fernand Windels.
Typescript copy with corrections. 4 l.

Review of *The milennium of Hieronynus Bosch* by Wilhelm Frän-
ger, translated by Eithne Wilkins and Ernst Kaiser.
Typescript copy with corrections. 4 l.
Preface.
Typescript copy. 2 l.
Word and image.
Typescript copy with corrections. 4 l.
Review of *An apology for the art of our time* by F. A. Wilson.
Typescript copy. 2 l.
The significance of "De Stijl".
Typescript copy with corrections. 1 l.
Report. Review of *Design for colour* by Hilaire Hiler.
Typescript copy. 3 l.
Review of *Notes on the technique of design and colour* by Hilaire
Hiler.
Typescript copy. 3 l.
Review of *Artist potters in England* by Muriel Rose.
Typescript copy. 1 l.
Review of *Staffordshire chimney ornaments* by Reginald G.
Haggar.
Typescript copy. 2 l.
The portrait of an artist. Review of *Paul Nash* by Anthony
Bertram.
Typescript copy with corrections. 3 l.
Review of *Deutsche Kunst im 20. Jahrhundert.* by Ludwig Grote.
Typescript copy. 1 l.
Review of *Meaning and symbol in three modern artists — Edvard
Munch, Henry Moore, Paul Nash* by George Wingfield Digby
and *Poet and painter: being the correspondence between Gor-
don Bottomley and Paul Nash, 1910-1946.*
Typescript copy with corrections. 5 l.
British lithographs.
Typescript copy. 2 l.
The present state of design and its relation to the industrial system.
Typescript with corrections. 16 l.
The making and the unmaking of books.
Typescript copy with corrections. 5 l.
Letter to Sir Herbert Read from M. G. Barber, dated March
12, 1951. Typescript. 1 l.
Letter to J. D. Newth from A. D. Peters, dated March 3, 1951.
Typescript copy. 1 l.
Letter to A. D. Peters from J. D. Newth, dated March 1, 1951.
Typescript copy. 2 l.
Review of *De profundis: the complete text* by Oscar Wilde.
Typescript copy. 4 l.

Foreword.
Typescript copy with corrections. 4 l.
A modern gnostic.
Typescript copy. 3 l.
Review of *The flies (Les mouches)* and *In camera (Huis clos)* by Jean-Paul Sartre, translated by Stuart Gilbert and *Existentialism* by Guido de Ruggiero, edited and introduced by Raynor Heppenstall.
Typescript copy with corrections. 4 l.
John Donne.
Typescript copy with corrections. 5 l.
Review of *Elected silence* by Thomas Merton.
Typescript copy with corrections. 3 l.
Plato — dialogues on education.
Typescript copy. 4 l.
Dublin unrevisited.
Typescript copy with corrections. 7 l.
Report. Review of *Dissertation on Vico's theory of poetry* by H. S. Davies.
Typescript copy with corrections. 4 l.
An open letter to the new director of the British Broadcasting Corporation.
Typescript copy with corrections. 3 l.
Review of *Byron: a self-portrait. Letters and diaries*, edited by Peter Quennell.
Typescript copy with corrections. 4 l.
Review of *Down the long slide* by Tom Hopkinson.
Typescript copy. 2 l.
Foreword (to *The flea of Sodom* by Edward Dahlberg).
Typescript with corrections. 3 l.
Typescript copy with corrections. 3 l.
Review of *Gerard Manley Hopkins* by the Kenyon Critics.
Typescript copy with corrections. 4 l.
1984.
Typescript copy with corrections. 4 l.
Americanism. Review of *The American democracy* by Harold J. Laski, *An inquiry into the principles and policy of the government of the United States* by John Taylor and *Pioneers of American freedom* by Rudolf Rocker.
Typescript copy with corrections. 5 l.
Review of *What is literature?* by Jean-Paul Sartre, translated by Bernard Frechtman.
Typescript with corrections. 4 l.
Review of *The forgotten language* by Erich Fromm.
Typescript copy with corrections. 3 l.

Review of *A preface to Eighteenth Century poetry* by James
Sutherland.
Typescript copy with corrections. 3 l.
Communication.
Typescript copy with corrections. 4 l.
Herbert Read writes.
Typescript copy. 2 l.
Letter from Eric W. White of the Poetry Book Society, dated
September 21, 1955. Typescript copy. 1 l.
The poet's eye. Review of *The fire and the fountain* by John Press.
Typescript copy. 2 l.
The creative imagination. Review of *The fire and the fountain* by
John Press and *The making of a poem* by Stephen Spender.
Typescript copy with corrections. 4 l.
Proposals for a Scottish philanthropist.
Typescript with corrections. 7 l.
Newspaper clipping from *The Manchester Guardian*, December
9, 1932. 1 l.
Review of *Freedom and culture*, compiled by UNESCO.
Typescript copy with corrections. 4 l.
Review of *Literature and psychology* by F. L. Lucas.
Typescript copy with corrections. 3 l.
Review of *Mill on Bentham and Coleridge*.
Typescript copy. 3 l.
One man show. Review of *Rude Assignment* by Wyndham Lewis.
Typescript copy with corrections. 4 l.
Report on a visit to France and Switzerland, November 1945.
Typescript copy with corrections. 5 l.
Wordsworth.
Typescript copy with corrections. 9 l.
I speak of the ungodly. Review of *Bosch's garden of delights* by
Nicolas Calas.
Typescript copy. 3 l.
Kicks and ha'pence.
Typescript copy with corrections. 5 l.
Review of *L'homme revolté* (The rebel) by Albert Camus.
Holograph and typescript copy with corrections. 7 l.
Review of *Coleridge* by Humphrey House.
Typescript copy with corrections. 4 l.
Review of *My host the world* by George Santayana.
Typescript copy. 2 l.
Review of *The responsibilities of the critic* by F. O. Mathiessen
and *Books in general* by V. S. Pritchett.
Typescript copy with corrections. 3 l.

Review of *Language as gesture* by R. P. Blackmur.
Typescript copy with corrections. 5 l.

Review of *A reading of George Herbert* by Rosemond Tuve.
Typescript copy with corrections. 3 l.

Review of *The art of Wordsworth* by Lascelles Abercrombie.
Typescript copy with corrections. 1 l.

Review of *Selected writings of John Ruskin*, edited with an introduction by Peter Quennell.
Typescript copy. 3 l.

Review of *The note-books of Mathew Arnold*, edited by Howard Foster Lowry, Karl Young and Waldo Hilary Dunn.
Typescript copy. 3 l.

Review of *The wisdom of the stars* by Antoine de Saint-Exupéry, translated by Stuart Gilbert.
Typescript copy with corrections. 3 l.

Review of *The letters of Samuel Taylor Coleridge*, selected with an introduction by Kathleen Raine.
Holograph. 1 l.

Review of *The Victorian temper* by Jerome Hamilton Buckley.
Typescript copy with corrections. 2 l.

Review of *Epistles to several persons (Moral essays)* by Alexander Pope, edited by F. W. Bateson and *Pope and his critics* by W. L. Macdonald.
Typescript copy. 1 l.

Review of *The common pursuit* by F. R. Leavis.
Typescript copy with corrections. 3 l.

Who was the ancient mariner? Review of *The wake of the bounty* by C. S. Wilkinson.
Typescript copy. 3 l.

Review of *The invisible writings* by Arthur Koestler.
Typescript and typescript copy with corrections. 4 l.

Review of *Wordsworth: a re-interpretation*, by F. W. Bateson.
Typescript copy with corrections. 4 l.

Foreword (of Rudolf Rocker's *Auto-biography*).
Typescript copy. 3 l.

Bonamy Dobrée.
Typescript copy with corrections. 6 l.
Letter to Sir Herbert Read from I. S. Scott-Kilvert of the British Council dated June 30, 1955. Typed. 1 l.
Biography of Bonamy Dobrée. Typescript. 1 l.

A cobalt bomb. Review of *The crowning privilege* by Robert Groves.
Typescript copy. 4 l.
With holograph notes. 1 l.

242

The hovering fly. Review of *Critical approaches to literature* by David Daiches and *The man of letters in the modern world*.
Typescript copy with corrections. 4 l.

Review of *Red, black, blond and olive* by Edmund Wilson.
Typescript copy. 1 l.

Review of *The English sense of humor and other essays* by Harold Nicolson.
Typescript copy with corrections. 2 l.

Review of *Heaven and hell* by Aldous Huxley.
Typescript copy. 1 l.

Review of *English literature of the Nineteenth Century* by R. C. Churchill.
Typescript copy with corrections. 3 l.

The return of a native.
Typescript copy with corrections. 3 l.

The future of painting: a reply to my critics.
Typescript copy. 6 l.
(Contains letter to Sir Herbert Read from Ian Finlay, undated. Typescript copy with corrections by Sir Herbert Read. 2 l.)
Notes from Professor Karl Hofer. Typescript with corrections. 3 l.
Notes from Professor Paul Strecker. Typescript with corrections. 2 l.
Notes from Professor Alexander Gouda. Typescript. 1 l.
Notes from Wolfgang Grözinger. Typescript. 1 l.
Notes from Siegmund Lympasik. Typescript. 2 l.
Notes from Professor Hermann Beenken. Typescript. 1 l.

Everyman as artist.
Typescript copy with corrections. 6 l.

Untitled (about ideological directives).
Typescript with corrections. 4 l.

Foreword (to a book by Professor Michelis).
Typescript with corrections. 3 l.

Tragic art.
Typescript copy with corrections. 6 l.

Ben Nicholson.
Typescript copy. 2 l.

Preface (to *Stained Glass* by Sowers).
Typescript copy with corrections. 2 l.

Foreword (about Gyorgy Kepes).
Typescript copy with corrections. 2 l.

Report. The question of taste: a study in visual art.
Typescript copy. 3 l.

Foreword (about Guiseppe Santomaso).
Typescript copy with corrections. 2 l.

Willi Baumeister.
Typescript copy with corrections. 3 l.

Review of *A history of modern criticism: 1750-1950* by René Wellek.
Typescript copy with corrections. 4 l.

Untitled (introduction to an exhibition of the works of sufferers from schizophrenia).
Typescript copy with corrections. 2 l.

Review of *The art of Indian Asia: its mythology and transformations,* by Heinrich Zimmer, completed and edited by Joseph Campbell.
Typescript copy with corrections. 3 l.

Le Corbusier.
Typescript copy with corrections. 3 l.
Typescript with corrections. 3 l.

L'architetto come uomo universale.
As printed in a magazine. 4 l.

The critic and the art market.
Typescript copy. 3 l.

Eröffnungsrede.
Typescript with corrections, holograph. 6 l.
Two notes in German, both typescript with corrections. 2 l.

Untitled (about younger sculptors).
Typescript copy. 6 l.

Contemporary British sculptors.
Typescript copy with corrections. 5 l.

New aspects of British sculpture.
Typescript copy. 4 l.

Introduction (about prehistoric Australian art).
Typescript copy with corrections. 5 l.
Postcard to Sir Herbert Read from the *Burlington Magazine,* postmarked June 18, 1954. Holograph. 1 l.
Letter to Sir Herbert Read from Peter Bellow of the Arts and Letters Division of UNESCO, dated June 14, 1954. Typed with holograph notes. 1 l.

The museums scandal.
Typescript copy with corrections. 11 l.

An aboriginal academician.
Typescript copy with corrections. 4 l.

First aid for the arts.
Typescript copy with corrections. 5 l.

Review of *Juan Gris: his life work* by Daniel-Henry Kahnweiler, translated by Douglas Cooper.
  Typescript copy with corrections. 5 l.
Primitive and modern art.
  Typescript copy. 2 l.
Felix Kelly.
  Typescript copy. 2 l.
  2 letters to Sir Herbert Read from Felix Kelly, undated. Holograph. 6 l.
Review of *The poetical works of William Wordsworth*, edited by E. de Selincourt and Helen Darbishire.
  Typescript copy. 2 l.
Review of *The gate of horn* by G. R. Levy.
  Typescript copy with corrections. 6 l.
The crisis in bookcraft.
  Typescript with corrections. 12 l.
Novelism at the Royal Academy.
  Typescript copy with corrections. 13 l.
A general impression.
  Typescript copy. 6 l.
Mexican art.
  As printed in a magazine. 2 l.
  Typescript copy with corrections. 4 l.
Foreword (*Chinese calligraphy* by Chiang Yee).
  Typescript copy with corrections. 4 l.
The British Pavilion.
  Typescript copy with corrections. 6 l.
Psychologie de l'art anglais jusqu'à la jeune peinture.
  Typescript copy with corrections. 8 l.
A postscript to posterity.
  Typescript copy with corrections. 5 l.
Art and aggression.
  Typescript copy with corrections. 9 l.
  Typescript copy. 5 l.
  Typescript with corrections. 6 l.
Review of *Aesthetics and history* by Bernard Berenson.
  Typescript copy with corrections. 3 l.
Letter to the editor of *The Listener* about his review of *Aesthetics and history* by Bernard Berenson.
  Typescript copy. 2 l.
The spirit of 20th Century painting.
  Holograph. 6 l.
The Duveen era (Review of a book of S. N. Behrman).
  Typescript copy with corrections. 5 l.

Review of *Art and social life* by G. V. Plekhanov.
Typescript copy with corrections. 4 l.

Keep Whitehall out (pencilled title).
Typescript copy with corrections. 5 l.

Review of *Criticism and the Nineteenth Century* by Geoffrey Tillotson.
Typescript copy with corrections. 3 l.

Review of *Paul Klee* by Carola Giedion-Welcker, translated by Alexander Gode.
Typescript copy with corrections. 3 l.
Second typescript copy with corrections. 4 l.

Preface (about Graham Sutherland). In French.
Proof sheets with corrections. 2 l.

Review of *Matisse: his art and his public* by Alfred H. Barr, Jr.
Typescript copy with corrections. 3 l.

Review of *The conduct of life* by Lewis Mumford.
Typescript copy with corrections. 3 l.

The burden of renewal. Review of *Art and technics* by Lewis Mumford.
Typescript copy with corrections. 5 l.
Holograph notes. 2 l.

Review of *The liberal imagination* by Lionel Trilling.
Typescript copy with corrections. 3 l.

The York Mystery Plays.
Typescript copy with corrections. 3 l.

The making and unmaking of books.
Typescript with corrections. 5 l.
Proof sheets with corrections. 2 l.

Preface (to *Aspects of form*, edited by L. L. Whyte).
Typescript copy with notes and corrections. 2 l.

Review of *The dilemma of the arts* by Wladimir Weidle. European Service General News Talks Weekly Book Summary, No. 185.
Typescript copy with corrections. 4 l.

Review of *De Stijl: 1917-1931* by Hans Ludwig Jaffé.
Typescript with corrections. 2 l.

38   Truth is more sacred: The Dahlberg-Read epistles.
Typescript, typescript copy and typescript copy with corrections.
177 l.

39   Art and industry.
Unbound copy. London, Faber and Faber, 1944. Second edition. With notes, both holograph and typescript attached, loose corrected proof sheets and a new preface, typescript with corrections for the third edition (revised).

Unbound copy. London, Faber and Faber, 1943. Second edition. Holograph notes and corrections.

4 letters to Sir Herbert Read from Richard de la Mare of Faber and Faber, all typed, October and November 1942 (one letter dictated by de la Mare but signed by someone else of Faber and Faber). 4 l.

2 letters from Sir Herbert Read to Richard de la Mare dated November 7, 1942 and February 24, 1943.
Typescript copies unsigned. 2 l.

Key to redistribution of blocks for the new edition.
Typescript copy. 4 l.
Holograph. 6 l.

Preface to the fifth edition. Typescript with corrections. 17 l.
Inside the loose cover of the new edition.

Conflicts in contemporary art. County Council of the West Riding of Yorkshire Education Committee, Breton Hall.
Printed pamphlet with holograph additions and corrections and attached typescript additions and corrections.

The grass roots of art.
Unbound copy. Lindsay Drummond, 1947. With holograph corrections and additions throughout.
Unbound proof copy. Faber and Faber, 1955. New edition. With holograph corrections and additions throughout.
Typescript with corrections and a printed piece attached. 9 l.
Letter to Sir Herbert Read from Phyllis A. Reinhardt, Slide and Photograph Librarian, Yale University Division of the Arts, dated January 6, 1955. Typed. 1 l.
5 letters to Sir Herbert Read from C. Dahl, Librarian to Aerofilms Limited, 1954-1955. Typed. 5 l.
2 despatch notes from Aerofilms Ltd. 2 l.
2 letters from Sir Herbert Read to Mr. Shaw, 1954 and 1955. Typescript copy unsigned. 2 l.
List of slides. Typescript copy with corrections. 2 l. Holograph. 1 l.
2 letters to Sir Herbert Read from the Art Department of *Country Life*, December 1954. Typed. 2 l.
Letter from Sir Herbert Read to the Librarian of Aerofilms Ltd., dated January 10, 1955. Typescript copy unsigned. 1 l.

The grass roots of art.
Letter to Sir Herbert Read from Joseph Hill, Vice-Principal of The Training College, dated March 19, 1954. Typed. 2 l.
Receipt and invoice from *Country Life*. 2 l.
2 letters to Sir Herbert Read from M. Shaw of Faber and Faber, December 1954. Typed. 2 l.
Letter to Sir Herbert Read from Victoria and Albert Museum, dated December 10, 1954. Holograph. 1 l.

Letter from Sir Herbert Read to The Librarian at Yale University School of Fine Arts, dated December 8, 1954.
Typescript copy, unsigned. 1 l.
Postcard to Sir Herbert Read from Reg., dated March 10, 1955, with a photograph of sculpture attached. 1 l.
2 letters to Sir Herbert Read from Faber and Faber, March 1955. Typed. 2 l.
Photograph. 1 l.
Unbound proof copy with corrections. Loosely inside printed cover of book.

40 This way delight. Delight, a first book of poems for children. Chosen by Herbert Read.
Holograph in notebook. 69 pp. With loose newspaper clippings.
Holograph notes and a postcard. 15 l.
Unbound proof copy on newsprint paper.
Earlier unbound proof copy on heavier paper.
Proof sheets of poems included with corrections. 45 l.
Typescript copy of the poems with notes. 58 l.
Typescript. 63 l.
Letters connected with the publication of *This way delight*:
2 letters from Alida Monro, the widow of Harold Monro, 1 typed, the other holograph. 2 l.
50 letters to Sir Herbert Read from various publishers. Typed. 58 l.
45 letters from Sir Herbert Read to various publishers. Typescript copy unsigned. 49 l. (3 of these are from Sir Herbert Read's secretary.)
Various lists of the poems to be used. Typescript copy with corrections and typescript with corrections. 9 l.
Index of first lines. Typescript copy with corrections. 4 l.
Acknowledgements. Typescript copy with corrections. 4 l.
Material about copyright fees. Typescript copy with corrections, typescript with corrections, holograph. 32 l.
What is poetry?
Typescript with corrections and holograph. 11 l.
Typescript copy with corrections. 7 l.
Permission forms from various publishers. 3 l.
Blurb. Typescript copy. 3 l.
Sample page. Printed. 1 l.
Some poems.
Typescript. 6 l.
Typescript copy. 6 l.

41 Lecture.
Typescript with corrections. 31 l.
Lecture materials.
Holograph, typescript, typescript copy and printed material. 54 l.

248

Journal de psychologie. 15 Janvier - 15 Février, 1931.
With holograph notes.

British Museum. Lantern slides catalogue.

Announcement in Danish of a lecture by Sir Herbert Read, April 26, 1935. 2 l.

Art and crisis.
Typescript copy with corrections, holograph, and typescript with corrections. 71 l.
Notes. Typescript copy with corrections and holograph. 5 l.

Letter to the editor from C. P. Snow about a review by Sir Herbert Read of Snow's Rede Lecture. Proof copy with corrections. 1 l.

Letter to the editor from Sir Herbert Read in answer to the above. Typescript copy with corrections. 3 l.

Threshold of a new age.
Proof sheets with corrections. 3 l.

Philosophy of change.
Proof sheets with corrections. 2 l.

The informal image in modern art.
Typescript with corrections. 20 l.
List of slides. Holograph. 1 l. Typescript with corrections. 1 l.

60 American painters: 1960. Walker Art Centre, April 3 - May 8, 1960. Brochure.

Excerpts from article by Jean Dubuffet, *Daedalus*, Winter 1960.
Typescript with notes. 2 l.

Contemporary British art.
Typescript with corrections and notes. 65 l.
Typescript copy with corrections. 42 l.
Proof sheets with corrections. 14 l.
List of artists. Typescript, typescript copy and printed on small pieces of paper with corrections and notes pinned to the back of proof sheets of *The Flea of Sodom*. 5 l.
Proof sheets of the plates. 10 l. Some plates cut from sheets, some loose.
14 letters to Sir Herbert Read about the publication *Contemporary British art*, from artists, their representatives and publishers. Holograph and typed. 17 l.
Blurb. Typescript copy. 1 l.
Miscellaneous notes on artists and coloured plates. Typescript, typescript copy and printed. 28 l.

42 Kenyon lectures. English prose style. (June 23 - August 6, 1949).
Typescript with corrections. 75 l.
(Inserted clippings, pamphlets, proof-sheets, and printed pages.)
Typescript copy. 80 l.

Typed letters from A. W. Ready regarding *English prose style*.
2 l.
Reply, unsigned, typescript copy. 1 l.
The modern epoch in art.
Typescript with corrections. 41 l.
Paul Nash.
Typescript. 16 l.
Paul Nash.
Typescript copy. 4 l.
List of illustrations.
Typescript copy. 2 l.
4 letters signed "Margaret".
Holograph. 4 l.
Instructions for the trustees of the Paul Nash estate.
Typescript copy. 3 l.
Remarks on the Memorial Volume selected by Paul Nash.
Typescript. 19 l.
Supplementary list of pictures.
Typescript with corrections. 9 l.
Unseen landscapes by Paul Nash. (Published in *Country Life*,
May 21, 1938).
Typescript copy. 4 l.
For, but not with.
Typescript copy. 6 l.
Art and war by Paul Nash.
Typescript copy. 15 l.
15 letters about Paul Nash's autobiography.
Typescript, typescript copy, and holograph. 15 l.
Typescript. p. 14-20. "duplicate copy".
A metaphysical artist. Geoffrey Grigson or Paul Nash.
Clipping from *The Listener*, April 1, 1948. 2 l.
Chronology. "Final copy".
Typescript copy. 4 l.
Editor's preface.
Typescript copy. 5 l.
List of illustrations to accompany "Outline".
Typescript and typescript copy. 4 l.
43 Anarchy and order.
Unbound proof copy with corrections.
Reason and romanticism.
Proof copy bound in plain paper wrapper. Incomplete with
some loose leaves.
Proof copy with corrections bound in plain paper wrapper.
Unbound proof copy. Incomplete.

250

Annals of innocence and experience.
  Proof copy unbound of title page and introductory pages.
    Contains, loosely inserted, corrections to the page proofs of
    The innocent eye.
  Typescript copy and holograph. 3 l.
Collected poems.
  Unbound proof copy with corrections.
The politics of the unpolitical.
  Unbound proof copy with corrections, in loose printed wrapper.

44 Coleridge as critic.
  Unbound proof copy with corrections.
Art now.
  Unbound proof copy with corrections.
  Unbound proof copy with new preface to this new edition
    attached and corrections throughout.
  Proof copy of the index with corrections.
  Notes on some painters. Typescript copy with corrections and
    holographs. 11 l.
  Letter to Sir Herbert Read from Curt Valentin, dated Decem-
    ber 10, 1946. Typed. 1 l.
  Letter to Sir Herbert Read from Frank McE., dated February
    9, 1948. 2 l.
Icon and idea.
  Unbound proof copy with corrections and the plates.
Selected writings: poetry and prose.
  Unbound proof copy with corrections. In printed paper wrapper.
  Proof copy of title page and foreword of the English (Faber)
    edition with American (Horizon) notice attached to title
    page and American printing information on verso.

45 Collected essays in literary criticism.
  Unbound proof copy with corrections.
  Preface to the Italian edition. Typescript copy with corrections.
    4 l.
  Contents. Typescript copy. 1 l.
  Letter to Sir Herbert Read from Faber proof-reader J. C. Jen-
    nett. Typed with notes and corrections. 2 l.
  Corrections. Holograph. 1 l.
Unbound proof gatherings of various books, many pencil marks
  throughout.
Loose in an exercise-book cover:
  2 letters to Sir Herbert Read from Irene Maguiness, dated Jan-
    uary and February 1945. Holograph. 8 l.
  Art through education. Holograph. 23 l.
  Information from the Leeds Girls' High School. Typescript copy
    with notes. 4 l.
  C.L.C. Art Syllabus. Typescript copy with corrections. 5 l.

Herbert Read und die englische Kunsterziehung von Herbert Klingst. In German.
Typescript copy with corrections. 6 l.

Letter to Sir Herbert Read from Kathleen Bartlett, dated June 18, 1946. Holograph. 1 l.

Biology in art and education. Review of Sir Herbert Read's *Education through art* by Hans Syz.
Typescript copy with pencil underlinings. 13 l.

Letter to Ian Caha from Sir Herbert Read, dated January 19, 1948.
Typescript copy with corrections. 1 l.

Letter to Sir Herbert Read from Ian Caha, dated December 30, 1947.
Typescript. 2 l.

Letters and lists of corrections from Faber and Faber.
Typescript, typescript copy and holograph. 10 l.

Letter to Sir Herbert Read from Cpl. Smith.
Holograph. 2 l.

Review of Sir Herbert Read's *Education through art* by Hans Syz. Reprinted from *Psychiatry: Journal of the Biology and Pathology of Interpersonal Relations*, Volume ten, number one, February 1947. 7 pp., 5 copies.

Newspaper clipping in German dated May 15, 1949 mentioning Sir Herbert Read's *Education through art.* 1 l.

Brochure from The Museum of Modern Art's Art Classes, Fall-Spring, 1944-1945.

Letter to Sir Herbert Read from Emay Twining, dated November 8, 1944. Typed. 1 l.

Two newspaper clippings from *The Times.* 2 l.

Pamphlet No. 8 from Incorporated Association of Preparatory Schools. Drawing and painting by A. M. Carr.

Pamphlet from the Eighth Grade Fine Arts, 1946. Thomas Jefferson Jr. High, Cleveland, Ohio.

46 The contrary experience.
Corrected proof sheets with 3 leaves of typescript and holograph. 136 l.

Letter to Sir Herbert Read from Eileen Brooksbank of Faber and Faber, dated January 16, 1963. Typed. 1 l.

Letter from Sir Herbert Read to Eileen Brooksbank, dated February 2, 1963.
Typescript copy with carboned signature. 1 l.

Henry Moore Exhibition for American universities, 1965. Introduction.
Typescript copy with corrections. 6 l. (2 copies)

Contents. Typescript. 1 l.
5 letters from Sir Herbert Read about the Henry Moore Exhibition (one to Henry Moore). Typescript copy. 5 l.
7 letters about the exhibition to Sir Herbert Read or copies for his attention. Typed and typescript copies. 7 l.
Memorandum. Typescript with corrections. 2 l.
A telegram to Sir Herbert Read from Robert Richman.
Typescript and typescript copy. 2 l. (2 copies)

47 Jacob Kramer.
Holograph. 5 l.
Catalogue of the *Exhibition of the work of Jacob Kramer, 8 September - 9 October 1960, Leeds City Art Gallery.*
Presentation copy to Herbert Read.
Letter to Jacob Kramer, dated 6.4.18. Pencilled holograph. 3 l.
Drawing to Read, dated 23.8.19. 1 l.

Correspondence

48 Letters to Sir Herbert Read from:
Ackerley, Joe. 20. Holograph.
Aldington, Richard. 72. Holograph and typed.
Bill, Clive. 3. Holograph.
Benda, Julien. 1. Holograph.
Berber, John. 10. Holograph and typed. (A poem tit'ed "War Pastoral" dedicated to Read included. Holograph. 1 l.)
Blunden, Edmund. 1. Holograph.
Boulton, Marjorie. 5. Holograph.
Bowes Lyon, Lilian. 11. Holograph.
Breton, André. 5. Holograph.
Bunting, Basil. 1. Typed.
Burri, Minka. 1. Holograph.
Butler, Reg. 1. Holograph.
Calder, Sandy. 1. Holograph.
Cairns, Huntington. 4. Typed.
Cary, Joyce. 1. Holograph.
Childe, Wilfred Rowland. 22. Holograph.
Church, Richard. 14. Holograph and typed.
Clark, Kenneth. 4. Holograph and typed.
Coghill, Nevill. 1. Holograph.
Comfort, Alex. 7. Holograph and typed.
Connolly, Cyril. 2. Typed.
Cooper, D. 13. Holograph and typed.
Dahlberg, Edward. 229. Typed (1 holograph).
Davie, Alan. 1. Holograph.
Day-Lewis, Cecil. 1. Holograph.
de la Mare, Walter. 2. Typed.

Dickinson, Lowes. 8. Typed.
Dobrée, Bonamy. 50. Typed.
Dobrée, Valentine. 13. Holograph and typed.
Dubuffet, Jean. 1. Typed.
Duthuit, Georges. 7. Holograph.
Eliot, Thomas Stearns. 158. Holograph and typed.
Elouard, Paul. 10. Holograph.
Erni, Hans. 4. Holograph and typed.
Evans, Merlyn. 1. Holograph.
Faber, Enid. 1. Holograph.
Faber, Geoffrey. 3. Holograph and typed.
Finlay, Ian Hamilton. 1. Typed.
Flint, F. S. 6. Holograph and typed.
Ford, Ford Madox. 10. Holograph and typed.
Forster, Edward Morgan. 2. Holograph.
Frost, Terry. 2. Holograph.
Fry, Roger. 1. Holograph.
Gabo, Naum. 47. Holograph and typed.
Garnett, Edward. 1. Holograph.
Gill, Eric. 6. Holograph and typed.
Giono, Jean. 4. Holograph.
Gollancz, Victor. 2. Typed.
Graves, Robert. 1. Holograph.
Greene, Graham. 2. Typed.
Grierson, H. J. C. 1. Holograph.
Grigson, Geoffrey. 3. Holograph.
Grohmann, Will. 8. Typed.
Gropius, Walter. 4. Holograph and typed.
Hanley, James. 5. Holograph and typed.
Hanley, Timothy. 1. Holograph.
Hayward, John. 1. Holograph.
Hayter, S. W. 1. Typed.
Hélion, Jean. 9. Holograph and typed.
Heppenstall, Rayner. 21. Holograph and typed.
Hepworth, Barbara. 76. Holograph and typed.
Heron, Patrick. 8. Holograph.
Hitchens, Ivon. 7. Holograph.
Housman, A. E. 1. Holograph.
Hughes, Ted. 1. Holograph.
Hugnet, Georges. 4. Holograph.
Hull, Richard. 16. Typed.
Hutchings, Patrick. 1. Holograph.
Huxley, Julian. 1. Typed.
John, Augustus. 1. Holograph.
Jones, David. 11. Holograph.
Jung, C. G. 5. Holograph and typed.
Kandinsky, Wassily. 5. Typed.
Knight, G. Wilson. 5. Holograph.

Kokoschka, O. 10. Holograph and typed.
Kramer, Jacob. 12. Holograph.
Lanyon, Peter. 4. Holograph.
Lawrence, T. E. 2. Holograph.
Le Bas, Edward. 1. Holograph.
Le Corbusier. 1. Holograph.
Leavis, F. P. 1. Holograph.
Lewis, Wyndham. 14. Holograph and typed.
Lowry, L. S. 1. Holograph.
McWilliam, F. E. 3. Holograph.
Mason, Bateson. 1. Holograph.
Mathieu, Georges. 1. Holograph.
Meadows, Bernard. 2. Holograph.
Miller, Henry. 12. Holograph and typed.
Miró, Joan. 3. Holograph.
Mitchison, Naomi. 1. Typed.
Moholy-Nagy. 2. Holograph.
Moore, Henry. 17. Holograph and typed.
Morley, F. V. 48. Holograph and typed.
Muir, Edwin. 11. Holograph and typed.
Muir, Willa. 3. Holograph.
Murry, J. Middleton. 9. Holograph and typed. (In addition:
    2 holograph letters by John Bailey to Murry.)
Myers, Leo. 4. Holograph.
Nash, John. 3. Holograph.
Nash, Paul. 5. Holograph. (Paper by Read on Paul Nash in-
    cluded. Typescript copy with corrections. 17 l.)
Newson, John. 2. Holograph and typed.
Nicholson, Ben. 134. Holograph.
Orage, A. R. 32. Holograph.
Orwell, George. 3. Typed photocopies. (6 letters concerning
    photo-copies included.)
Pasmore, Victor. 2. Holograph.
Payne, Robert. 27. Typed.
Piper, John. 1. Holograph.
Plomer, William. 2. Holograph.
Pound, Dorothy. 1. Holograph.
Pound, Ezra. 3. Holograph and typed.
Rackham, B. 2. Holograph.
Raine, Kathleen. 28. Holograph and typed.
Remarque, Erich Maria. 6. Holograph and typed.
Richards, I. A. 2. Holograph.
Richter, Hans. 5. Holograph and typed.
Roberts, William. 1. Holograph.
Romains, Jules. 2. Holograph.
Rothenstein, Michael. 2. Holograph.
Rothenstein, William. 2. Holograph.
Russell, Bertrand. 2. Typed.

Russell, Peter. 5. Typed.
Sackville-West, Edward. 1. Holograph.
Sadler, M. E. 13. Holograph.
Sassoon, Siegfried. 5. Holograph.
Scott, Tom. 1. Typed.
Sell, Joseph. 1. Holograph.
Shahn, Ben. 1. Typed.
Sickert, Walter. 1. Holograph.
Simenon, Denise. 1. Typed.
Simenon, Georges. 1. Typed.
Sitwell, Osbert. 1. Holograph.
Sitwell, Sacheverell. 2. Holograph.
Spark, Muriel. 4. Holograph.
Spender, Stephen. 32. Holograph and typed.
Stein, Leo. 1. Holograph.
Steinberg, Saul. 1. Holograph.
Stokes, Adrian. 21. Holograph.
Stravinsky, Igor. 1. Typed.
Sutherland, Graham. 2. Holograph.
Tapié, Michel. 1. Holograph.
Tàpies, Antonio. 1. Typed.
Tate, Allen. 18. Holograph and typed.
Tate, Isabella. 1. Holograph.
Thomas, Dylan. 3. Holograph.
Thompson, D'Arcy W. 1. Typed.
Tippett, Michael. 1. Typed.
Townsend, William. 1. Holograph and typed.
Treece, Henry. 45. Holograph and typed.
Waley, Arthur. 1. Holograph.
Webb, Beatrice. 4. Typed.
Wedgwood, Josiah. 2. Holograph.
Wells, H. G. 7. Holograph and typed. (Including one signed by
    Marjorie Wells (Mrs. G. P. Wells), his secretary.)
Wells, John. 1. Holograph.
Wharton, Edith. 2. Holograph.
Wheen, Arthur Wesley. 14. Holograph.
Wilson, Colin. 8. Typed.
Wingfield, Sheila. 5. Holograph and typed.
Woodcock, George. 3. Typed.
Woolf, Leonard. 2. Typed.
Woolf, Virginia. 1. Holograph.
Worringer, Marta. 1. Holograph.
Worringer, Wilhelm. 18. Holograph and typed.
Yeats, William Butler. 1. Typed.
Miscellaneous. 141 letters. Holograph, typed, typed copy.

49 Letters, unsigned carbons, from Sir Herbert Read to:
    Alford, John. 1. (Letter from Alford to John S. Keel included.)

Berger, John. 4 (Proof copy of a review by Berger of *The Grass roots of art* included.)

Dahlberg, Edward. 16.

Dickinson, Lowes. 1.

Dubuffet, Jean. 1.

Eliot, T. S. 10. (includes 1 pencilled holograph)

Erni, Hans. 2. (2 photographs and a paper on Erni by Read, typescript copy, 3 l., included.)

Faber, Geoffrey. 1.

Gabo, Naum. 3.

Grohmann, Professor Will. 7.

Hepworth, Barbara. 1.

Higham, David. 1.

Hitchens, Ivon. 2.

Hull, Richard. 3. (Change of address included)

Jung, Dr. C. G. 3. (Includes letters from Jung's secretary and typescript copy of *The legend of the green children.*)

Koestler, Arthur. 1. (Includes telegram from Arthur Koestler, Georges Mikes, Stephen Spender and three-page statement on Russian invasion of Hungary.)

Moore, Henry. 1. (Includes letter to Read from J. R. M. Brumwell.)

Muir, Edwin. 2.

Newsom, John. 1.

Nicholson, Ben. 3. (Includes typescript copy with corrections, 8 l.; paper by Read on Nicholson.)

Raine, Kathleen. 2.

Richards, I. A. 1. (holograph "copy")

Russell, Peter. 1.

Spender, Stephen. 2. (2nd letter has holograph additions in red pencil.)

Wells, H. G. 3.

Wilson, Colin. 3.

Miscellaneous. 23.

50 Freedom Defence Committee.

Constitution. Typescript copy and mimeograph. 5 l.

Draft letters to sponsors and friends. 6 l.

21 letters replying to appeal for funds. Typescript and holograph.

Replies from:

E. M. Forster. 2. (initialled postcard and signed holograph)

George Orwell. 1. (signed holograph)

Bertrand Russell. 2. (signed holograph and typescript reply from Read)

Stephen Spender. 1. (signed holograph)

Graham Sutherland. 1. (signed post card)

Julian Symons. 1. (signed typescript)
Leonard Woolf. 2. (signed typescript)

51 Freedom Press.
Copy of circular letter dated October 25, 1944. Typescript. 1 l.
Freedom press defence. Typescript copy. 9 l.
Letter from *The Times*, John Webb, to Read. Typescript. 1 l.
Letter from Read "To the editor". Typescript copy. 2 l.
Letter from Read to "Commander Stephen King-Hall, M.P."
    Typescript copy. 1 l.
Newspaper clippings.

Notes on Contributors

SIR HERBERT READ (1893-1968)

HERBERT EDWARD READ was born on his father's farm, Muscoates Grange, at Kirbymoorside in Yorkshire on December 4, 1893. He spent the first ten years on the farm and then went to a Halifax boarding school. On leaving school he worked in a bank for three years before entering Leeds University, where his studies were interrupted by the outbreak of the First World War. He served in the Yorkshire Regiment (the Green Howards) from 1915 to 1918, earning the D.S.O. and the M.C. From 1919 to 1922 he worked at the Treasury and from 1922 to 1931 was Assistant Keeper of the Victoria and Albert Museum. From 1931 to 1933 he was Watson Gordon Professor of Fine Art in the University of Edinburgh, and from 1935 to 1939 he was Editor of the *Burlington Magazine*. In 1935-1936 he was Sydney Jones Lecturer in Art at the University of Liverpool, in 1940-1942 Leon Fellow of the University of London, in 1953-1954 Charles Elliot Norton Professor of Poetry at Harvard, and in 1954 the A. W. Mellon Lecturer in Fine Arts at Washington, D.C. In 1962 he was made Senior Fellow of the Royal College of Art and an honorary Professor of the University of Cordoba, Argentine, and awarded an honorary doctorate in Fine Arts by the University of Buffalo. He received the degree of Litt.D. from the Universities of Boston and York and that of D. Litt. from the University of Leeds. He was President of the Society for Education through Art, of the Institute of Contemporary Arts, of the Yorkshire Philosophical Society, and of the British Society of Aesthetics. He became a trustee of the Tate Gallery in 1965, and in 1966 with Rene Huyghe, he was awarded the Erasmus Prize. He was knighted in 1953.

GEORGE BARKER (1913-   ) was born in Essex. He has taught in Japan as a Professor of English Literature, and is the author of two novels and many books of poems. His *Collected Poems* (1930-55) were published by Faber & Faber in 1957. Later volumes include *Two Plays* (1958), *The View from the Blind I* (1962), and *Dreams of a Summer Night* (1966).

SAM BLACK (1913-   ) was born in Scotland, and educated there and in France and Belgium. He was a schoolteacher in the years before the Second World War, and after his war service became one of Her Majesty's Inspectors of Schools, and, later, Principal Lecturer in Art at Jordanhill Teachers College, Glasgow. He is a Founder Member of The International Society for Education Through Art, and a member of the Royal Scottish Society of Painters in Water Colours, the Canadian Society of Graphic Art, the Canadian Society of Painters in Watercolour. He was a Commonwealth Visiting Fellow to Australia in 1963 and is currently Professor and Acting Head of the Art Education and Fine Art Department of the Faculty of Education, University of British Columbia. His paintings are represented in many public collections in Europe and North America. He is married and has four daughters.

EDWARD DAHLBERG (1900-   ) was born in Boston, Massachusetts, and educated at the University of California at Berkeley and at Columbia University. He is the author of many works of fiction and criticism, including *Bottom Dogs* (1929), *Those Who Perish* (1934), *Do These Bones Live* (1940), *The Flea of Sodom* (1950), *The Sorrows of Priapus* (1957), and, in collaboration with Herbert Read, *Truth is More Sacred* (1961). His autobiography, *Because I was Flesh*, was published in 1964.

DONALD DAVIE (1922-   ) was born in Barnsley, Yorkshire, and educated at Cambridge. He has published two books of criticism, *Articulate Energy* (1957) and *Ezra Pound, Poet as Sculptor* (1964), and three collections of poetry, *Brides of Reason* (1955), *A Winter Talent* (1957) and *Events and Wisdoms* (1963). From 1964 to 1968 he was Chairman of the Department of Literature at the University of Essex. He is at present Professor of English at Stanford University.

BONAMY DOBREE (1891-   ) was educated at Haileybury, Woolwich, and Cambridge, and published his first book, the classic study *Restoration Comedy*, in 1924. Since that time he has published many biographies, books of criticism, anthologies, and scholarly editions as well as a number of imaginary dialogues and some fiction. Generally regarded as a leading scholar of the eighteenth century (his *Early Eighteenth Century* is the most brilliant volume in the *Oxford History of English Literature* of which he was a General Editor) he is also an authority on several modern writers. Of his more than thirty books perhaps the most outstanding are *Essays in Biography* (1925), *John Wesley* (1933), *As Their Friends Saw Them* (1933), *Alexander Pope* (1951), *The Broken Cistern* (1954). He was Professor of English Literature at the University of Leeds from 1936 to 1955, and Gresham Professor in Rhetoric from 1955 to 1961. His wife Valentine (nee Brooke-Pechell) is a painter and author. He was awarded the O.B.E. in 1929.

ROY FULLER (1912-   ) was born in Failsworth, Lancashire, and educated at private schools. He is a solicitor and since 1958 has been Legal Advisor to the Building Societies Association. He is the author of eight novels and nine collections of poems, including *Poems* (1939), *The Middle of a War* (1942),

Counterparts (1954), *Collected Poems 1936-61* (1962) and *Buff* (1965). He is married with one son, the poet John Fuller, and is a Fellow of the Royal Society of Literature. In 1968 he was elected Professor of Poetry at Oxford.

HOWARD B. GERWING (1932-   ) was born in Kelowna, British Columbia, and educated at the University of British Columbia. He is the Special Collections Librarian of the University of Victoria, and editor of *British Columbia Library Quarterly.*

WALTER GROPIUS (1883-1969) .was born in Berlin, and studied at the Technische Hochschule there and in Munich. Before the First World War he designed factories, residences, furniture, and locomotives. He served with the Ninth Hussars during the War and was awarded many decorations. In 1918 he created the Staatliches Bauhaus at Weimar, later moving it to Dessau where the school he himself had designed was dedicated in 1926. Between 1926 and 1934 when he voluntarily left Hitler's Germany, he created many designs for residences, theatres, factories, prefabricated houses and car bodies. In England from 1934 to 1937 he designed buildings in collaboration with Maxwell Fry. In 1937 he became a permanent resident of the United States and senior Professor of Architecture at Harvard. Together with Moholy-Nagy he established the New Bauhaus (later called the Chicago Institute of Design). In 1938 he became chairman of the Department of Architecture in Harvard's Graduate School of Design. He designed the Harvard Graduate Centre (completed in 1950) and many other buildings for government and industry. He received many honorary degrees and other marks of distinction from universities and organizations in Europe and America.

MICHAEL HAMBURGER (1924-   ) was born in Berlin, Germany but moved to England at an early age. His first book, a translation of Hölderlin, was published in 1943 when he was serving in the British Army. He has published five collections of poems, of which the most recent are *Weather and Season* (1963) and *In Flashlight* (1965). His translations include *Hölderlin: Poems and Fragments* (1966), and, in collaboration with Christopher Middleton, *Modern German Poetry 1910-1960.* He has published three books of criticism, and has lectured in German at University College, London, and at the University of Reading. In 1966-67 he was Purington Lecturer at Mount Holyoke College, Mass. At present he lives in London.

BARBARA HEPWORTH (1903-   ) was born in Wakefield, Yorkshire, and studied at Leeds Royal College of Art. She was awarded a C.B.E. in 1958 and a D.B.E. in 1965 and has received the honorary degree of D.Litt. from the Universities of Birmingham, Leeds, and Exeter. Her sculpture has been awarded many international prizes including the Grand Prix of the 5th Sao Paolo Biennial in 1959, and her work is represented in public collections throughout the world. A one-man exhibition of her work was presented at the 25th Venice Bienniale in 1950, and retrospective exhibitions of her work were held in 1954 and 1962. She has been a Trustee of the Tate Gallery since 1965. Sir Herbert Read contributed a foreword to her 1952 volume, *Barbara Hepworth: Carvings and Drawings*, published by Lund Humphries. Her most recent publication is *Drawings from a Sculptor's Landscape* (Corey Adams & Mackay, 1966). She lives in St. Ives, Cornwall.

JOHN HOLLOWAY (1920-   ) was educated at New College, Oxford. He was a Fellow of All Souls from 1946 to 1960, and currently teaches at Queens

College, Cambridge. He is the author of many works of criticism, including *Language and Intelligence* (1951), *The Victorian Sage* (1953), *The Chartered Mirror* (1960), and *The Story of the Night* (1961). He has published three collections of poetry, *The Minute* (1956), *The Fugue* (1960) and *The Landfallers* (1962). He is married, with one daughter, and is a Fellow of the Royal Society of Literature.

ANTHONY KERRIGAN (1918-   ) was born in Massachusetts and studied Sino-Japanese at the University of California in Berkeley. He is the editor of Borges' *Personal Anthology* (Grove, 1967) and is the editor with Herbert Read and Martin Nozick of the currently appearing *Selected Works of Miguel de Unamuno*. He divides his time between Dublin and Spain.

THOMAS KINSELLA (1928-   ) was born in Dublin, Ireland, and educated at University College, Dublin. He worked as a Civil Servant until 1965, when he became Poet in Residence at the University of Southern Illinois. He has published a number of translations from the Irish; and his books of poetry include *Poems* (1956), *Another September* (1958), *Moralities* (1960), *Downstream* (1962), *Wormwood* (1966) and *Nightwalker and Other Poems* (1968). A group of his worksheets were featured in *Malahat 3*.

G. WILSON KNIGHT (1897-   ) was educated at Dulwich College and St. Edmund Hall, Oxford. A Shakespearean producer and actor as well as scholar, he has directed, in England and Canada, productions of *Hamlet, King Lear, Othello, Romeo and Juliet, Timon of Athens*, in all of which he has played the leading role. His first books on Shakespeare revolutionized Shakespearian criticism; in *The Wheel of Fire* (1930), *The Imperial Theme* (1931), *The Shakespearean Tempest* (1932), he established a totally new way of examining and interpreting poetic drama. His later Shakespearean books, *Principles of Shakespearean Production* (1936, reissued and enlarged as *Shakespearean Production* in 1964), and *The Mutual Flame* (1955) were equally perceptive and imaginative. In addition to his work on Shakespeare, he has written several books on Byron and commented vividly upon the work of John Cowper Powys, Alexander Pope, John Milton and the Romantics. His autobiographical *Atlantic Crossing* was published in 1936 and his one play, *The Last of the Incas*, in 1954. He was Professor of English at Trinity College, Toronto from 1931 to 1940, and later occupied a chair in English Literature at the University of Leeds of which he is now Emeritus Professor. His latest book, a collection of essays spanning forty years of his explorations, entitled *Shakespeare and Religion*, has just been published by Routledge & Kegan Paul. He was awarded a C.B.E. in 1968.

JACOB KRAMER (1892-1962) was born in Klincy in the Ukraine. The family left Russia in 1900 and settled in Leeds. He taught at Bradford and Leeds Schools of Art for many years, and in 1960 was honoured with a retrospective exhibition by Leeds City Art Gallery. The catalogue of this exhibition included a long introduction by Herbert Read who had been a friend since before the First World War.

DENISE LEVERTOV (1923-   ) was born in Ilford, Essex, and settled in the United States shortly after the close of the Second World War. Her collections of poetry include *The Double Image* (1946), *Overland to the Islands* (1958), *With Eyes at the Back of Our Heads* (1960), *The Jacobs Ladder* (1961). She is married to Mitchell Goodman and lives in New York.

262

HENRY MOORE (1898-   ) is now generally regarded as the world's greatest living sculptor. He was born in Castleford, West Yorkshire, and, after serving in the First World War, studied at the Leeds School of Art, and then the Royal College of Art in London. His work is represented in over fifty public collections in Europe, the Americas, and Australasia. His most recent public commission was the creation of a Reclining Figure for the Unesco building in Paris (1957-58). He has received the honorary degree of D.Litt. from the Universities of Leeds, London, Reading, Hull and Oxford. He has a doctorate in Arts from Harvard, a Doctorate in Law from Cambridge and a Doctorate in Engineering from Berlin. He has been a member of the Royal Fine Art Commission since 1947, and a member of the National Theatre Committee since 1962. He was a member of the Arts Council from 1963 to 1967, and a Trustee of the Tate Gallery from 1941 to 1956. He was a Trustee of the National Gallery from 1955 to 1963 and from 1964 to the present. He was made a Companion of Honour in 1955 and received an O.M. in 1963.

BEN NICHOLSON (1894-   ) was born in Denham, Bucks, England, and studied at the Slade. His paintings and reliefs have brought him many international prizes, and his work is represented in most of the major public collections throughout the world. Sir Herbert Read introduced the two volumes surveying his work from 1911 to 1948 and from 1948 to 1955, which were published in 1948 and 1956 respectively. In 1954 he received the "Ulissi" Prize at the Venice Biennale, in 1956 the Governor of Tokyo prize at the 3rd International, in 1956 the Grand Prix at the 4th Lugano International, and in 1957 the 1st International Prize at the 4th Sao Paolo Biennial. In 1957 he also received the first Guggenheim Foundation Award. He lives in Switzerland. He received an O.M. in 1968.

NORMAN NICHOLSON (1914-   ) was born in Millom, Cumberland, where he still lives. He is the author of the standard work on Cumberland and Westmoreland in *The County Books* series, and of *The Lakers: The Adventures of the First Tourists* (1955). He has celebrated the life of the small provincial town in his touching and witty *Provincial Pleasures* (1959) and has written two critical works about William Cowper. His verse plays (*The Old Man of the Mountains* (1946), *Prophesy to the Wind* (1950), *A Match for the Devil* (1955), *Birth by Drowning* (1960)) have been widely performed in Britain, but he is chiefly known for his three books of poems, *Five Rivers* (1944), *Rock Face* (1948), *The Pot Geranium* (1954). His *Selected Poems* appeared in 1966.

VICTOR PASMORE (1908-   ) studied at the Central School of Arts and Crafts. He was Master of Painting in the Department of Fine Art of Durham University from 1954 to 1961, and has been consulting architectural designer for Peterlee New Town since 1955. His paintings and reliefs are represented in many public collections in Europe, Australia, and North America. He was a Trustee of the Tate Gallery from 1963 to 1966. In 1959 he was awarded a C.B.E.

SIR ROLAND PENROSE (1900-   ) was educated at Queen's College, Cambridge, and in France. He organized the International Surrealist Exhibition in London in 1936 and painted and exhibited with the Surrealist group in London before the outbreak of the Second World War. He was a founder of the Institute of Contemporary Arts in London, and has been its chairman since 1947. He was a Trustee of the Tate Gallery from 1959 to 1966, and organized that Gallery's Picasso Exhibition of 1960. His publications include *The Road is Wider than Long* (1939), *In the Service of the People* (1945) and *Picasso, His Life and Work* (1958). He was awarded a C.B.E. in 1961 and a knighthood in 1966. He lives in Sussex.

MICHAEL W. PIDGEON (1945-   ) was born in Rochford, Essex, and educated at the University of Victoria, British Columbia, where he is at present pursuing graduate studies in linguistics.

KATHLEEN RAINE (1908-   ) was born in London and educated at Girton College, Cambridge. She has published six collections of poetry, *Stone and Flower* (1943), *Living in Time* (1946), *The Pythoness* (1949), *The Year One* (1952), *Collected Poems* (1956), and *The Hollow Hill* (1965). Her collection of critical essays, *Defending Ancient Springs*, was published in 1967, and her Andrew Mellon lectures on Blake have just been published in two lavishly illustrated volumes by the Bollingen Foundation under the title *Blake and Tradition*.

STEPHEN SPENDER (1909-   ) was born in London and educated at University College, Oxford. One of the leading poets of the thirties in England, he became, in the forties and fifties, also a prominent critic and editor. He was co-editor of *Horizon* from 1939 to 1941 and of *Encounter* from 1953 to 1967. He has held senior academic appointments at Northwestern University and the Universities of Cincinatti and California. In 1966 he delivered the Clark Lectures at the University of Cambridge, and in 1968 the Mellon Lectures in Washington, D.C. In 1967 he was a Fellow of the Institute of Advanced Studies at Wesleyan University. He is the author of over thirty books including an autobiography, *World within World* (1951), the critical works, *The Creative Element* (1953) and *The Making of a Poem* (1955), and numerous volumes of poetry. His *Collected Poems* appeared in 1954. In 1962 he was awarded the C.B.E.

REGINALD C. TERRY (1932-   ) was born in England and educated at the Universities of Leicester, Bristol and Michigan. After working for some years as a journalist and in the field of Adult Education he emigrated to Canada and in 1965 joined the English Department of the University of Victoria. He is at present on leave in London where he is completing a Doctoral dissertation on Anthony Trollope.

FELICITAS VOGLER (1922-   ) lives with her husband, Ben Nicholson, in Switzerland. Her photographs have been represented in many international exhibitions and she has presented several one-man shows.

GEORGE WOODCOCK (1912-   ) was born in Winnipeg and educated in England where, from 1940 to 1947, he edited the magazine *Now*. He returned to Canada in 1949. He has published biographical studies of William Godwin (1946), Peter Kropotkin (1950) and Pierre-Joseph Proudhon (1953), and critical studies of the work of Aphra Behn (1948), Oscar Wilde (1950) and George Orwell (1966). *The Writer in Politics* appeared in 1948, *Anarchism: A History of Libertarian Ideas and Movements* in 1962, and *Civil Disobedience* in 1966. He is the author of four collections of verse, *The White Island* (1940), *The Centre Cannot Hold* (1942), *Image the South* (1949) and *Selected Poems* (1967). Since 1956 he has taught English and Asian studies at the University of British Columbia where he edits the quarterly, *Canadian Literature*.